THE NEW GERMAN CINEMA

John Sandford

THE NEW GERMAN CINEMA

A DACAPO PAPERBACK

Library of Congress Cataloging in Publication Data

Sandford, John, 1944-
  The new German cinema.

  (A Da Capo paperback)
  Bibliography: p.
  Includes index.
  1. Moving-pictures — Germany (West)
I. Title.
PN1993.5.G3S3 1982   791.43′0943   82-8981
ISBN 0-306-80177-9   AACR2

Published by Da Capo Press, Inc.
A Subsidiary of Plenum Publishing Corporation
233 Spring Street, New York, N.Y. 10013

CONTENTS

Preface

The West German Cinema entered the 1960s in a state of almost total collapse: as far as the world at large was concerned, it was non-existent, and its standing at home had sunk so low that at the 1961 Berlin Film Festival it was announced that the annual prize for the best German film could not be awarded that year, as there simply was no best German film. At the beginning of the 1980s the West German Cinema stands in the limelight of international attention, its leading directors are familiar names to cineastes both at home and abroad, and its films have reaped critical acclaim – not to mention prizes – all over the world. Behind this transformation in the West German film scene lies a phenomenon that, by analogy with the other 'new' national cinemas of the past decade or so, has come to be known as the 'New German Cinema': one of the most remarkable, enduring, and promising developments in the cinema of the 1970s. It is the aim of this book to provide an introductory survey of that 'New German Cinema'.

'The New German Cinema' is a collective term for the work of a number of very different directors, nearly all of whom have grown up in the post-war years. It is not a 'movement' or a 'school', nor is it a self-consciously 'underground' or 'alternative' cinema. It occupies the ill-defined but fruitful mid ground between the underground proper – which flourished briefly in the late sixties – and the commercial cinema of the old film establishment. Nor is the New German Cinema an heir to the 'old' German Cinema – the renowned German film of the Weimar years. The Third Reich and its aftermath left a gap in German film culture that was largely filled by imported films, and in particular films from America. The young directors of the New German Cinema grew up largely ignorant of the German films of the twenties, but well-versed in the ethos of Hollywood. The films they were later to make themselves bear witness above all to these early impressions.

The term 'New German Cinema', which has its equivalents in many languages, but is in fact little used in German, is in many ways a questionable one. The 'German' Cinema it refers to is, of course, the West German Cinema. There is in the German Democratic Republic an equally flourishing young cinema, but one whose preconditions have nothing to do with the rebirth of the cinema in the German Federal Republic. There are other terminological problems. *Is* this a 'New' Cinema? Is it, given its roots in the traditions of Hollywood and more recent moves towards an 'internationalization' of its products, a 'German' Cinema in any real sense, even if only a *West* German Cinema? And indeed, given its close links with television, are its products really 'Cinema'? These are fundamental issues, and any attempt to define and assess the New German Cinema must bear them in mind. Much of what I have written in the following pages is therefore informed by the threefold question: 'Is it New? Is it German? Is it Cinema?'.

Part One of this book is a historical outline of the West German Cinema, indicating the conditions out of which the New German Cinema arose. Part Two looks at the work of seven representative directors, its chapters arranged in roughly the chronological order in which each one first made his impact in the New German Cinema. In Part Three I have tried to define what is distinctive about the New German Cinema, firstly by examining the more prominent thematic concerns of the films, and secondly by looking at the economic and political factors that have determined the shape of the directors' work.

In keeping with the book's aim of providing an 'introductory survey', the approach to the individual directors in Part Two is descriptive rather than evaluative. The virtues of the 'auteurist' approach are debatable, but in the case of such a disparate phenomenon as the New German Cinema, and in particular in an *introduction* to the New German Cinema, it is a particularly helpful way of coming to grips with the topic in hand. Any selection of directors for special attention is bound to be invidious and contentious. My choice has been guided more than anything by the *international* reputation of the directors concerned. The New German Cinema, it has often been remarked, has for long been better appreciated abroad than in West Germany itself, and the seven directors to whom the bulk of this book is devoted are internationally the 'big names' of the New German Cinema. They also between them give some idea of its thematic and formal range and variety. One of them, Rainer Werner Fassbinder, has played a disproportionately major role, and for many outsiders his name is virtually synonymous with the New German Cinema as a whole. His output of films is prodigious, and without parallel in its diversity. He has accordingly been given a special place in Part Two. As a general principle I have surveyed all the work of the major directors: to do equal jusice to Fassbinder has meant writing a chapter that is longer and different in format from those allotted to the other directors.

Concentration on the 'big seven' has inevitably meant that the Berlin directors, whose important work has been little shown abroad, have not been given the same attention they might have received had my perspective been a German one. The Berlin directors, whose work is briefly discussed in Chapter 9, occupy the 'documentary wing' of the New German Cinema; there are also major talents on the 'underground wing' – Herbert Achternbusch, Niklaus Schilling, and Werner Schroeter, for instance – whose role in the New German Cinema might also be rated more highly from a German perspective. Even in the mainstream of the New German Cinema as it is experienced in West Germany there are major directors, such as Peter Lilienthal, whose work is virtually unknown abroad. Chapter 9 discusses some of these 'other' directors: the epithet is not intended slightingly, only as a reminder that these are filmmakers whose work – often because of the fortuitous whims of international film distribution – still awaits discovery in the world at large.

I have not assumed that readers will necessarily have seen the films discussed, and have accordingly given some indication of contents in all appropriate cases. I have also not assumed a knowledge of German. All translations from German and other foreign sources are my own. In translating, I have preferred accuracy to elegance (an intriguingly high proportion of the quotations from filmmakers were in any case formulated originally in a distinctly verbose or wooden manner). Some German terms – especially the names of institutions – have been retained; in this case they are explained when first used, and may in any case be found in the Glossary of German Terms at the end of the book. Film titles have been given in English, followed, at the first significant mention, by the German title in brackets. The English titles are those in common use; normally they are the titles under which

films have been released in Britain. They should therefore not be read as necessarily *translations* of the German titles: where the German title is significantly different from the English one this has been noted in the text. Where films do not yet have an 'official' English title (usually because they have not been released in Britain or America) I have simply translated the German title, and indicated this by the use of quotation marks. The date given for each film is that of the year of completion of production.

I would like to thank the many people and organizations that have provided me with help and information. Particular thanks are due to Sheila Lattimore for her helpful comments and advice, Elizabeth Oliver of the British Universities Film Council, Frau Eva Orbanz of the *Stiftung Deutsche Kinemathek*, Herr Hans Helmut Prinzler of the *Deutsche Film-und Fernseh-Akademie*, Frau Helga Rulf of the *Goethe-Institut London*, Mrs Ilse Wolff of Oswald Wolff Ltd, and to the staff of the libraries of the *Deutsche Film- und Fernseh-Akademie* in West Berlin and the British Film Institute in London, as well as – for help received in Germany – to Horst Breuer, Adrian Hannah, Volker Honemann, and Volker Mertens. Information, advice, and comments have been forthcoming from friends and acquaintances too numerous to mention here: I am grateful to them all. I would also like to thank the British Academy for supporting a vital research visit to Germany with money from the Small Grants Research Fund in the Humanities, and the editors of *German Life and Letters* for permission to use material originally published in their number of April 1979.

Grateful thanks too to Jan Dawson and Andi Engel for permission to reprint extracts from their interviews with Wim Wenders and the Straubs respectively, and to Günter Grass for permission to reprint his engraving of David Bennent. Permission to use the illustrations in chapter three was given by the Straubs' British distributors, the Artificial Eye Film Company. (Further acknowledgments for illustrations may be found at the end of the Index of Film Titles.)

Finally, I would like to express my gratitude to Mrs Dina Lom, the UK Representative of the German Federal Film Board, who supplied not only the bulk of the illustrations, but also much invaluable advice and information.

PART ONE : THE BACKGROUND

1 THE DEVELOPMENT OF THE WEST GERMAN CINEMA

i The Post-War Years

The last film premiere of the Third Reich took place on 31 January 1945, when Veit Harlan's KOLBERG was shown to the embattled German troops on the Atlantic Front at La Rochelle. The following day came the film's official opening in Berlin, before an audience of Party members and prominent names from the acting world. Three months later the Third Reich came to an end. Germany was now under the control of the four Allies – the Soviet Union, the United States, the United Kingdom, and France – each responsible for administering one of the four zones of occupation into which the country had been divided. All took immediate steps to control the media of information and entertainment, including the cinema. The devastation of production and distribution facilities that the war had caused, not to mention the destruction of most of the country's cinemas, rendered the Allies' initial blackout of the media virtually superfluous. The occupying powers were determined that the Germans should be sealed off from everything that could be remotely construed as belonging to the Nazi past. In the cinema, as in the other media, this meant firstly providing the Germans with material that they, the Allies, had produced, and then secondly granting licences to carefully vetted Germans to produce their own newspapers, magazines, radio programmes, and films, all of which would for some time still be subject to careful censorship.

The policies adopted by the Allies towards all the German media were to have lasting consequences, and nowhere more so than in the cinema. For the Russians, Nazism had been the natural development of monopoly capitalism into the most nakedly aggressive and chauvinistic imperialism. Their attitude towards the German *people*, and particularly towards the working class, was initially more conciliatory than that of the Americans. As far as the Russians were concerned there were far more good Germans than the Americans were willing to concede. And so, in the Eastern Zone, film production was allowed to flourish relatively soon again after the Nazi defeat. It was, however, a highly centralized industry, and has remained so to this day, partly for ideological reasons, party for the very practical reason that centralized major production facilities that had survived the war were situated in the Soviet Zone, particularly at Babelsberg near Berlin. The Western Allies were more wary, and especially the Americans, who saw Nazism more in terms of an illness from which the Germans could only recover if they were isolated from dangerous influences from their past, and then carefully screened, and finally 're-educated' in the ways of Western democracy.

It was a grandiosely idealistic ambition, but in their initial determination to carry it out, the Americans bequeathed to the West Germans a sickly film industry that has to this day never managed to stand on its own two feet. The reasons were an unholy mixture of the ideological and the economic. It was an axiom of the American 're-education' programme that if Germany were flooded with the products of American culture, the Germans would, by some mysterious process of osmosis, be transformed into shining exemplars of Truth, Justice, and the American Way. Hollywood was delighted: here was a vast market, potentially the biggest in Europe, that had been closed to them throughout the war years. A great backlog of films that had already paid their way elsewhere could now be re-released at prices that would undercut any competition. The Germans, not unnaturally, were pleased too, and flocked to see the films they had been denied access to by the Nazis. The first few films were subtitled, but soon dubbing established itself as the solution to the language problem. And so it was that the post-war generation of West German cinema-goers (and that was to include the future directors of the New German Cinema) quickly came to accept dubbed old Hollywood movies as standard fare in their picture-houses.

The Americans were, of course, not guided entirely by idealism in their handling of the German cinema. When the market was opened to Hollywood, steps were taken to ensure that things remained that way. The West Germans, it was stipulated, must not impose an import quota on American films. The failure to protect the domestic product that this implied – something virtually unique among film-producing countries – was to have dire consequences for the West German film industry. The major American companies were able to establish a stranglehold on the West German cinema from which it has never recovered: indeed, American domination has grown greater and greater as the years have passed.

As if Hollywood's disingenuous endorsement of the re-education programme were not enough, the Americans also set about dismembering the centralized and closely coordinated structure of the film industry that the Nazis had left behind. Again their intentions were, ostensibly, honourable. In place of ideologically contaminated monopoly there was to be healthy diversity. Unfortunately it did not work that way. The splitting up of the film industry simply weakened it, particularly at the primary level of production. The producers were too small to be viable, few survived beyond their first or second film, and all were in thrall to the distributors. But even the distributors were for the most part unable to withstand the inherent superiority of their American competitors, and it has long been the major American distributors who between them have almost totally dominated the West German market. As if to add insult to the injury that had already been done to the West German cinema, the one concern that resisted Hollywood's onslaught was UFA, the giant pre-war and then Nazi conglomerate that had been the object of the Americans' trust-busting crusade in the first place. UFA refused to lie down, and despite ostensible attempts to dismantle it, it was resurrected in a new guise in the mid-fifties to become for a while the biggest film complex in Europe, only then, this time of its own accord, to collapse in 1961 into relative insignificance.

It was against this unfavourable background that the West German cinema floundered through its first decade, and had to all intents and purposes sunk without trace by the beginning of the sixties – at any rate as far as the production of even marginally presentable films was concerned. Curiously enough, it was the early years that were the most promising – the period of desperate privation and close supervision by the Allied authorities. The films of these occupation years did their best to present an appraisal of what had just happened to Germany, though none really managed to explain just *how* it had happened. This was to be a failing that none of the handful of 'quality' films made in West Germany in the 1950s was able to shake off. The hero of the early post-war films was the 'little man': the problem was that he was all too conveniently and comfortably innocent. The 'little man' (and presumably most audiences found no difficulty in identifying with him) was the victim of history; the Nazis were 'the others', the villains, demonized or satirized into a safe distance. Nazism was all too often presented as Evil Incarnate, a malevolent Fate whose dark mysteries were not worth probing: the horrible fact that it had descended on the 'little man' was material enough for an archetypal struggle of good and evil.

Until 1949, when the two separate German states came into being, it was still possible to speak of a single 'German' cinema. The first, and most memorable postwar German film was in fact made for the Soviet Zone's state film corporation DEFA by Wolfgang Staudte in 1946.[1] THE MURDERERS ARE AMONG US (DIE MÖRDER SIND UNTER UNS) used the ruined landscape of Berlin as an almost expressionistic background to the story of a man who seeks to bring to justice his former captain, responsible for atrocities in Poland, and now a 'decent, honest citizen'. The other outstanding film of this period was made in the West: Helmut Käutner's IN FORMER DAYS (IN JENEN TAGEN, 1947), which traced in seven episodes the fortunes of the changing owners of an old motor-car during the Nazi years. Of the filmmakers who portrayed not so much the implications of the Nazi past as the desolation of the present, it was to be an Italian, Roberto Rossellini, who captured some of the most remarkable images of life among the ruins of Berlin in GERMANY YEAR ZERO (GERMANIA ANNO ZERO, 1947).

There had been some grounds for hope in the years from 1946 to 1949 that post-Hitler Germany might be developing a cinema that could bear comparison with the neo-Realism that had emerged from post-Mussolini Italy. The foundation in 1949 of the German Federal Republic in the Western zones, and of the German Democratic Republic in the East, quickly dispelled this illusion. Now there were two German cinemas. The East German cinema went its own way in the service of the new communist state. In the West, after an initial flurry of pessimistic soul-searching, epitomized in THE LOST MAN (DER VERLORENE, 1951), which Peter Lorre both directed and starred in, there was a remarkable change of mood. Optimism was the keynote of public life now that the 'Economic Miracle' was getting under way; escapism became the keynote of the cinema: the grim past was finished and done with.[2]

Now that staple of German cinematic sentimentality, the *Heimatfilm*, raised its picture-postcard head again. The racist and mystically nationalistic implications it had acquired during the Nazi years were conveniently forgotten, though they were too closely bound up with the genre to be totally eliminated. The world of the *Heimatfilm* was ordered and unproblematic, a world of happy countryfolk in idyllic surroundings. The classic of the 1950s was Hans Deppe's 'GREEN IS THE HEATH' (GRÜN IST DIE HEIDE, 1951), which inspired countless imitations. Later, between 1955 and 1957, a new variant was added to the genre in the shape of the Romy Schneider 'Sissi' films, set in imperial Austria. The market was flooded with shallow entertainment: the *Heimatfilme* were joined by operettas, reviews, romantic comedies, and, later, a series of Edgar Wallace thrillers and Karl May Westerns – the latter shot largely in Spain and Yugoslavia. These were films that, in their avoidance of all contemporary relevance, let alone political statements or awkward questioning, reflected the mood of the 1950s in West Germany. Their protagonists were essentially passive and 'decent', and were rewarded accordingly. A few films even reverted to the hero worship of the Nazi cinema, portraying great men whose destiny it was to lead lesser mortals to better things. This was especially true of Rolf Hansen's SAUERBRUCH (1954), the story of a brilliant surgeon whose patients have only to submit themselves utterly to his genius. An even closer reflection of the authoritarian 'grand old man' that Konrad Adenauer personified was presented in Alfred Braun's STRESEMANN (1957), which misrepresented its historical subject as a wily father-figure pestered and hampered by an unreasonable and obstructive parliamentary opposition.

A few films, however, did stand out as being a cut above the general escapist sentimentality. Some were so unlike the commercial mainstream as to look decidedly experimental. In retrospect such films as Herbert Vesely's 'FLEE NO MORE' (NICHT MEHR FLIEHEN, 1954) and Ottomar Domnick's JONAS of 1957 look more like isolated precursors of the New German Cinema than products of the 1950s. The mid fifties, the period of West German rearmament, saw a spate of war films, which, on closer inspection, turn out to do little more than resurrect the immediate post-war myth of the honest German serving his fatherland in good faith, but betrayed by the evil little clique who have taken hold of the reins of power. This was true not only of the opportunist and run-of-the-mill war films of the period, but also of such well-intentioned classics as Helmut Käutner's THE DEVIL'S GENERAL (DES TEUFELS GENERAL, 1954), based on Carl Zuckmayer's play of 1946. The year before, Käutner had made a more convincing, though somewhat sentimentalized, war film, set this time in occupied Yugoslavia: THE LAST BRIDGE (DIE LETZTE BRÜCKE). It was, however, not until 1960 that a film with a similar title, Bernhard Wicki's THE BRIDGE (DIE BRÜCKE), managed to establish itself as *the* classic anti-war film of the West German cinema. Yet therein lay its major weakness: it was a film against war in general, and despite its documentary pretensions, it failed – like all its inferior predecessors – to show where this war had come from. The *effects* of National Socialism were painted in their full horror; its *causes* remained unquestioned.

A few films also returned to the theme of THE MURDERERS ARE AMONG US, and asked how the Nazis of yore were faring in the Federal Republic. They were doing quite nicely, was the general answer. Staudte himself, now working in the West, made two major films on this ticklish topic: ROSES FOR THE STATE PROSECUTOR (ROSEN FÜR DEN STAATSANWALT, 1959) and FAIRGROUND (KIRMES, 1960), in both of which former SS officials are shown to hold high office in the Federal Republic. The former Nazi who becomes a wealthy industrialist was another popular figure, notably in Kurt Hoffmann's THE PRODIGIES (WIR WUNDERKINDER, 1958). Indeed, the fabulously wealthy industrialists who had made rapid fortunes out of the boom of the 1950s exerted a dubious fascination on the public at large. This mixture of envious admiration, hostility,

ROSES FOR THE STATE PROSECUTOR Martin Held as the State Prosecutor

national pride, and prurient curiosity was exploited in a number of films of the period, one of the most successful being Rolf Thiele's THE GIRL ROSEMARIE (DAS MÄDCHEN ROSEMARIE, 1958).

For all their commercial success, these would-be topical films that still all too often missed the point were the rare exception amidst the general paralysis of inspiration and talent that befell the West German cinema in the 1950s. In quantitative terms, however, these were the boom years. Feature film production reached a peak of 128 in 1955; the following year audience attendance too reached a peak of 817 million cinema visits, a figure that represents an average of 16 visits per person; and in 1959 the number of cinemas reached *its* peak at 7,085.[3] The boom in film production had been partly inspired by the credit guarantees that the government provided between 1950 and 1956, initially to distributors, and then from 1952 to producers. These had done nothing to impove the quality of the West German cinema, they merely inflated out of all proportion the number of films made – especially as producers had to promise a 'package' of up to eight films in a row.

Moves to encourage the production of films of a higher standard had had little effect. From 1951 onwards producers were able to submit their films for assessment with a view to relief from entertainment tax. This relief was to be granted if the film obtained a quality rating from the Film Assessment Office – the FBW, which awards the grades 'valuable' (*wertvoll*) and 'especially valuable' (*besonders wertvoll*) to films it adjudges to be of merit.[4] The relative conservatism of the FBW in the 1950s, however, merely encouraged the production of 'safe' and often banal films. Prizes awarded annually by the Federal Ministry of the Interior were also meant to encourage quality, but they too were all too often awarded according to what looked more like criteria of 'audience appeal', or even political acceptability.

The boom of the mid fifties did not last long, and by the end of the decade the bottom had fallen out of the film market. Many factors were to blame, but one in particular stood out: television. Like most Continental countries, West Germany acquired the television habit later than had been the case in Britain, not to mention the United States. The big build-up in television set ownership began in the late fifties, and whereas in 1957 there had been only a million sets in West Germany, there were four million by 1960;[5] by the end of the sixties there were 16.75 million. Cinema attendance figures dropped sharply, cinemas began closing, and film production shrank.

The film industry discovered, however, that there was one area that television, as a 'family medium', could not enter into, and that was sex. Coincidentally, a new audience was emerging who did not want family entertainment, and who were not interested in German television: the hundreds of thousands of immigrant workers from the puritan Mediterranean countries. And so the West German cinema turned to sex, at first under the guise of 'education'. Later, as the moral climate became more permissive, it moved into the field of semi-pornographic 'revelations', with endless series of 'Schoolgirl-' and 'Housewife-Reports', and bizarrely-titled slapstick Bavarian sex comedies (a peculiarly German genre that looks like some mad variant of the *Heimatfilm*). Though somewhat crestfallen by now, the sex wave still rolls on, and even today sex films make up the bulk of West German film exports.[6]

ed like an official proclamation
y of the West German cinema.
val the Federal Minister of the
 no Federal Film Prize would
s no film had been made that
 filmmakers had failed to deli-
e was now a new generation
vinced that *they* could – if only
These young directors were
 wanted to make features as
ibited their work each year in
usen. At the eighth Oberhaus-
1962, twenty-six of them gave
as well as to their ambition, in
e down in film history as the

out it the flavour of the much
at West Germany had now
e and revolutionary in tone, it
that the old order had finally
d the determination and con-
interests it had ignored would
ew and better. Above all, it
ew wave of filmmakers – here
sixties is apparent – and it
declared their intention of seizing this chance of
graduating from short to feature films:

> The collapse of the conventional German cinema
> finally removes the economic basis from an attitude
> of mind that we reject. With it, the new cinema has a
> chance of coming to life.
>
> German short films by young *auteurs*, directors, and
> producers have in recent years received a great
> number of prizes at international festivals, and have
> met with approval by international critics. These
> works and their success show that the future of the
> German cinema lies with those who have shown that
> they speak a new language of the cinema. As in other
> countries, so too in Germany the short film has
> become both training ground and laboratory for the
> feature film. We declare our object to be the creation
> of the new German feature film.
>
> This new cinema needs new freedoms. Freedom

> from the customary conventions of the trade. Free-
> dom from the influence of commercial partners.
> Freedom from the tutelage of vested interests.
> We have a concrete notion of the production of the
> new German cinema at the intellectual, formal, and
> economic levels. We are collectively prepared to take
> economic risks. The old cinema is dead. We believe
> in the new one.
> Oberhausen, 28 February 1962.[7]

The Oberhausen Manifesto is generally regarded as
the starting point of the New German Cinema,
although its twenty-six signatories included only one –
Alexander Kluge – who was later to become known to
the world at large as a major film-maker. It also looked
for some time as if the Manifesto was going to turn out
to be a damp squib: despite its resounding proclamations, nothing much happened in the years that followed to alter the desolate face of West German film
production.

One thing was achieved, though, and that was the
setting up in 1965 of a body to help subsidize new films
by young directors. This was the *Kuratorium junger
deutscher Film*, which came into being as a direct result
of the Oberhausen Manifesto and subsequent lobbying
by its signatories and supporters. With the help of
government funding the *Kuratorium* provided interest-
free loans (which averaged 300,000 DM) on the basis of
scripts submitted by non-established directors.

And then came the breakthrough. 1966 was the
annus mirabilis of the New German Cinema. It was also
perhaps more truly the year of its birth than 1962 had
been, for 1962 had produced only the Oberhausen
Manifesto; 1966 on the other hand produced both films
and, for the first time, international recognition. When
Alexander Kluge's first feature film YESTERDAY GIRL
(ABSCHIED VON GESTERN, 1966) gained eight awards,
including a Silver Lion, at the 1966 Venice Biennale, it
was the first time since the war that a German film had
managed to win an official Venice award. West Germany also did well at Cannes in 1966, where three films
in particular were most favourably received: Ulrich
Schamoni's IT (ES, 1965), Volker Schlöndorff's
YOUNG TÖRLESS (DER JUNGE TÖRLESS, 1966), and Jean-
Marie Straub's NOT RECONCILED (NICHT VERSÖHNT,
1965). Later the same year, at the Berlin Film Festival,

Ulrich Schamoni's brother Peter also won an international prize, the Silver Bear, for his film 'CLOSE SEASON FOR FOXES' (SCHONZEIT FÜR FÜCHSE, 1966).

Suddenly, then, in 1966 a new and different German cinema seemed to have arrived, and it attracted the admiring attention of the world outside, which had up till then regarded West Germany as a non-starter in the field of serious cinema. When one reads the articles, pamphlets, and books that accompanied this rebirth, one is struck by the almost universal mood of optimism or even euphoria. Already by the spring of 1967, Constantin, the largest and, at the time, the most enterprising film distributor in the country, had mounted an exhibition and published a booklet under the title *Der junge deutsche Film* – a title that pointed not only to the freshness of the new cinema, but also to the youth of its creators. In October 1967 the Mannheim Festival presented a survey of the New German Cinema, and in the months that followed seasons of new German films were shown in London, Prague, Bratislava, Rome, and Paris. Evidence that the New German Cinema had really arrived came in December 1967, when the news magazine *Der Spiegel*, in its final number of the year, deemed the phenomenon worthy of a cover story.

The optimism and euphoria were to be short-lived. The established film industry – '*Opas Kino*', or 'Grandad's Cinema', as it was now being called by the younger directors – had not taken kindly to the *Kuratorium junger deutscher Film*, whose sponsorship of no fewer than twenty films in its first three years looked to them like unfair competition. Now *they* began lobbying parliament, and found sympathy in particular with a Christian Democrat member called Hans Toussaint. Toussaint ('the gravedigger of the young cinema', according to Alexander Kluge) pushed through a bill that finally became law at the beginning of 1968. This was the 'Film Promotion Law': the *Filmförderungsgesetz*, or 'FFG'.

Doubtless some members of the Bundestag supported the FFG proposal in the misguided belief that they would thereby be furthering the widely acclaimed New German Cinema, but the effect (and undoubtedly the intention) of the FFG was to reinforce the dominance of the commercial cinema and to encourage the marketing of 'safe', trivial formulae. The law provided for a levy of 10 pfennigs on every cinema ticket sold (the so-called '*Filmgroschen*'), this money to be collected by the Film Promotion Office – the *Filmförderungsanstalt*, or 'FFA' – in West Berlin. At the same time, the budget of the *Kuratorium*, responsibility for which now passed from the Federal authorities to the *Länder*, was reduced by over a half to around 750,000 DM per annum.[8]

The bulk of the FFA's income was to be made available in the form of grants to promote the production of new feature films, but the criteria by which the grants were allotted were decidedly unfavourable towards directors who were young or experimental: a producer could automatically obtain a grant of up to 250,000 DM if he had already produced a film – a so-called '*Referenzfilm*' – which had brought in a gross revenue of 500,000 DM within two years. Admittedly this threshold was lowered to 300,000 DM if the film had been designated 'valuable' or 'especially valuable' by the FBW, or if it had gained a main prize at a major international festival, but these meagre concessions to quality were little comfort to the bulk of the new directors. They had made films of a demanding nature that simply did not pull in the audiences necessary to trigger the mechanism of the FFG. Worse still, some had not yet made a feature film at all, and now – particularly with the slashing of the *Kuratorium*'s budget – saw little prospect of ever obtaining the promotion they needed if they were even to make a start in their career.

Meanwhile, *Opas Kino* began to reap the benefits of the new law. It was delightfully simple if all you were interested in was making money: you found a sure-fire formula to attract a reasonable-sized audience, and after your takings had grossed 500,000 DM you went along to the FFA and collected up to 250,000 DM, with which you made another film to the same well-tried formula . . . and so on, and so on, into a tedious infinity of banality and drivel. It was in this way that the bulk of the West German films of the 1970s were made – the films of the commercial cinema, as opposed to those of the New German Cinema. Unlike the New German Cinema, they were, mercifully, confined almost exclusively to the home market, and have, with the notable exception of the sex films, not been shown abroad.

The mechanism of the FFG encouraged series rather than individual films, and series galore were accordingly made. The great majority were sex films, but, notwithstanding their teutonic matter and manner, this was an international phenomenon. Other series were more peculiarly German: the *Heimatfilm* still survived, as did the Euro-Western, the Edgar Wallace thriller, the romantic love story, and the horror-film. But there were also great strings of corny situation comedies that flogged their moribund subject matter well beyond death. One series, the 'Mad Aunts' and 'Uncle Willy' films, dealt with barmy relatives; another, the 'Reverend' series, involved a funny priest. Perhaps the most peculiar of all seemed to come straight from the pages of a schoolboy comic: these were the '*Lümmel*' (lout) and '*Pauker*' (swot) films, set in schools, and portraying the antics of harassed teachers and classroom pests.

The crisis in the cinema that had led to the Oberhausen Manifesto, to the *Kuratorium*, and then to the FFG and the subsequent boom in triviality, had been brought to a head by the advent of television. It is a measure of the inroads made by television that where in 1956 there had been sixteen cinema visits per head of population, twenty years later in 1976 the figure had sunk to 1.9, the lowest in the European Community.[9] There is thus some irony in the fact that it was television that in the end came to the rescue of the new cinema that had been so cruelly nipped in the bud in 1968. Television, originally the arch-enemy of the cinema, holds much of the credit for the existence of the New German Cinema as we know it today.

The structure of West German television is a complicated mixture of regional and network programmes, all operating on the BBC-style public corporation principle. There are three services. The simplest in structure is the 'second channel', the *Zweites Deutsches Fernsehen*, or 'ZDF', which broadcasts a single national programme. At the other extreme there are the minority-appeal 'third channels', five in number, each serving a particular region or group of regions. And then in the middle is the 'first channel', usually referred to as the 'ARD', which are the initials of the coordinating body that networks the various programmes originated in its nine constituent regional corporations.[10] These regional corporations (which are also responsible for radio) vary greatly in size, and, notwithstanding a general obligation to 'neutrality', some

are recognizably more to the right, others more to the left on the political spectrum.

There is thus in West Germany a greater range of outlets than in practically any other European country to artists working in the medium of television. This is particularly true of the film: feature films play a very important role in television programming in West Germany, where an average of over two a day are broadcast, and more films are now screened on television than in all the country's cinemas. Many of these are of course old cinema films, but a sizeable number are newer films, produced with the help of the television corporations themselves. Here then was the source of funding and the outlet for their work that the young directors turned to. Accepting help from television did however mean accepting aesthetic and political limitations; it also, especially in the early years, brought economic drawbacks. A film premiered on television rarely does well in the cinemas, for the potential audience has already watched it free of charge at home. It was this simple but important lesson that led in November 1974 to the signing of a major agreement between the television corporations and – on behalf of the film-makers – the Film Promotion Office.

This 'Film/Television Agreement' (*Film/Fernseh-Abkommen*) was designed to bring to an end the haphazard, uncoordinated, and contradictory arrangements that had meant that television was on the one hand assisting the production of new films, but on the other hand throttling their distribution prospects. The Agreement's most important provision is for co-productions between the television corporations and film producers: 34 million marks were set aside for this for the four years from 1974 to 1978. Also provided for is the allotment of production subsidies in exchange for broadcasting rights. Furthermore, the broadcasting authorities agreed to donate a million marks a year to the FFA to be distributed on a 'no-strings' basis to support the realization of worthy filmscripts. Meanwhile, outside the scope of the Film/Television Agreement, television continues to produce, and co-produce, films under the aegis of the corporations' various drama departments. Only in this latter case are films still likely to be premiered on television, for co-productions made under the Agreement must be allowed to run for two years in the cinemas before they may be transmitted, and in the case of films supported by the advance purchase of broadcasting rights, five years must elapse before they can be shown on television.

The Film/Television Agreement of 1974 came at the same time as an important amendment to the Film Promotion Law. This provided for the first time for '*Projektförderung*' – the provision of grants for the realization of promising filmscripts. This was something the young film-makers had been lobbying for for some time: a subsidy system that, like that of the *Kuratorium*, did not favour established directors and producers.[11]

Now, once more, things were beginning to look more promising for the New German Cinema. The mid seventies also saw the consolidation of its reputation abroad, not least through the enterprise of the Goethe-Institut, the semi-official body entrusted with the cultural representation of West Germany in foreign countries. Already in the spring of 1972 the New York Goethe-Institut had helped arrange a season of seventeen features and twelve shorts under the then novel title 'New German Cinema' at the Museum of Modern Art. The international interest that had been aroused in 1966 was rekindled in 1974 when Fassbinder's FEAR EATS THE SOUL won the International Critics' Prize at the Cannes Festival, and it was this film that later the same year became his first to be released commercially in London.

In 1976 and 1977 the New German Cinema finally established itself as something worthy of attention in the outside world. The common tenor of the articles and reviews that began appearing in some numbers in those years was surprise and admiration. *Newsweek* started the ball rolling in February 1976 with a cover-story on the 'German Filmboom'. In December 1976 the BBC presented a television feature on the new directors called 'Signs of Vigorous Life', accompanied by an article in the *Radio Times* that talked of the 'amazing renaissance' of the German cinema, a phrase echoed in the 'remarkable resurrection' hailed in the guide to 'Who's Who in the fashionable German films' that the *Sunday Times* published in July 1977.[12] 'The New German Cinema is the liveliest in Europe,' proclaimed an article in *Time* magazine on 20 March 1978, whilst three months later the London *Times* headed a report on the New German Cinema with the words

'Exciting new cinema shows the way'. German films were by now staple fare in the art house circuits and film clubs, and even found their way onto television in a number of countries. Something that had not happened since the 1920s was at last happening again: German films were being shown, talked about, and admired all over the world.

Interest focussed in particular on a number of directors. Such unfashionable 'auteurism' is uniquely appropriate in the case of the New German Cinema, which has from the outset been pre-eminently a '*cinéma des auteurs*', an '*Autorenkino*', where each film, in content and technique, bears the distinctive stamp of its director.[13] This has been the inevitable result of a system where young, unestablished film-makers have had to be scriptwriter, director, and producer in one, realizing their visions on low budgets, with small teams and tight schedules, yet free of many of the constraints of commercial production company demands and trade union regulations familiar in the more developed film industries of Britain and the USA. It has been both the strength (artistically) and the weakness (commercially) of the New German Cinema.

Who, then, are the *Autoren* of the New German Cinema? Directors have come and gone over the past one and a half decades, and any list must inevitably be somewhat arbitrary in its selection. There are, however, seven directors who began making films in the sixties, and who, more than any others, during the seventies established the reputation of the New German Cinema abroad. Firstly, there is of course Rainer Werner Fassbinder, the most prolific and best-known of the group. By now perhaps Werner Herzog and Wim Wenders are equally familiar names. These three have attracted much attention abroad; four other directors are slightly less well known, but equally important figures: Jean-Marie Straub, Alexander Kluge, Volker Schlöndorff (all members of the 'first generation' of the New German Cinema), and Hans Jürgen Syberberg. It would be difficult to imagine a more varied group of artists, each making films with most distinctive and individual flavours. One thing is certain about the New German Cinema: unlike the French *Nouvelle Vague*, with which it has often been misleadingly compared, it is not a cohesive 'movement' or 'school'.

PART TWO = SEVEN DIRECTORS

2 ALEXANDER KLUGE

Alexander Kluge's role in the New German Cinema has been wide-ranging and of major importance. He is the intellectual among the new directors, a lawyer by profession, an Honorary Professor of the University of Frankfurt am Main, a writer of semi-documentary fiction, as well as of theoretical works in that fruitfully indeterminate borderland between politics, sociology, psychology, philosophy, and aesthetics that was pioneered by the neo-Marxists of the Frankfurt School. To call Kluge the 'father' of the New German Cinema might seem inappropriate in view of his comparative youth, although, born in February 1932, he is the oldest of the new directors. But it was Kluge's films that – along with Straub's – first brought international admiration to the West German cinema in the 1960s, and it is his name that today remains the most familiar among the twenty-six signatories of the Oberhausen Manifesto. He has moreover in the intervening years

acted both as spokesman and theoretician of the New German Cinema in his writings on the aesthetics and economics of the cinema, in his role as head of the *Institut für Filmgestaltung* in Ulm, and in his activities as a resolute campaigner for a better deal for the West German film-makers.[1] And, of course, on top of everything else, he has made some outstanding films.

Kluge's approach to film-making is aptly characterized by that much-abused epithet 'Brechtian'. His films analyse and demonstrate, deliberately challenging conventional forms of perception and expression; they seek to stimulate the audience's awareness, to provoke and question rather than to soothe and confirm. In some respects this brings them close to the work of Straub, but the two directors have made films with a very different feel to them. Kluge's films have a pace and variety, a rapidity and range of montage, and a wry irony that are far removed from the 'austerity' associated with much that Straub has done. Like Brecht, Kluge has subjected his work time and again to analysis, criticism, and revision; and like Brecht he has grounded his analysis and criticism in a Marxist debate about the nature of his medium, about the preconditions and potential of art in capitalist society.

Kluge's theoretical writings do not make for easy reading: like all radical texts they grapple with ideas that, by definition, run counter to received modes of thought. Like his films they are tentative and experimental, a jostling succession of aperçus, elaborations, images and arguments that is both stimulating and daunting, and always impressive for its vitality and imaginativeness.[2] Kluge has not produced a convenient, concise, and comprehensive theory of film, but in all his writings, with a quite remarkable consistency, certain key ideas surface time and again.

Underlying everything is Kluge's theory of realism,

a theory that derives ultimately from Marx, but is indebted more than anything to Bertolt Brecht. There are, according to this theory, two types of realism. The one involves the superficial reproduction of outward reality; it merely confirms – and thereby affirms – the existence of what it shows. It is exemplified in the cinema by conventional documentaries. The other form of realism is critical and subversive, seeking out the truth beneath the deceptive surface of things. It is closely associated for Kluge with protest, for it involves an active confrontation with the world rather than passive receptivity: 'The motive for realism,' he says, 'is never confirmation of reality, but protest.'[3] Or again: 'For a realistic attitude a certain degree of energy is needed, for realism must be produced, realism is not a state of nature. The natural state is ideology, dreams.'[4]

Ideology and dreams are the province of the commercial cinema, which treats its audience like Pavlovian dogs, serving them up an unending routine of stereotyped stimuli in exchange for equally stereotyped responses. Such an audience gains nothing: 'Money, time, and their own experience are simply taken from them.'[5] It would be wrong, however, to assume that Kluge is adopting an attitude of killjoy snobbery towards the cinema. On the contrary, he sees one of the great virtues of the cinema in its 'plebeian' origins, its roots in fairground entertainment. He is sceptical about the earnestness with which the educated classes approach the cinema: 'I really believe in triviality. I believe that audiences who haven't enjoyed much in the way of schooling can often be smarter and have more experience than someone who's always imposing his culture-grid and then not being able to see very much.'[6]

Education and culture are emphatically not preconditions for the cinema audience that Kluge envisages. Education has been too one-sided, stressing the logical, intellectual faculties in Man, ignoring the senses and the imagination. Kluge has a favourite image for this, that of the school break, the playtime between lessons: it is here that the cinema is situated, not in the classroom. Here he finds possibilities of perception that, in opposition to the official apparatus of consciousness as cultivated in the classroom, represent an 'oppressed class'.[7] And what better way of liberating this neglected and subversive potential than through the cinema? For

the cinema has the great advantage of circumventing our pre-programmed 'logical' faculties, and speaking instead to our senses and our imagination.

The senses, Kluge says, are wrongly dismissed as somehow inferior to our consciousness. In fact they are fundamental not only to perception but to the organization of that perception into knowledge – and in support of this contention he cites Karl Marx.[8] Here we are approaching the heart of Kluge's theory, for through the senses the cinema stimulates the audience's *imagination*, and it is this – '*Phantasie*' is the German word he uses – that seems to be the key term in his writings. It is fundamental to Kluge's view of the way the cinema works that the film is potentially there already in the audience's imagination; it is the director's job to activate this potential:

For some tens of thousands of years film has existed in people's minds – stream of association, daydreams, experience, sense impressions, consciousness. The technical invention of the cinema has simply added reproducible counterparts to this.[9]

The important point, and Kluge has stressed this on many occasions, is that the relationship of film-maker to audience must not be one of domination: the film-maker is not to manipulate his audience, nor should he impose his message or his visions on them. Kluge's ideal cinema is not a monologue, but 'cinema as dialogue, as something the audience can respond to – and, in fact, not just respond, but *make* the cinema. There's more contained in the audience's heads, in their imagination, than a director can ever think of.'[10] This is a cinema that, to use a nice image of Kluge's, provides a 'climbing frame' for the imagination.[11]

What, then, does all this mean in practice? Kluge is under no illusions about the difficulties of winning audiences over to a new kind of cinema:

A dialogue with the real experiences of the audience demands a new filmic language, and this new language initially withdraws from the audience, because they're not used to it, and because all the rest of the language of film is stuck in the habitual grooves. . . . Anybody who has been wrongly trained at any time – in piano lessons, for instance –

knows that they need a bit of practice if they want to become 'natural' again.[12]

It is, for Kluge, important that the audience should behave 'naturally'. His reply to the many interviewers who have, politely but unmistakably, suggested that they found his films baffling is disarmingly simple: stop worrying, sit back and watch. Here again, Kluge's faith in the power of film to activate the audience's imagination is very much in evidence:

> A very easy method would be for the audience to stick to the individual shots, to whatever they happen to be seeing at any given moment. They must watch closely. Then they can happily forget, because their imagination does all the rest. Only someone who doesn't relax, who is all tensed up, who searches for a leitmotif, or is always finding links with the 'cultural heritage', will have difficulties. He's not watching closely any more. What he sees is semi-abstract and not concrete. It would be a help if he quietly recites to himself what he hears and sees. If he does that it won't be long before he notices the sense of the succession of shots. That way he'll learn how to deal with himself and his own impressions.[13]

Kluge is quite insistent about the vital role of the imagination and of the senses. The cinema cannot talk in abstractions, but must stick to concrete images. The individual case will take on meaning in the audience's minds; it is not the film-maker's job to try to formulate that 'meaning' in advance. Clearly for Kluge 'the truth' – as Brecht said – 'is concrete':

> In my opinion it's impossible to turn the cinema into an institution for moral education. People go to the cinema in order to be entertained, 'attentively but relaxed', as Walter Benjamin put it, in other words with a certain carefree casualness. If you take people's imagination, libido, and thirst for knowledge seriously, you can set their thoughts in motion. So I'm not trying to impart any abstract ideas about the Federal Republic, science can do that better. The general principles must be contained in the individual case. As soon as I stray from the concrete, I begin to talk gibberish.[14]

It is difficult to discuss Kluge's work on the basis of a neat filmography. It has much of the nature of an open-ended experiment: the material he shoots, and the material contained in his copious archives, may be re-used from one film to another, sometimes repeating, sometimes varying what has gone before; similarly, some films refashion entirely his earlier work. Kluge has been involved in the making of a score or so of films, in most cases – and particularly more recently – both as scriptwriter and director. About half of his films are shorts, and of the features only a handful have become well known. Kluge would almost certainly reject the idea of a hierarchy in his œuvre, but it is probably not unfair to say that the core of his work is made up of three feature films, each of them landmarks in the New German Cinema: YESTERDAY GIRL, ARTISTES AT THE TOP OF THE BIG TOP – DISORIENTATED, and OCCASIONAL WORK OF A FEMALE SLAVE.

Kluge's first film, made with Peter Schamoni in 1960, is a twelve-minute short called 'BRUTALITY IN STONE' (BRUTALITÄT IN STEIN), an investigation of the ideological implications of Nazi architecture. It is a film that already exemplifies remarkably well both the techniques and the theory of film-making that Kluge was to develop over the coming years. Its concern with Germany, with German history, and particularly with the Nazi years, is typical of most of Kluge's work, but more significant are the technical devices it uses for putting that concern across. In its attempt to capture the essence of the Nazi dictatorship by portraying the buildings and architectural plans of the period, it exemplifies perfectly Kluge's desire to present the concrete rather than the abstract, to approach the viewer through his senses rather than his intellect. Similarly in its suggestive mingling of texts, documents, and documentary footage it not only speaks 'for itself', but, as Kluge intended, to the viewer's imagination as well, stimulating associations and ideas.

BRUTALITY IN STONE was followed by a number of other shorts, including, in 1964, 'PORTRAIT OF ONE WHO PROVED HIS METTLE' (PORTRÄT EINER BEWÄHRUNG), which introduced one of Kluge's favourite genres, the character-sketch in which an individual is allowed, often ironically, to speak for him- or herself. In this particular case the subject is a (fictitious) German policeman who has, alarmingly, managed to serve loyally under six very different regimes. Later Kluge was to make analogous (though much more sympathetic) portraits of his grandmother and his father respectively in 'FRAU BLACKBURN, BORN 5 JAN. 1872, IS FILMED' (FRAU BLACKBURN, GEB. 5. JAN. 1872, WIRD GEFILMT, 1967) and 'A DOCTOR FROM HALBERSTADT' (EIN ARZT AUS HALBERSTADT, 1970). A similar family portrait followed in 1973 with 'A WOMAN FROM THE PROPERTY-OWNING MIDDLE CLASS, BORN 1908' (BESITZBÜRGERIN, JAHRGANG 1908). Apart from these shorts, whose titles all suggest their ambition to capture on film what portrait painters have traditionally captured on canvas, Kluge has included character sketches in many of his other films. Indeed, his main feature films are themselves at one level extended character portraits of their protagonists.

This is very much the case with Kluge's first feature, YESTERDAY GIRL (ABSCHIED VON GESTERN, 1966). The script for the film is based on the story 'Anita G.' from Kluge's 1962 prose volume *Life Stories*. Anita G., whose biography is that of a real woman Kluge heard about through a friend, is a girl of Jewish descent who arrives in West Germany from the GDR with no possessions but the clothes she stands up in and the suitcase that accompanies her wherever she goes. In an elliptical sequence of episodes that switch from fiction to documentary, from the surreal to the naturalistic, we see her stumbling through various encounters with the reality of life in the Federal Republic, to end up, an unmarried mother, in prison.

As the film begins, Anita is in court, accused of stealing a cardigan from a colleague at work. She is put on probation, and gets a job selling language-course records. It is not long before she is sacked by her boss, who hopes thus to prove to his wife that he was not having an affair with Anita. After a menial job in a hotel – from which she is again dismissed on suspicion of petty theft – Anita, now expelled from her lodgings too, has a fleeting affair with a student, and then decides to go to university herself. But this does not work either, as she has none of the requisite qualifications. Again she is unable to pay her hotel bills, and begins an affair with a certain Pichota, a senior official

YESTERDAY GIRL Alexandra Kluge as Anita G.

in the education ministry, who takes it upon himself to 'educate' her. When this relationship comes to an end as well, Anita, now pregnant, wanders the highways and streets, and then finally gives herself up to the police. In prison she helps draw up the dossier of the accumulated offences for which she is wanted in different parts of the country.

Such a bald summary does not do justice to the film. The narrative sequences, from which any summary must of necessity be gleaned, are intermittent and often highly oblique; the overall mood of the film is moreover less bleak than a mere recital of events suggests. Kluge uses many devices to break up and vary the progression of the narrative, as well as to distance the viewer. Firstly there are the intertitles that serve almost as chapter headings, but that are also comments on the events shown, set off in their turn by the verbal commentary that accompanies some sequences. Then there is the use of the sound track, with occasional discrepancy between sound and vision, and music that is often ironically inappropriate to the sequence it accompanies. The classic dramatic alienation device of a direct address to the audience is also used, together with more filmic devices such as speeded-up and surrealist sequences, and the insertion of illustrations – old photographs, books, and prints.

The narrative sequences themselves are sometimes carefully rehearsed, sometimes improvised, and in some cases even a 'candid camera' technique is used (as in the shot of Anita trying to sell her records to passersby in a shopping street). The typical Kluge-esque 'portraits' also occur, with the characters concerned self-consciously expounding their occupations and life stories direct to the camera. Sometimes these take the form of semi-documentary inserts, like the bizarre dog-training display to which Pichota takes Anita, and where the real centre of attraction is clearly the trainers themselves and their philosophy, rather than the dogs.

Holding all these disparate elements together is the figure of Anita G. She was played by Kluge's sister Alexandra, and her performance was immediately hailed as the best the post-war German cinema had seen. Indeed, when YESTERDAY GIRL was premiered at the 1966 Venice Film Festival, a straw poll among 82 critics selected Alexandra Kluge as the most outstanding female player, giving her 65 votes, as against nine for Ingrid Thulin, five for Julie Christie, and three for Jane Fonda. The amazing range of moods conveyed by Alexandra Kluge's expressive face is more than anything responsible for keeping the film above the potentially sentimental sombreness that the actual story line suggests. Anita G.'s fate is little short of tragic, but it does not *feel* tragic, such is the resilience and determination, the wide-eyed curiosity and vitality with which Alexandra Kluge shows her confronting her misfortunes.

What, then, is YESTERDAY GIRL about? Kluge has impressed upon us the perils of searching too earnestly for meanings in his films, but if, as he proposes, one lets the film work upon one's imagination, meanings do suggest themselves – and Kluge himself has not been too reticent, outside the film, or inside it for that matter. For a start, the German title is much more helpful than the English one. '*Abschied von gestern*' – 'Farewell to Yesterday', or, more clumsily but more accurately, 'Taking leave of Yesterday' – is an ironic comment on the relationship between past and present. It is confronted not only by the film itself, but by the quotation from Camus with which it opens: 'We are separated from yesterday not by a yawning abyss, but by the changed situation.' Here then is the film's 'secret' title; its ostensible one in fact refers to Anita's illusion. Like so many refugees from the East she has come to the Federal Republic naively expecting to 'make a clean break', to 'build a new life'. But, and this is a favourite theme of Kluge's, past and present are inseparable, for the past is the precondition of the present, and its weight is by definition inescapable.[15] Anita's family had suffered under the Nazis because they were Jews, and then after the war they suffered under the communists because they were capitalists.[16] Anita's past is that of an unwanted outsider, and that is what she remains in the present.

Kluge develops the theme of the inseparability of past and present not only at the individual level (we see photographs of Anita's childhood; memories of childhood Christmasses, and children's books and stories crop up; and there is always the nostalgic tango music sentimentally echoing the good old days); the theme is presented too at the national level, with the implication that individual history and national history are also inseparable, and both in this particular case are peculiarly German. YESTERDAY GIRL is thus also a film about West Germany, a society that has not taken leave of yesterday as much as it would like to think. The film's individual comments on West Germany are, at one extreme, flamboyantly grotesque, as in the dreamlike sequence in which two men, who have asked a mother which of her two children is to have its brain removed, proclaim: 'This system cannot be compared with any previous totalitarian system. That's what new about it.' (Again the false insistence that we have taken leave of the past!) Other sequences are more restrained, though still unambiguous, as in the dog display where the trainer proclaims the authoritarian philosophy of his profession: the dogs will be grateful to him, for only through training can they find freedom. And then there are the many shots that are allowed to speak for themselves by virtue of their visual impact alone. These come thick and fast during Anita's final odyssey through the Federal Republic, but one above all epitomizes her fate: Anita sits on her suitcase, alone on what is virtually a little meadow in the middle of the *Frankfurter Kreuz*, the great central intersection of the West German Autobahn network; the cars speed past silently all around, night is coming on, and overhead the planes come in to land at Rhein-Main airport.[17] It is not a positively hostile society, it is not even uncaring, for the people Anita encounters try, in their misguided ways, to help her. But none of them, including Anita herself, take account of the weight of the past. Kluge had begun with a monitory epigram from Camus, he closes with a utopian vision from Dostoevsky: 'Everyone bears the guilt for everything, but if everyone knew that, we would have paradise on earth.'

YESTERDAY GIRL, the first post-war German film to win an official award at a major international festival, marked the high point of the breakthrough of the New German Cinema that so suddenly occurred in 1966. It was, of course, not a 'commercial' film, though it did manage to attract impressively large audiences; time and again it was compared with Godard's work, and in particular with VIVRE SA VIE, and some critics went so far even as to confess that they found it not a little perplexing. Kluge's next film was to be even less 'accessible', and its title made it clear that he regarded confusion as by no means the prerogative of the audience.

ARTISTES AT THE TOP OF THE BIG TOP – DISORIENTATED (1967), which was made as a more or less spontaneous reaction to the violent rejection of Kluge's 'elitism' by radical students at the Berlin Film Festival, is one of the most difficult, but at the same time one of the most fascinating and suggestive films of the New German Cinema. It is a film that is moreover *about* the very difficulties with which it presents its audience: the first, and still really the only, film that both exemplifies and discusses the problems of 're-functioning' (to use a popular term of the period) an established and heavily commercialized art-form into something radical and subversive. A film, in other words, about the problems of the New German Cinema.

The story is that of Leni Peickert, daughter of a circus performer who died trying to perfect his art. Leni is determined to create a circus worthy of her father's memory – a *'Reformzirkus'* as it is called at one point. She makes little headway until an unexpected inheritance comes her way. But even though she now has the performers, the animals, and a location, she is still not sure they can realize her ideals. In the end she abandons the project without ever giving a performance, and decides to try her hand in television instead.

As with YESTERDAY GIRL, the narrative of the film is much less easy to follow than a brief summary suggests. The story is approached from many different angles, and with an even wider range of techniques, and is constantly intercut with extraneous material, some of it of no apparent relevance (speculations on the sex life of space travellers, for instance), whilst other sequences more clearly supplement and complement the main strand of events. One of the film's major difficulties is its failure to make clear just what Leni's *'Reformzirkus'* actually *is* – but this inability to define what she wants to do is of course a major cause of her own 'disorientation'.[18] The nearest thing we get to a statement of intent comes, characteristically, not from Leni herself, but from a woman reporter who has tried to summarize her plans: 'You want to involve the audience, you want to interest them. You want to see the audience feel itself really face to face with these animals, and not stupefied by dull sensations.' It is not exactly a concrete plan of action, but it does bear similarities with Kluge's own ideas about a reinvigoration of the cinema. What little we see of the abortive preparations once Leni has got her troupe together is even less enlightening: a routine *is* discussed, but, apart from the bizarre nature and vaguely revolutionary implications of many of the numbers, the '*Reformzirkus*' remains more of a grand ideal than a practical proposition.

The *difficulties* that Leni encounters are, on the other hand, much easier to pin down: they are partly artistic, and partly financial. The artistic problem is implicit in the film's title, and is elaborated in an opening caption, in the commentary to the film, and in a number of sequences, especially the early ones. The circus, we are told, came into being at the time of the French Revolution as a celebration of the limitless capabilities of the New Man. Many of the opening sequences are a homage to the great and not so great circus performers who have pushed their achievement to its absolute limits. But now an impasse has been reached: 'They had worked their way up to these heights. And now right up at the top of the big top they didn't know what to do next. Effort alone is of no use at all.' 'The inhuman situation,' we are told at another point, 'leaves the artist with no choice but to raise still further the level of difficulty of his work.'

The 'inhuman situation' that Leni encounters is made up of the harsh realities of capitalism: the need to have money if she is to start up a new circus, and the almost impossible task of winning over an audience whose tastes have been shaped by the commercial fare to which they are accustomed. Here too Kluge serves up some epigrammatic home truths: 'It's only as a capitalist that one can change that which is'; 'She cannot remain an artiste if she wants to be an entrepreneuse'; 'If the capitalist does what he loves and not that which is useful to him, then he gets no support from that which is.' The message is all too clear, and it is aptly ironic that Leni's millionaire friend Gitti Bornemann, whose sole heiress she becomes, is herself the daughter of the former head of a 'socialist research institute in Frankfurt' who emigrated in 1932 to the USA, only to find that he could make his way there as an entrepreneur, but not as a socialist.

The recurrent references to television underline all the more the implications Leni's crusade has for the cinema. Curiously, though, they also date the film: television in 1967 was still the enemy and not yet the partner of the West German cinema. Kluge, with some prescience, registers both the threat and the potential represented by television. The televised circus is not the ideal, but it is better than nothing. Quite early in the film we hear of Leni, 'She is prepared to make compromises, and has signed a contract with television.' It is a remark that one might expect to be made of a film director, and when Leni's earnest intellectual friend Dr Busch holds forth on the attractions of the televised circus as opposed to the 'real thing', his argument is precisely the one that was used time and again to explain the attractions of television compared with the inconvenience of the cinema. How can you expect people, he says, to bother to dress up, to go out, to pay, and to sit on a wooden bench at the circus, when they can see it all in the comfort of their own home on television?

Interwoven with the problems of the artist is a theme that had been central to YESTERDAY GIRL: the theme of time, of the past and of our memories of it. In fact the film opens with some old documentary footage of a Nazi rally, appropriately the 'Day of German Art' in 1939, which, with its medieval pageantry, looks back to an even earlier stage of German history.[19] This reminder of an even more disorienting time for German artists, the 'yesterday' of Leni's world, is accompanied by Kluge's whimsically appropriate choice of music: a Spanish version of the Beatles' song 'Yesterday'. The virtues of not forgetting, and in particular not forgetting the horrors of the past, are extolled in the image of the elephants, for whom Kluge manifests a singular affection and respect throughout the film.[20]

The temptingly simple equation 'Leni Peickert = Alexander Kluge' must, in the end, be rejected. For Kluge the film's conclusion shows a road he did not take:

Leni Peickert abandons her '*Reformzirkus*' before the premiere has even occurred because she realizes that the programme she has put together isn't going to sweep the audience off their feet. She doesn't want a '*Reformzirkus*' to damage the chances of the really utopian circus that she sees in her mind's eye. Time and again she seeks concrete ways out of the dilemma of having either to integrate or isolate yourself.[21]

As a pendant to ARTISTES AT THE TOP OF THE BIG TOP – DISORIENTATED, Kluge put together a sixty-minute film called 'THE INDOMITABLE LENI PEICKERT' (DIE UNBEZÄHMBARE LENI PEICKERT). First shown on West German television in 1970, it uses material that had originally been shot for ARTISTES, but reverses the progression of Leni's career as shown there: this time she begins in television, but is dismissed for smuggling in an uncensored film, and returns to the circus. Much less predictably, Kluge went on in the early seventies to make three science-fiction films: the two features 'THE BIG DUST-UP' (DER GROSSE VERHAU, 1970) and 'WILLI TOBLER AND THE WRECK OF THE SIXTH FLEET' (WILLI TOBLER UND DER UNTERGANG DER 6. FLOTTE, 1971), and the short 'WE'LL BLOW 3 × 27 BILLION DOLLARS ON A DESTROYER' (WIR VERBAUEN 3 × 27 MILLA. DOLLAR IN EINEN ANGRIFFSSCHLACHTER, 1971). Unusually for this typically a-political genre, they are films that reflect issues of modern capitalism in the milieu of space travel. They too were made as a reaction to the hostile reception Kluge had received from the students of the protest movement. They were, Kluge insists, not intended as a concession to popular taste, but were made in the relative peace and quiet of Ulm as a joint experiment with a number of collaborators – an experiment with a genre Kluge feels has great potential, but which has been little exploited in Germany.[22]

In 1973 Kluge returned to more familiar ground. OC-CASIONAL WORK OF A FEMALE SLAVE (GELEGEN-HEITSARBEIT EINER SKLAVIN) is in the line of YESTERDAY GIRL and ARTISTES AT THE TOP OF THE BIG TOP – DISO-RIENTATED: again the story of a woman's efforts to make her way in a more or less hostile Federal Republic. As in YESTERDAY GIRL, the lead role was taken by Kluge's sister Alexandra, who plays Roswitha Bronski, a young Frankfurt housewife. Roswitha runs an illegal abortion practice in order not only to keep herself, her children, and her offensively selfish husband, but in order to afford to have yet more children. Then things change: her abortion practice is closed by the police, and her husband, who had formerly stayed at home studying, gets a job as a chemist in a local factory. Roswitha rethinks her position, and decides to become politically active. She discovers that her husband's firm has secret plans to transfer its operations to Portugal, laying off its Frankfurt employees. Ros-witha's attempts to agitate among the threatened workers are of little avail: the firm decides independently not to close the Frankfurt plant. Her husband, moreover, is fired because of her activities, and Roswitha, like Pelagea Vlassova in Brecht's *The Mother*, ends up selling sausages wrapped in political pamphlets outside the factory gates.

Anita G. had blundered along without any clear plan; Leni Peickert had a plan but moved in a rarefied artistic realm; Roswitha Bronski, by contrast, has a plan and attempts to implement it in the everyday world. And yet, ultimately, like her two predecessors, she fails. Her failure is not tragic, nor is it patronisingly ridiculed as some feminist critics objected. Roswitha is very much a positive figure, spontaneous, alert, concerned; she stands out as the sympathetic heroine in a gallery of villains – again Kluge presents some delightfully satirical portraits of the representatives of the world of law, order, injustice, and hypocrisy. Roswitha's failure results from the application of all-too-human ideals to an all-too-inhuman reality.

OCCASIONAL WORK OF A FEMALE SLAVE is not primarily a film about abortion, although this was a major issue in West Germany at the time. There is, early in the film, a shockingly realistic reconstruction of an abortion, and this, combined with the major role played by Roswitha's work in these early sequences, led some to feel that this was the issue at stake. For Kluge, however, the real issue lies in the paradoxical relationship between Roswitha's activities as an abortionist and her role as wife and mother: she helps other women *not* to have families so that she can support and increase her own family. Kluge regards this as symbolic of the selfishness that for him is epitomized in the phenomenon of the family: protectiveness towards its own members, hostility towards outsiders. Or, as the commentary accompanying the opening image of the Bronski family looking out of the window at the snow puts it: 'Inside it's warm, outside it's cold.'[23]

The film is, then, primarily about the family, and in particular about Woman's role in a society based on the hermetic family unit. That role, the title proposes, is that of a slave – a kept, and unpaid, worker. Roswitha's mistake lies in her projection of the problems of her own condition onto the outside world; the film portrays

OCCASIONAL WORK OF A FEMALE SLAVE Franz Bronski as
Franz Bronski and Alexandra Kluge as Roswitha Bronski

Roswitha's actions, including her failure to make an
impact, which results from the fact that she transfers
her essentially private experience onto social struggles, and moves further away from the root of her
problems the more she becomes involved in the outside world.[24]

Yet despite – indeed, perhaps *because of* – her failure
and her lack of insight, Roswitha Bronski remains a
singularly appealing figure. Quixotic and mistaken she
may be, but one cannot help admiring the way she has

applied her zeal and determination to *practical* ends: a
fact that for Kluge makes her the most hopeful of his
heroines.

Although Kluge still uses his familiar techniques of
commentary, titles, intercutting, and montage, the
story of Roswitha Bronski is told less unconventionally
than those of Anita G. and Leni Peickert had been. OC-
CASIONAL WORK OF A FEMALE SLAVE was followed, however, by a film in which 'deconstruction' is taken to
new extremes. THE MIDDLE OF THE ROAD IS A VERY DEAD
END (IN GEFAHR UND GRÖSSTER NOT BRINGT DER MIT-
TELWEG DEN TOD), which Kluge made in 1974 with
Edgar Reitz, interweaves a number of disparate fictitious and documentary strands into a nightmarish
picture of life in the contemporary Federal Republic,

and in particular in Frankfurt am Main, where shots of the carnival celebrations are set off against the violent eviction of squatters by riot police. At the film's centre (if indeed it can be said to have a centre) is the story of a female spy who is sent from the GDR. Although her report is rejected by her boss as too 'lyrical', the impressionistic collage that makes up the film is, ironically, precisely the damning dossier he was hoping for.

At the end of OCCASIONAL WORK OF A FEMALE SLAVE a factory security officer, peering through binoculars at Roswitha's subversive sausage-stand, had uttered the priceless remark 'We regard these sausages as a threat to industrial peace'. The institution of 'works security' had already played a minor role in the science-fiction world of 'THE BIG DUST-UP', and in STRONG-MAN FERDINAND (DER STARKE FERDINAND, 1976) Kluge devotes a whole film to what he sees as one of the most alarming – because largely unheeded – growth industries in the Federal Republic. The Ferdinand of the title is an ex-policeman who is appointed to run the works security in a large factory. Ferdinand sets to work with paranoiac zeal, installing himself in a 'command centre' overlooking the factory floor, and even taking his little army of security officers on field combat exercises. Disappointed at the company's failure to appreciate his efforts (which have included arresting one of the directors), he goes out and shoots a government minister to prove to the world just how necessary security officers are.

STRONG-MAN FERDINAND is more or less contemporaneous with Schlöndorff/von Trotta's KATHARINA BLUM, and the two films are both expressions of concern at the excessive growth of the law-and-order mentality in West Germany in the 1970s. But whereas KATHARINA BLUM deals with already widely discussed issues, Kluge's film, in exploring the activities of *private* police operations, opens up new ground. A vast amount of research went into the making of STRONG-MAN FERDINAND, but it nonetheless lacks the documentary sequences familiar in most of Kluge's work – they would have been virtually impossible to make in any case, given the subject matter. In fact, STRONG-MAN FERDINAND lacks many of the characteristics that had come to be associated with the 'typical' Kluge film. The portrait of quixotic ambition, as exemplified in Leni Peickert and Roswitha Bronski, is now presented in a much more conventional narrative manner. But the combination of cool presentation and mildly zany contents remains. Ferdinand is a figure of fun, at once disturbing and hilarious; he is not, in that respect, in the same class as the sympathetic Anita, Leni, and Roswitha. What Kluge has done here is rather to place in the centre of his stage one of those figures who had previously occupied the satirical periphery of his films.[25]

KATHARINA BLUM was famously successful; STRONG-MAN FERDINAND was not. Although, more than any other of Kluge's works, it has all the elements of popular appeal, it made little headway in the cinemas. Kluge was furious: the blame, he claimed, lay with conservative cinema owners who either would not show it, or who withdrew it after only a few showings, despite good attendance figures. It is an all too familiar situation, another skirmish in the New German Cinema's struggle for recognition and support in the domestic market. That it should involve Alexander Kluge is not without its unhappy irony. The man who, more than any others, has represented and fought for the interests of the new directors, spoke in 1966 of the determination and vision that have guided his activities ever since:

I would fight to the end of my life to ensure that this kind of expression in the medium of film remains firstly necessary and secondly possible. Anyone who wants to put a stop to it is our enemy. . . . This fundamentally idiotic habit of telling the same stories over and over again, things that our senses already know, things that the audience has already been programmed for: it's nothing but contempt for the audience. Their imagination is much richer and goes far beyond the things we risk expressing.[26]

The setback with STRONG-MAN FERDINAND took much of the wind out of Kluge's sails: notwithstanding his grand proclamations of a decade before, he declared he had now had enough, and he was not going to make any more feature films. OCCASIONAL WORK OF A FEMALE SLAVE was prefaced with a declaration of faith in the cinema's abilities: 'Roswitha Bronski feels an enormous power within her, but she knows from films that this power really exists.' It is hard to believe that Kluge will keep to his threat for long.[27]

Straub and Huillet during the filming of MOSES AND AARON

3 JEAN-MARIE STRAUB

'Difficult' is one of the easiest epithets to apply to Straub's work; it is also, along with 'austere' and 'uncompromising', one of the commonest. And nor are the difficulties confined to the films: to locate Straub himself in the national context of the New German Cinema is much more problematic than is the case with the other major directors. Straub is in fact one of the most international of film makers. He was born and grew up in France, made his first films in West Germany, to which he moved in 1958 to escape conscription to the Algerian War, and since 1969 has lived and worked in Italy. Although he has made films with French and Italian dialogue, the bulk of his work has been in German, and he has often derived his material from German sources. The philosophical and technical aspects of his work too have roots in German Marxism

and in the aesthetic theories and dramatic practice associated primarily with Bertolt Brecht (though Straub himself has pointed out that he had at first read few of Brecht's theoretical writings).

The origins of Straub's association with the cinema are, however, very French, and a major part of his contribution to the New German Cinema has been his introduction into Germany of some of the spirit of French cinematic culture, and in particular the enthusiasm and analytical rigour of the *Nouvelle Vague*. Straub's home town is Metz, a city that, during his childhood, underwent at the hands of the occupying Nazis one of those periods of Germanization that have been a recurrent feature of the history of Alsace-Lorraine through the centuries. After the war Straub ran a film club there from 1950 to 1954 in an attempt to raise the miserable standard of the city's film culture. His ambition at the time was to write film criticism, and he would hitch-hike to Paris to see films, and to look in on various directors at their work. In 1954 he moved to Paris and worked as an assistant on a number of films for five of them: Abel Gance, Renoir, Rivette, Astruc, and Bresson. Bresson seems to have been *the* decisive experience for him, and of Bresson's films it was LES DAMES DU BOIS DE BOULOGNE, which Straub had earlier studied at his film club in Metz, that made the deepest impression. Straub himself lists Renoir, Lang, Murnau, Griffith, Grémillon, Mizoguchi, and Ford as equally important mentors, but the cool control, the minimalist visuals, sound-tracks, and acting techniques, the refusal to make concessions to the dictates of commercial appeal, that are the hallmark of Straub's much-cited 'austerity', reveal more than anything his overriding debt to Robert Bresson.

By the time of his move to Paris in 1954, Straub had decided he wanted not just to write about films, but to make them too, and he already had a specific project in mind: a film about Bach. Thirteen years and two other films were to intervene before the Bach project was finally realized. In the meantime in Paris Straub met Danièle Huillet, who was to become his wife and co-director. In 1958, threatened with conscription to the colonial war in Algeria, he left Paris for Germany, where at first he busied himself with gathering material for the Bach film. At the end of 1959 he and Danièle married and settled in Munich.

It was proving impossible to find financial backing for the Bach project: the thankless slog of fund-raising was to be the bane of Straub's life in the years to come. A friend in Paris had suggested that Straub should go and see the writer Heinrich Böll: he did, and he also began reading his works. He now decided to make a film of Böll's novel *Billiards at Half Past Nine*. Two years were spent looking for a producer, but again in vain. So Straub turned to a more modest project, a version of Böll's short story *Bonn Diary*, and it was this, under the title MACHORKA-MUFF – the name of its protagonist – that, released in 1962, was to be the first Straub-Huillet film.

The political thrust of Heinrich Böll's satire has been repeatedly directed at the post-war 'restoration' in West Germany, at the sorry resurrection of the military-industrial ethos in a country that, in 1945, had the chance to become the first country in Europe without an army. West Germany was rearmed against the wishes of much of the population, and Böll's *Bonn Diary* appeared in 1956, when the country's new armed forces were integrated into NATO. Straub had been a student in Strasbourg at the time, and felt his 'first bout of political rage' at what he saw as 'a rape, the rape of a country on which an army has been imposed, a country which would have been happier without one'.[1]

Colonel Erich von Machorka-Muff (the name translates roughly as 'tobacco fug') spends a momentous few days in Bonn: he is not only promoted to general, and able, after laying the foundation stone of the Academy of Military Memories, to clear at last the name of one of Hitler's marshals, but he also becomes the eighth husband of his aristocratic mistress, Inniga von Zaster-Pehnunz (*innig* in German means 'intimate' or 'heartfelt', and both *Zaster* and *Penunzen* are slang terms for 'money'). The story is clearly rich material for an elaborately satirical film. MACHORKA-MUFF, however, resists the temptation to self-indulgent caricature, and turns Böll's humorous character-portrait into a fast-paced, acerbic and spare little documentary. Machorka-Muff's commentary provides a kind of 'story-line' for the film, but it is a narrative that is almost peripheral to the little details picked up by the camera and the microphone, and the implications conveyed by the unaccustomed angles of the shots, and the combinations of sound and vision: the film is, in the words of the title sequence, 'an abstract-pictorial dream, not a story'. Machorka-Muff is a symbol of the restoration in West Germany, but we realize this not from what he *says* – he is indeed almost sympathetic in his sarcastic, wry cynicism – but from what he *is*: his role in this society is dubious in the extreme, and he moves through it with the disquieting smooth self-assurance of the reinstated 'rightful' rulers.

MACHORKA-MUFF had little critical or commercial success. Like Böll's story, it displeased the Right with its desecration of long-cherished virtues, but it also displeased critics on the Left, who felt that Straub, with his cool objective style, had missed the opportunity for parodying all that Machorka-Muff stood for. The selection committee for the Oberhausen Short Film Festival in 1963 – the year after the Oberhausen Manifesto – initially rejected the film, and it was only with great difficulty that the Straubs managed to get it shown at all in the cinemas.

Their next work, NOT RECONCILED (NICHT VERSÖHNT ODER ES HILFT NUR GEWALT, WO GEWALT HERRSCHT, 1965), again addressed itself to the darker side of German history, and again it was based on a work by Heinrich Böll. The novel *Billiards at Half Past Nine* (1959) is a classic study of what is called in German *die unbewältigte Vergangenheit* – the past that has not been come to terms with. It is a sombre portrait of half a century of German history as reflected in the lives of three generations of a Rhineland family. Although the foreground action is confined to a single day in 1958, much of the book is devoted to the characters' reflections and memories, which, in a complex and shifting pattern of narratorial devices, reveal a world where personal loss and sorrow are occasioned by political history, a peculiarly German history that has bruised and broken a whole nation down through the generations. The central figure of the novel, Robert Fähmel, cannot forget and cannot forgive; he refuses the easy way out of closing one's eyes to the past: he is, as he repeats, 'not reconciled'. 'Not Reconciled' was the title the Straubs adopted for their film, adding as a subtitle the desperate revolutionary insight of Brecht's St Joan of the Stockyards: 'Only violence serves where violence reigns' – a reference to the end of the film where Robert's 'mad' mother Johanna, placed in an asylum for her dissident humanity, fires a shot at a smug, time-serving politician who stands for all the things that Machorka-Muff had symbolized.

Just as Straub's first film had been the 'story of a rape', so, he stated, NOT RECONCILED was the 'story of a frustration, . . . the frustration of a people who had muffed their 1848 revolution, who had not succeeded in freeing themselves from Fascism'.[2] The theme of the fascism latent beneath the surface of *all* of Germany's recent history is Straub's central concern: 'by putting the past (1910, 1914, 1934) on the same level as the present, I have made a film which is a reflection on the continuity of Nazism both with what preceded it (first anti-Communism, then anti-Semitism) and what followed it.'[3] In doing so, Straub whittled away all that he felt superfluous and anecdotal in Böll's novel. *Billiards at Half Past Nine* was already an opaque and elliptical work, its ever changing patterns of consciousness determined by the very isolation of its characters, each locked up in himself, alone with thoughts and memories common to all but, tragically, openly confessed by none. Straub's reductionist technique resulted in a film that demanded even more of its audience, and offered them none of the comforting visual and oral entertainment they were accustomed to in the cinema. They were not amused, and at the premiere on 4 July 1965 there was uproar. Although the film was stoutly defended by a small group of admirers, it met with no commercial success, and was even threatened at one point with a destruction order by Heinrich Böll's publisher.

In 1967 the Bach project, with which Straub had intended to begin his career in 1954, was at last realized. Unlike MACHORKA-MUFF and NOT RECONCILED it was not based on a pre-existing literary text: THE CHRONICLE OF ANNA MAGDALENA BACH (CHRONIK DER ANNA MAGDALENA BACH) is a fiction – Bach's wife never wrote this journal of her marriage – but it is at the same time a most accurate documentary reflection of the last twenty-seven years of the composer's life. The film is partly a love story: 'a woman talking about her husband whom she loved unto his death'.[4] It is also a portrait of the struggles and sorrows of Bach's life: personal sorrows in the successive deaths of his children that punctuate the film, and public struggles for recognition and the barest means of subsistence. In this latter respect Straub sees parallels between Bach and himself: the

uncompromising artist hampered by a society that wants to be comforted rather than challenged. Indeed, Straub even called the film his 'contribution to the fight of the South Vietnamese against the Americans', drawing a parallel between the artist's fight for his right to integrity and the struggle for liberty in a broader political arena.[5]

Above all, THE CHRONICLE OF ANNA MAGDALENA BACH is a celebration of Bach's music, which is played throughout the film live and on original instruments: 'The point of departure for our CHRONICLE was the idea of attempting a film in which music is used neither as accompaniment nor as commentary, but as aesthetic material.'[6] To this end the film avoids the sentimentality and gimmickry of the conventional biographies of 'great composers'. Its technique is humble, modest, and cool; the musical pieces retain their integrity as music, and are played for themselves and often in their entirety. Structurally the film itself works like a classical composition, with shots and sequences ordered in a careful pattern that mirrors the world of Bach's work. There is of course an element of self-consciousness in all this, but this too is a deliberate device. For all the wigs, the costumes, and period settings, THE CHRONICLE OF ANNA MAGDALENA BACH is a record of twentieth-century musicians playing eighteenth-century music, and it makes no secret of the fact.

Perhaps because of the beauty and inherent attraction of the musical performances, the Bach film was much better received than the Straubs' preceding works, and it remains today probably the best-known of their films. Their next film, THE BRIDEGROOM, THE COMEDIENNE AND THE PIMP (DER BRÄUTIGAM, DIE KOMÖDIANTIN UND DER ZUHÄLTER, 1968), was a 23-minute short that grew out of a request by Fassbinder's *action-theater* that Straub should direct a play for them. In the event he put on Ferdinand Bruckner's 1926 play *Sickness of Youth* – but in his own pared-down version that reduced the two hours of the original to eight and a half minutes. Straub had, he proclaims, removed all meaning from the play: 'It simply shows relations whereas in Bruckner's play there is psychology – there one knows what it is all about – but in my piece there are only constellations, people who have certain relations with each other which dissolve and reappear.'[7] The *action-theater*'s barely-audible performance was

filmed in one take with a static camera placed at an angle to the minimal stage, on the back wall of which there is a partially illegible quotation from Mao Tse Tung, and the rest of the film was built up around this central sequence. It opens with a piece of graffitti the Straubs had discovered in the Munich post office. Inscribed presumably by the wife or the daughter of a G.I., it read 'stupid old Germany/ I hate it over here / I hope I can go soon / Patricia' – an echo of the Straubs own discontent with a society they were soon to leave. There then follows a long tracking shot along the dark Landsbergerstrasse, where prostitutes wait for their motorized clients. Then comes the play, and after it a wedding ceremony, followed by a slow pan across an empty field into which a car drives, a car chase, and finally, after some verses from St John of the Cross, a conclusion in which the comedienne of the title shoots the pimp so that she may be free to love her bridegroom.

Such an apparently arbitrary, chaotic, and meaningless film was hardly likely to endear the Straubs to an already sceptical public. THE BRIDEGROOM, THE COMEDIENNE AND THE PIMP has remained a little-known work, rarely performed, and even more rarely discussed. Yet for some it is Straub's masterpiece. Consider, for instance, Richard Roud's lyrical conclusion:

> Straub once said that the only truly mystical film was LES DAMES DU BOIS DE BOULOGNE. If by mystical he meant a film that achieves that exalted plane on which form *becomes* content, where the ethical and the aesthetic merge, and where the light from an open window brings to the human face an illumination that goes beyond all understanding, then there is now another such film: THE BRIDEGROOM, THE ACTRESS AND THE PIMP.[8]

At a more analytical level, Tony Rayns sees it as a film that

> broaches an extraordinary range of issues: the conventions of theatre staging, the form and syntax of narrative film, 'realism' and 'melodrama' as modes in both theatre and film, a specific socio-political situation in West Germany (vis-à-vis what was happening elsewhere in May 1968), the inherited weight of the nineteenth century's social morality in contemporary Europe.[9]

For Straub himself it was 'the most aleatory of my films and the most political', but it was also, he said, a 'film film'.[10]

It is this idea of a film not only about itself but about film in general that is taken up in a most illuminating article by Martin Walsh. For him the sequences in THE BRIDEGROOM are 'a meditation upon the . . . stylistic possibilities of the cinema and in their sequential organization they constitute the history of that cinema', a history that runs from the initially static, and then moving, silent and uncommented opening shots, which are like the birth of the cinema itself, through the filmed 'talkie' play and the 'thriller' chase, to the 'cinéma-vérité' wedding sequence. And then comes the final sequence that is the Straubs' very own:

> film art . . . in the course of these 23 minutes has evolved through its principal historical stages, until reaching its liberation in the materialist presentation that is Straub's own. The killing of the pimp is, metaphorically, the killing of German's (sic) decadent cultural heritage – the specifically German implication being raised in the graffitti that opened the film. . . . Straub has laid 'stupid old Germany' to rest, the cinema has been liberated from its stifling conventions, and the film's movement from the sordid opening to the celebratory close cements the significance of this new beginning.[11]

The 'new beginning' made little impact on the German cinema, and the following year the Straubs left to live in Italy, in the hope – soon to be disappointed – that there 'the power of the film industry would not be so entrenched'.[12] The first film they made in Italy was a new departure: it was their first colour film (though still shot in 16mm), and its dialogue was in French. It also had what must be one of the longest titles in film history: LES YEUX NE VEULENT PAS EN TOUT TEMPS SE FERMER OU PEUT-ÊTRE QU'UN JOUR ROME SE PERMETTRA DE CHOISIR À SON TOUR (1969). It was in fact a version of a little-known play by Corneille – *Othon* –

THE CHRONICLE OF ANNA MAGDALENA BACH Christiane Lang-Drewanz in the title ‮le‬

and that is the title that, for the sake of convenience, is usually given to the film as well.

Othon's complex plot deals with intrigues in ancient Rome, with personal and political relationships, above all with the tensions and confusions that link love and power. For Corneille the play's implications had strong contemporary relevance. Straub felt its relevance applied equally to the twentieth century, and cited in particular the power struggles that have characterized the history of post-war France. The title he chose is programmatic: it is a conflation of two quotations from the third act of the play, pointing to the possibility of a better future where the people, whose eyes cannot remain forever closed to the way things are, may become masters of their own affairs. The film remains faithful to Corneille's text, but, as one might have expected, the Straubs did not produce a conventional rendering *à la Comédie Française*. The actors do indeed wear togas, but no other concessions to tradition are made.

In the first place, only three of the actors were French native-speakers (Straub himself was one of them); the rest, mainly Italians, all spoke with a more or less pronounced foreign accent. Normally a director would use post-dubbing to overcome such a problem (especially in Italy, where post-dubbing is the norm for *all* films); for Straub, however, far from being a 'problem', the foreign accents were an integral part of the whole project: they were just one of the many 'alienation effects' to which he was subjecting Corneille's play. Not only did the actors have foreign accents, they also for the most part talked very quickly, in a staccato monotone, turning many of the speeches into a barely intelligible stream of sounds and rhythms. Intelligibility was further reduced by the fact that the film was shot – with original sound – out of doors: not among some tranquil Roman ruins, but in the heart of the modern city, with the sights and sounds of twentieth-century Italy, the cars and scooters, buses and planes, busy in the background.

Such a shocking demystification of an ancient Roman subject pointed the way to the Straubs' next film, which took as its text a work by the patron saint of the 'epic theatre', Bertolt Brecht; a text moreover set ostensibly in imperial Rome. *The Business Affairs of Mr Julius Caesar* was a fragmentary novel that Brecht wrote whilst in exile in Denmark in the late thirties. Both Brecht and the Straubs were interested in the contemporary relevance that a materialist approach could extract from the politics of ancient Rome, and for both the parallels between politics and business were particularly enlightening. Both of these themes are exemplified in HISTORY LESSONS (GESCHICHTSUNTERRICHT, 1972), in which the Straubs returned to German dialogue. As in OTHON characters in togas are seen against the background of modern Rome: indeed, they are confronted by a young man in modern dress, who interviews them. The film, which is built up out of the alternation of these interviews and three extensive travelling shots through the streets of Trastevere, shows how the façade of democracy is used to legitimate privilege and injustice. It is, according to Straub, 'all Marx, but . . . not from Marx';[13] about 'trade and democracy, that is to say in the last analysis about imperialism'.[14]

Shortly after HISTORY LESSONS the Straubs embarked on the first part of their 'Jewish Triptych', a fifteen-minute short entitled INTRODUCTION TO ARNOLD SCHOENBERG'S ACCOMPANIMENT TO A CINEMATIC SCENE (EINLEITUNG ZU ARNOLD SCHOENBERGS BEGLEITMUSIK ZU EINER LICHTSPIELSCENE, 1972). Described by Straub as his first 'agitational film',[15] it focuses on a piece by Schoenberg that bears the inscription 'Danger threatening, fear, catastrophe'. At its centre is the theme of anti-semitism – a letter by Schoenberg on the subject is read – illustrated with verbal and visual documents on fascism, capitalism, and imperialism.

At the centre of the 'Jewish Triptych' came another film based on a work by Schoenberg: the Straubs' 1974 version of the opera *Moses and Aaron*. Straub had seen the first stage production in Berlin in 1959, and immediately wanted to make a film of it, but a film that, in contrast to the production he had just seen, would be set in the open air. And that, fifteen years later, and after two years of preparation, was precisely what he and Danièle Huillet did: the setting chosen was the remote and barren countryside of southern Italy. Most of the action takes place in the amphitheatre of Alba Fucense, near Avezzano, with a few additional sequences by the Lago del Matese and three weird and beautiful panning shots of the band of fertile land between the Nile and the desert.

MOSES AND AARON Moses (Günter Reich) finally triumphs over Aaron (Louis Devos)

Within these locales the film shows the three-sided debate and struggle between Moses, Aaron, and the people, represented by the chorus. MOSES AND AARON (MOSES UND ARON) again makes no concessions to popular assumptions of what one may expect of the cinema: the characters' poses are statuesque, their disposition in the amphitheatre formal and geometrical; the sequences are long, and the individual shots too are lengthy and immobile. As the film proceeds, however, the 'austerity' is relaxed somewhat: there is more to look at in the way of events, things, and animals; and in the last sequence of all – a debate without music between Moses and the captive Aaron (lying at his feet in the mud) – the constricting circle of the amphitheatre has been left behind as the Promised Land is approached.

The struggle between Moses and Aaron for the leadership of the people takes on archetypal dimensions: it represents the polarity between the intellect and the senses, between mind and body, word and image. Moses' problem is to present a radically new and difficult concept to his people: the concept of monotheism and an invisible god. By so doing he can liberate them from bondage and lead them to freedom with a new sense of identity and pride. He is thus a revolutionary leader of an extreme and puritan kind – though not without his contradictions, for the film makes clear that the struggle is partly within Moses himself. The people are all too ready to fall back into the familiar, easy, and attractive old ways, and in this they are seconded by the 'revisionist' Aaron.

It is not difficult to see the relevance of this central theme of MOSES AND AARON to the Straubs' own lives and work: their new, sober, ascetic, and rigorous cinema must also constantly fight the temptations of the old, with its instant appeal and meretricious sensualism. That the theme has wider political implications is also apparent: Moses' problem is that of any revolutionary faced with the thankless task of winning a sceptical and unwilling people to a vision that offends the 'natural' norms they have absorbed. The Straubs undoubtedly had these associations in mind when they dedicated the film to their friend and colleague Holger Meins, who died in November 1974, shortly after the completion of MOSES AND AARON, as a result of a hunger strike; he had been in prison since June 1972 awaiting trial on charges of terrorist activity. The Straubs' handwritten dedication was later removed from the film at the insistence of the West German film censorship board and the television authorities.

The final part of the 'Jewish Triptych' was the Straubs' first film in Italian. FORTINI/CANI (I CANI DEL SINAI, 1976) is, according to Straub, 'something absolutely without precedent in cinema – a cinematographic essay'.[16] It is a film about the ideas and attitudes of the Jewish Italian writer Franco Fortini, and much of it is taken up with long sequences of Fortini reading from his book *The Dogs of Sinai*, an investigation of the attitudes of the Italian bourgeoisie to the Arab / Israeli conflict against the background of the fascist years and Fortini's own youth during that period. Fortini's stance is anti-Zionist, seeing in present-day pro-Israeli sentiment a most dubious anti-Arab racialism that is the old anti-semitism of the previous generation in a new guise. The readings by Fortini are interwoven with sequences that reflect and counterpoint his argument: a television news bulletin, articles from newspapers, a Jewish service, the streets of Florence, a dark seashore, and long peaceful shots of an Italian landscape – wooded hills with little villages, fields, vineyards, shimmering in the heat haze, silent but for the chirping of birds – but a landscape, we learn, where the Nazis had massacred resistance fighters during the war.

The Straubs followed FORTINI/CANI with another film built around the reading of a text. Fortini's argument is difficult to follow at a first viewing, but its opacity is relieved by the interposed 'contemplative' sequences that allow time for reflection. The French eleven-minute short EVERY REVOLUTION IS A THROW OF THE DICE (TOUTE RÉVOLUTION EST UN COUP DE DÉS, 1977) makes fewer concessions to the viewer's power of concentration. It is, quite simply, a reading of Mallarmé's notoriously 'difficult' poem 'Un coup de dés jamais n'abolira le hasard', but a reading this time by nine people. The setting is the Père Lachaise cemetery in Paris where, next to a plaque bearing the inscription 'Aux Morts de la Commune', the speakers sit in a semi-circle on the grass. Each speaker reads a section from the poem in an uninterrupted shot, and then at the end the camera looks out across a cityscape of modern apartment blocks.

EVERY REVOLUTION IS A THROW OF THE DICE has at least one thing in common with all the other films of Straub and Huillet: the fact that it is hardly designed to pull in mass audiences. Certain distinctive features were apparent from the outset in the Straubs' work, and subsequent films have brought not so much a 'development' in their work as an exploration of the applicability of their approach to different subject matter. That subject matter has been almost always supplied by pre-existing texts: only THE CHRONICLE OF ANNA MAGDALENA BACH has an entirely original script, but even that was made up out of various historical and biographical documents. In their choice of texts, Straub and Huillet have concentrated on works of a more or less historical import, sometimes works with contemporary subject matter, sometimes subject matter from

a previous stage in civilization. (In OTHON the text is at several removes from the audience: we are not just watching a 'film of a book', but a film of a seventeenth-century play which in its turn is based on the writings of Tacitus – themselves historical accounts of ancient Rome.)

In all the subjects treated by the Straubs the theme of power is central, its use and misuse in a more or less political context. Initially the subject matter of their films was ostensibly German, but German history is clearly used as a paradigm with much wider implications, as is the history of Rome, and then later that of the Jews. Subsumed beneath the general theme of power is a more personal element that surfaces most clearly in the Bach film and in MOSES AND AARON: the theme of the revolutionary, the revolutionary not just in a political sense, but the artistic innovator, the prophet without honour.

There is nothing unusual about such subject matter. What is of course unusual is the manner in which it is handled in the Straubs' films. The old debate – central to Marxist aesthetics – about the extent to which a radical message requires an equally radical package is exemplified in an acute form in these films, as well as in their reception by critics and filmgoers. It is partly a theoretical debate over the separability or otherwise of form and content, and it is partly practical: how *does* one put across one's ideas to a mass audience unless it be in a form to which that audience is accustomed? But what if that form implicates and reflects – and perhaps confirms – precisely the philosophy that one is trying to question? In the cinema there are few 'radical' film-makers who are able, or willing, to match their subversive messages with a filmic form that is equally subversive of the dominant tradition. Of the few who do, Jean-Luc Godard is undoubtedly the most often cited contemporary example, and one whose name is often linked with Straub's. Yet even Godard has made a name for himself with a whole series of (to use a term beloved of bewildered English critics) more 'accessible' films. Straub has not: he and Danièle Huillet have from the very beginning stuck uncompromisingly to their austere aesthetic.

This has meant films lacking in the readily digestible feast for the eyes and ears that audiences have come to expect of the cinema. At the visual level it has meant long-held shots and unconventional, 'off-centre' framing, as well as shots that often carry on until after the sequence has apparently 'finished'. It has meant a frequently immobile camera that often refuses to follow an action through in the way to which the audience is accustomed, a camera that often deliberately concentrates apparently inexplicably on 'peripheral' details. 'Background' elements also take on unaccustomed dimensions on the soundtrack: the noise of traffic, the chirping of birds, the cascade of a fountain, the hollow acoustics of an empty room are never 'doctored', but remain as reminders that the Straubs have always refused to use conventional post-dubbing and sound mixing techniques, whilst the 'foreground' dialogue is rarely allowed to assume the clarity and prominence of the conventional film: non-professional actors using unexpected tone, pitch, delivery, and accent all play their part in this.

It is hardly surprising that the Straubs' films have, as one of their strongest admirers readily admits, 'acquired a formidable reputation for opacity and tedium'.[17] Their career has been distinguished by a never-ending series of struggles with producers, distributors, and exhibitors simply to get their films made and shown, and with critics and audiences over their validity and value. Some dismiss the Straubs' films as simply incompetent, hasty and shoddy work cobbled together on inadequate budgets: an accusation to which Straub has reacted with indignation, pointing out that for NOT RECONCILED ten times as much film was shot as was finally used, whilst one scene alone was shot 31 times before they were satisfied with the result. From a French perspective, Francis Courtade explained Straub's opacity in racial terms: 'a native of Lorraine, he has moreover something very Germanic about him: the inability to put problems clearly, a love for the mists of abstraction.'[18] Other critics are more inclined to make accusations of sheer perversity: thus Dieter E. Zimmer, referring to OTHON, described the film as 'the winner in a competition to see who can hit a low-flying target in the most laborious and impracticable manner possible'.[19]

Zimmer was actually contrasting Straub most unfavourably with Schlöndorff, a comparison that is worth pondering, for between them – with Schlöndorff playing, as it were, Aaron to Straub's Moses – they are a paradigm of the divergent strategies of radical filmmakers: on the one hand the purist who insists that radical contents demand a radical form, on the other the entertainer who (and here there are close parallels with Fassbinder) operates within the conventions of the commercial cinema to spread his radical message more widely. Danièle Huillet's comments on Schlöndorff's KATHARINA BLUM are illuminating, for they go to the heart of her and Straub's rejection of the conventional cinema:

I think people who in twenty years' time look at films that have been made today, or people who come from another culture, won't understand them any more, because films like KATHARINA BLUM are made with a cinematographic code that is nothing but cinema. If you don't understand this code, then you have no idea what is going on. Just as you wouldn't understand the meaning of red and green on the road. We are trying to make films where people can understand what is happening even when they don't know this code.[20]

What the Straubs are attempting then is a 'deconstruction' of those conventions whose steady accretion has characterized the course of film history, leading the cinema ever further from reality. This means stressing the *documentary* element in film: each film is to be as accurate a document as possible not only of its subject matter, but also of itself – of the performance that went into its making. Inevitably this self-reflective technique invites the adjective 'Brechtian' and ideas of the 'alienation effect', and certainly Brecht's theories of the 'epic' as opposed to the 'Aristotelian' theatre offer. many parallels with the Straubs' vision of a new cinema in opposition to the old, even though Straub is careful not to be too closely identified with Brecht's ideas. There is a distinct element of puritanism in this recall to fundamentals, this aesthetic that Roud calls 'both Jansenist and Calvinist'.[21] The Straubs are quite deliberately trying to take the cinema back to its beginnings by eliminating 'all the artistic, filmic surface to bring people face to face with the ideas in their naked state'. 'The work we have to do,' Straub has said, 'is to make films which radically eliminate art, so that there is no equivocation.'[22]

The Straubs see their cinema as realist in the extreme, whilst the commercial cinema moves ever further from reality:

> Ten years ago . . . even the mediocre films from America . . . still had some links with reality. Now it happens less and less, and the films are getting more and more brutal and are trying to distance people further and further from reality – the gap between life and what is served up on the screen is getting bigger and bigger.[23]

'Deconstruction' means refreshing people's vision by refusing to satisfy the expectations they bring to the cinema, and by that very refusal making them aware of those expectations. It involves awakening people from stupidity, battling against 'the contempt, against the pimps of the film industry who believe, out of their own contempt and stupidity, that films are never stupid enough for the public'.[24] It is clearly an uncomfortable and unpopular process.

The Straubs' work raises many questions, and not least the question of its own effectiveness. The Straubs are under no illusions about the failure of their work to reach a mass audience – something, they feel, that can only be achieved on television. They blame this failure on the film distribution system, the commercial cinema that they see as having so besotted the audience that it becomes ever more difficult to get through to them.[25] They refuse to 'fight stupidity with stupidity',[26] yet there is precious little evidence that their way of 'fighting stupidity' is making any headway. Their films remain the preserve of a small band of converts. When one looks at the West German cinema over the past two decades one can only surmise that their influence has diminished. MACHORKA-MUFF and NOT RECONCILED were some of the first evidence of a radically new spirit abroad in the cinema. In the sixties there were many who looked to Straub for inspiration in their own work. Today the Straubs are still admired by many film makers, but few would want to emulate them. The big directors of the New German Cinema have drifted into precisely that mainstream that the Straubs so despise, and even they have as yet hardly attracted the mass audience.

4 VOLKER SCHLÖNDORFF

Like Jean-Marie Straub, Volker Schlöndorff belongs to the 'first wave' of the New German Cinema, and like Straub he came to the German cinema from an apprenticeship in France. Schlöndorff was born in Germany – in Wiesbaden in 1939, but his family moved to Paris in 1956, where he completed his secondary schooling and went on to study Political Science. During these student years he also studied at the Paris film school, the Institut des Hautes Études Cinématographiques. Here he met Louis Malle, and it was as Malle's assistant on ZAZIE DANS LE MÉTRO that he gained his first major experience of practical film-making. During the years from 1960 to 1964 he worked as assistant for a number of French directors, including not only Malle (whom he also helped with VIVA MARIA), but Melville and Resnais, assisting the latter with the directing of L'ANNÉE DERNIÈRE À MARIENBAD.

There are other outward similarities with Straub: a number of Schlöndorff's films, for instance, like most of Straub's, are in fact the product of a husband-and-wife partnership. Margarethe von Trotta, who married Schlöndorff in 1969, has both co-scripted and acted in his work, and was his co-director for THE LOST HONOUR OF KATHARINA BLUM. The critique of West German society contained in KATHARINA BLUM is part of a radical undercurrent that runs through all of Schlöndorff's work, and here too there are parallels with

Straub. But here too the parallels end, for any radicalism in Schlöndorff is restricted to the thematic level: at the formal, technical level it is hard to imagine two more different directors. Schlöndorff is not given to technical experiments, avant-garde mannerisms or innovations; his work is polished and entertaining, and his films contain in abundance the elements of audience appeal that Straub deliberately avoids. If Straub is (or was) to the German cinema what Godard is to the French, then Schlöndorff has been its Claude Chabrol. Schlöndorff's philosophy of film-making is unashamedly populist: 'I believe that it's only as a popular medium, as nickelodeon, that the cinema can really be justified.'[1]

Schlöndorff has accordingly long been one of the pioneers of 'commercial' developments in the New German Cinema. His A DEGREE OF MURDER, released in 1967, was, for instance, the first film by the new generation of directors to be made in colour.[2] It was followed by MICHAEL KOHLHAAS in 1969, which was, by a very long head, the first 'international' film of the New German Cinema: scripted by Edward Bond, with a cast made up of actors from Britain, France, Germany, and Czechoslovakia, MICHAEL KOHLHAAS was not only produced with American money – from the Columbia Corporation – but was actually made in English. Later in 1969, again in the vanguard of developments that soon came to typify the New German Cinema, Schlöndorff made a film for television – a version of Brecht's *Baal*. Perhaps the greatest vindication of Schlöndorff's popularizing approach to the cinema came in 1975 with THE LOST HONOUR OF KATHARINA BLUM, which not only managed to present sensitive major political issues to a wide audience, but was actually the first real commercial success of the whole New German Cinema. A similar box-office success seems likely for the six-million-mark version of Grass's *The Tin Drum* that Schlöndorff completed in early 1979.

Whilst assisting Resnais in Munich with the shooting of L'ANNÉE DERNIÈRE À MARIENBAD Schlöndorff read Robert Musil's massive novel of the decline of the Austrian Empire, *The Man Without Qualities*. On his return to Paris he assisted Pitoeff who was putting on a production of Musil's play *The Dreamers*, and it was there that he decided to make what was to be his first feature film: a version of *Young Törless*. Published in

1906, Musil's novel, set in a boarding school on the Slav fringes of the Habsburg Empire, reflects the crumbling of old values and beliefs as the twentieth century encroaches on an almost feudal world. The Törless of the title is a sensitive pupil who is drawn into uneasy complicity with two other boys who are subjecting one of their fellows to protracted and sadistic 'punishment' for a petty theft.

Musil's novel is a brief, but dense and intense study of a psychological crisis. Schlöndorff's adaptation – YOUNG TÖRLESS (DER JUNGE TÖRLESS, 1966) – is more forthright, and points up the political rather than the psychological implications of Törless's perturbations. His brief stay at the school takes from him the certainties with which he came and turns them into doubts: he learns that the borderline between good and evil is by no means clear, that men slip easily across it and are never permanently on one side or the other, and that all of us are capable of atrocities. Schlöndorff's critics found the message heavy-handed, and some condemned Törless's attitude as symptomatic of precisely that mixture of arrogance, indifference, and cowardice on the part of the intellectuals that enabled the atrocities of the Third Reich to occur – those very atrocities that Schlöndorff had seen prophesied in Musil's novel; the fact that Schlöndorff might actually be offering up Törless for our criticism seemed to escape those who condemned the *director* for the *protagonist's* behaviour. Some critics also had reservations about the unconvincing casting of Barbara Steele as a village prostitute, but one thing nearly all were agreed on, and that was the professionalism of Schlöndorff's technique. It was a piece of praise that was to be repeated many times in Schlöndorff's subsequent career, and there were other signs in the film that pointed to later developments in his work: notably the deliberate reduction of a complex literary text to a straightforward narrative, avoiding the temptation to find filmic equivalents for sophisticated literary devices. This was to be the approach Schlöndorff adopted to Böll's *Katharina Blum* and Grass's *Tin Drum*.

At one point in TÖRLESS, Beineberg, one of the two 'torturers', is sitting in a coffee house reading a newspaper report of a murder that turns out to have been an accident. This was the germ of the script for A DEGREE OF MURDER (MORD UND TOTSCHLAG, 1967), but this second film of Schlöndorff's, although it was also concerned with young people in crisis, seems far removed from the dark, austere world of the Austro-Hungarian boarding school. It is the story of a young waitress in contemporary Munich, who shoots her importunate lover and then engages two other young men to help her dispose of the body. At the time the film pleased its audiences and, on the whole, its critics, but today it looks derivative and shallow, making no attempt to parody or criticize the mannerisms it copies. The explanation for its contemporary appeal probably lies in its portrayal of the alienation and rebelliousness of young people in the guise of the manners of the 'swinging sixties': an image that undoubtedly flattered young German audiences with its implication that their country was also in the vanguard of the latest trends and fashions.[3]

As a historical document, however, A DEGREE OF MURDER is fascinating: it does indeed capture the mood of West Germany in 1967, the first year of that 'Grand Coalition' that so exacerbated the scepticism and sense of betrayal already vaguely felt by many of the younger generation. It was a year in which moral and social attitudes began to change – too quickly for some, not quickly enough for others. It was canny of Schlöndorff to engage Brian Jones, the former guitarist of the Rolling Stones, to write the music for A DEGREE OF MURDER, for the Stones, their way of life, and their music were a symbol, albeit a heavily commercialized one, of youthful disaffection. Schlöndorff's film has a number of little sequences that remind one of the very German outrage with which the older generation greeted the new casual attitudes that were emerging among the young (attitudes that were equally German in the thoroughgoing nature of their casualness): a little incident where upright citizens indignantly point out the protagonists have parked at a forbidden spot, or the nicely observed reactions of a family on the Autobahn when they discover that the car with which they have had a minor collision contains representatives of that Younger Generation of which they have clearly read lurid accounts in the popular press. Totally unnerved, they quickly take the generously proffered money and run.

But A DEGREE OF MURDER documents something else too, and that is the uncomfortably ambiguous attitude adopted by Schlöndorff, and many others at the time, to the youthful revolt of the late sixties. There are in fact parallels here with the much-criticized attitude of Törless to the events around him. The glamourized image of the 'lovable outsiders' à la Bonny and Clyde, who find no place in the boring constraints of the ordinary world, squares uneasily with the desperate melancholy and emptiness, redeemed only by occasional flashes of vitality, that Schlöndorff's 'bande à part' actually experience. It is a prescient ambiguity on Schlöndorff's part, anticipating later developments not only in his own work, but in German society as a whole; the romanticization of rebellion is, however, very much a product of its time. A DEGREE OF MURDER may not be a first-rate film, but it does fulfil the expectations Schlöndorff had of it even before its release:

I hope that in our work, in our words and gestures something that typifies the present time will be expressed. Analysis is not the aim. The object is something like the American action-films of the thirties, which, filmed in studios, deliberately avoided all contemporary references, and yet today tell us more about how it felt to be alive then than many documentaries do.[4]

The theme of rebellion and the reactions it provokes in a distinctively German context is, from A DEGREE OF MURDER onwards, the central theme of all of Schlöndorff's work. More specifically it often takes the form of rebellion by women, and in three of his films, A DEGREE OF MURDER, THE MORAL OF RUTH HALBFASS, and THE LOST HONOUR OF KATHARINA BLUM, he shows women driven to homicide as a result of the abuse they have suffered at the hands of men. In a short contribution to the Franz Seitz production THE KETTLE-DRUMMER (DER PAUKENSPIELER, 1967) – no connection, despite the similar title, with THE TIN DRUM – Schlöndorff, in a Kluge-like quasidocumentary, reconstructs the tragic outcome of what started as a playful rebellion, when a young boy takes potshots from an upstairs window with his father's gun. A crowd begins to gather, rumours spread, uncomfortably intolerant sentiments are voiced; the press are there, the fire brigade and police arrive, and now the boyish prank becomes a trial of strength with the massed representatives of law and order. The commentary-over, which had begun humorously, turns to dead earnest as the end approaches: the little boy, terrified and blinded by tear gas, shoots himself for fear of punishment. It all happened, we are told, in Munich, at number 3 Donnersbergerstrasse, in March 1964.

AN UNEASY MOMENT (EIN UNHEIMLICHER MOMENT), as Schlöndorff's little episode is called, is about the fatal ludicrousness of German over-reaction to innocent deviance: a remarkably close anticipation of ideas and even actual sequences to be developed seven years later in KATHARINA BLUM. In MICHAEL KOHLHAAS (MICHAEL KOHLHAAS – DER REBELL, 1969) he again portrayed over-reaction, but this time over-reaction on the part of the rebel. In his adaptation of Kleist's story of 1810 about the sixteenth-century horse dealer whose grievance at a petty injustice escalates into wholesale war on the entire social order, Schlöndorff presented material that looked very much like an allusion to contemporary events in West Germany. Terrorism was not yet an issue in 1969, but the student revolt was, and the film's references to closed universities and rioting students could hardly be overlooked. Schlöndorff himself was unwilling to be drawn, insisting that the story was not at all political, pointing out that it contains no abstract or analytical dialogues, but nonetheless conceding that one might even see the student leader Rudi Dutschke as a kind of Kohlhaas, and offering his own political verdict on Kohlhaas's rebellion:

Kohlhaas fails, because he tries to fight a system as an individual – something he could only manage as part of a collective movement. The necessary awareness of the historical situation was simply non-existent then.[5]

'Whoever seeks justice outside the laws of the state is a rebel' would, Schlöndorff proposed, make a good motto for the film.[6] One might, with hindsight, equally propose the subtitle of Böll's *Katharina Blum*: 'How violence can arise, and what it can lead to.' Kohlhaas indeed becomes dismayed at the violence, destruction, and terror his campaign has unleashed, for the movement he has begun gets out of hand and slips from his control. Here too, there seem to be close parallels with those many supporters of the West German protest

movement of the 1960s who were to watch aghast as their civil-rights campaign slipped into terrorism – although Schlöndorff at the time felt that Kohlhaas had not been radical *enough*: 'Kohlhaas founders over the compromise the state offers him. He accepts the proffered reform. And so he forfeits his terror effect and loses all influence.'[7]

For all its remarkable political relevance, MICHAEL KOHLHAAS had been conceived of initially as an entertaining 'action film' with the Western-sounding title 'Man on Horseback'. Schlöndorff had read Kleist's story in Mexico, while working on VIVA MARIA, and hit upon the idea of filming in Europe an exciting action-packed adventure of the sort normally associated with more distant lands. The international cast and team, the American backing and distribution, and the English dialogue, were all meant to ensure a commercial success. In retrospect, Schlöndorff feels the venture to have been a failure. Certainly in his desire to make use of international stars he sadly miscasted the daintily glamorous Anna Karina as Kohlhaas's wife (an error of judgment similar to the employment of Barbara Steele in TÖRLESS), but his principal doubts about the film are more fundamental, and of major import not only for his subsequent work, but for the whole New German Cinema. The problem with KOHLHAAS was that much of its potential power lay in its Germanness, and in the attempt to internationalize the film that strength had been lost:

A film should be as concrete as possible. That means that a German film, precisely in order to be competitive at the international level, must be especially German. I don't believe you can produce films synthetically by gathering together the best components from all over the place, and then thinking that you'll end up with something worthwhile.[8]

It was an important lesson, and one that Schlöndorff has not forgotten. When he came in 1978 to make his biggest film ever, THE TIN DRUM, he consciously avoided the temptation to gather a star cast together and make an 'international' film.

Another rebel, again from German literature, was the subject of BAAL (1969), a television adaptation of Brecht's early, semi-expressionist portrait of a sensual libertine. Schlöndorff's is a latter-day Baal, a kind of hippy drop-out, who haunts the fields and wrecked-car lots on the edge of Munich, wreaking social and emotional havoc with the bourgeois world whenever he comes in contact with it. Now deliberately avoiding star casting, Schlöndorff chose a relatively unknown young German actor to play the part: a certain Rainer Werner Fassbinder.

→ Fassbinder had a minor role in Schlöndorff's next film, THE SUDDEN FORTUNE OF THE POOR PEOPLE OF KOMBACH (DER PLÖTZLICHE REICHTUM DER ARMEN LEUTE VON KOMBACH, 1970). This was Schlöndorff's contribution to the 'kritischer Heimatfilm', of which there was a flurry in the early seventies. The Heimatfilm was a favourite German genre, idyllic, trite, and sentimental, presenting idealized portraits of country life. Schlöndorff and a number of other directors, quite independently of each other, made use of the popular rural setting to present a radical analysis of the true conditions under which country people – and others – live. As a token of his serious intentions, Schlöndorff made the film in black and white, telling the story (which is based on an old chronicle) of the oppressed peasants of Hesse who, in 1822, after five unsuccessful attempts, finally managed to rob the coach that so provocatively carried a coffer of money past their wretched village every two weeks. Their sudden wealth, of course, soon gave them away, and they were sentenced to death.

Although there are elements of the adventure film, of the Western even, in this tale of the conception, execution, and consequences of the waylaying of a passing coach, Schlöndorff is more interested in the desperate circumstances of the peasants that drove them to this hopelessly ill-conceived piece of rebellion. Above all it is the mentality of an oppressed people, who have internalized the very world-view that oppresses them, that Schlöndorff explores. His film shows how education, folklore, and religion all serve to blind them to the true nature of their enslavement. Their only possible escape seems to be to the promised land of America (one tenth of the population of Hesse emigrated in the nineteenth century, the commentary tells us), or into a never-never land of dreams, like the goosegirl who has heard that even the likes of her sometimes marry princes. The idea of concrete political change is simply not available to them. The robbery brings a brief mood of liberation

as the peasants prance and dance in the woods where the fabulous coach passes, but once they are caught they admit and rue their 'guilt', even mercilessly beating the one among their number who is unrepentant. They see only a crime in what they have done, and not a revolutionary act. Like Schlöndorff's other historical films, THE SUDDEN FORTUNE OF THE POOR PEOPLE OF KOMBACH has strong contemporary implications, touching as it does on the much-debated topic of the 'manipulation of consciousness', and on what was now becoming the acute issue of defining the borderline between criminal and political violence.[9]

THE MORAL OF RUTH HALBFASS (DIE MORAL DER RUTH HALBFASS, 1971) is Schlöndorff at his most Chabrolesque. Originally called 'The Wife', the film was inspired by an actual case, a sex-and-murder scandal in Düsseldorf known as the 'Minouche Affair', which, to the delight of the popular press, turned into a protracted trial that lasted for two years.[10] Schlöndorff sets his film among the nouveaux riches of the Frankfurt area, and manages some neat and witty digs at the contemporary mores of the trendier levels of West German society. The hills around Frankfurt are peppered with the villas of the new West German financial and industrial ruling class, and it was a milieu that particularly fascinated Schlöndorff:

These characters out of the popular magazines. They're not in the least bit evil, they're just naive and lacking in all culture. All they have is money. That's the difference between this Rhine-Main society, for instance, and the French haute bourgeoisie in Louis Malle's LE FEU FOLLET. There there's intellect and taste. Here there's just enormous luxury.[11]

This is a setting that Schlöndorff was to make use of again in KATHARINA BLUM, though there a veneer of culture seems to have crept over the wealthy milieu with which Katharina has connections. There are other links with KATHARINA BLUM too. Among all the deception and skulduggery of RUTH HALBFASS there is one innocent character, a minor figure who is abused by the others, all of whom totally ignore her feelings. Doris Vogelsang, the betrayed wife of Ruth Halbfass's lover, is the only real victim of the whole affair. Like Katharina Blum she takes recourse to a pistol in an attempt to avenge her outraged honour. Her victim, Ruth's husband Erich, in fact recovers; Doris, however, hangs herself in prison.

Doris Vogelsang is a tragically peripheral figure in THE MORAL OF RUTH HALBFASS. In SUMMER LIGHTNING (STROHFEUER, 1972) Schlöndorff places a woman in the centre of the stage in a film that anticipates by some years the feminist themes taken up by female directors in the second half of the seventies. Margarethe von Trotta plays a young woman called Elisabeth Junker during the uncomfortable period that elapses between her divorce and her remarriage. Her time is devoted to finding a role in life, a job, and fighting for access to her son Nikki, who is indignantly withheld from her by her ex-husband. From the outset – the opening shot shows her riding to the divorce court on her moped and being hooted at by an impatient (male) driver – Elisabeth finds the dice are loaded against her as a woman. Unable to find work that provides more than the most meagre income (let alone any dignity), she is obliged to adopt a lifestyle (second-hand Volkswagen, flat shared with a pregnant friend) that falls short of her husband's (smart new executive saloon, luxury villa). This in turn, in the eyes of the Law, makes her an unsuitable custodian for her son. When a new woman moves in with her husband the Law does not object: he has a big house, and the lady in question is a trained nanny; every independent action by Elisabeth, however, is taken as evidence of disorderly living.

SUMMER LIGHTNING is far from being a cold theoretical tract, however. It sparkles with humour and wit, not least at the ludicrous side of Elisabeth's plight, and even in the delightful interlude in which the Swiss Marxist Konrad Farner takes Elisabeth and her friend on a tour of the Alte Pinakothek to illustrate his theory of sexism in art, there is irony in the old man's own avuncular sexism: 'Keep beautiful, that's the main thing you must do', is his parting advice. Elisabeth gains some insight from her trials, but not enough, and the film is not just a critique of her society, but an explanation and a critique of her as well. She fails to appreciate that she actually invites treatment as an object with her miniscule skirts and dresses, and the wig she wears. She fails too to appreciate the machismo of Nikki's cowboy clothes and shooting games, and when, in the end, she falls in love with – and in – Italy,

she is quite oblivious to the fact that this sentimental idyll is an even more male-dominated world than Germany.[12]

Elisabeth's enlightenment is only partial, but her tribulations at least are relieved by laughter and a resilient sense of the sheer absurdity of it all. The next feature film that Schlöndorff made – this time with Margarethe von Trotta as co-director – was again to be about a young woman who is rudely awakened to the crueller realities of the world.[13] But for Katharina Blum there was to be no way back, no laughter, and no Italian idyll.

By the mid seventies sections of the right-wing press in West Germany had managed to generate a widespread popular mood of insecurity and near hysteria: a totally disproportionate overreaction to the terrorist activities attributed to the Red Army Faction. Much of the responsibility for the backlash that has soured West German public life in recent years lay with Axel Springer's *Bild-Zeitung*, the most widely read and most sensational of the country's daily papers. *Bild*, never at a loss for vilificatory innuendo, set out on a witch hunt, not for the terrorists, but for the men and women behind them, their alleged supporters and helpers: the 'Sympathisanten', as they soon came to be known. A democracy as unsure of itself as West Germany was easily panicked, and the unsavoury practice of 'sniffing out' the opinions of all and sundry spread with alarming speed from the commercially motivated sensationalism of the mass press to the computer banks and questionnaires of efficiency-minded bureaucrats. Now not only were 'Sympathisanten' to be identified and pinned down, but any possible advance of that 'long march through the institutions' that Rudi Dutschke had enjoined upon the students of the late sixties as the only alternative to the chimera of violent revolution was to be resolutely blocked.

Bild's gleeful philistinism led it to look especially carefully at the country's artists and intellectuals on its regular 'Sympathisanten'-forays. Heinrich Böll seemed an ideal target. Böll had had the temerity to write an article in *Der Spiegel* criticizing *Bild* for the irresponsibly hysterical coverage it was giving to the activities – real and imagined – of the 'Baader-Meinhof Gang'.[14] Heinrich Böll, winner of the Nobel Prize for Literature, a tireless campaigner for decency, humanity, and

moderation, became henceforth the target of a concerted and sustained campaign of denunciation, innuendo, and abuse: a campaign that was not without effect in official quarters too, for the whole Böll family were soon to join the other victims of police raids, searches, and phone tapping.

Böll's response was, typically, to write a novel, *The Lost Honour of Katharina Blum, or how violence can arise, and what it can lead to.*[15] The novel sets out to answer the question how it is that an innocent young woman, who goes out one evening to a harmless party,

can four days later become a murderess. The answer is quite simple: Katharina has been the victim of a vitriolic and mendacious onslaught on her dignity and integrity in the mass press. Katharina Blum is a shy, retiring young woman, who takes back to her flat one Ludwig Götten, a young man she has met at a carnival party. The next morning her flat is surrounded and invaded by scores of armed police, but Ludwig, whom they are seeking, has, with Katharina's help, escaped in the night. Eventually he is arrested in a holiday cottage belonging to a wealthy, and importunate, acquaintance of Katharina's. Götten's only crime, it appears, is to have deserted from the army, taking with him the contents of the regimental safe. Katharina, in the meantime, has been quickly adopted as ideal shock-horror-scandal material by a popular newspaper called the '*Zeitung*'. Overnight she becomes known to mil-

THE LOST HONOUR OF KATHARINA BLUM The public face: the distraught Katharina (Angela Winkler) is displayed like a captured wild animal for the benefit of the press photographers

The private face: Katharina is interrogated by Inspector Beizmenne (Mario Adorf)

lions as a terrorist and a whore; her life is wrecked, her friends are implicated, and her ageing and ill mother dies of shock. In the end, in outrage and desperation, she shoots the journalist responsible for her ruination.

Heinrich Böll actually sent a copy of the proofs of his story to Schlöndorff and von Trotta before the book appeared, and they were immediately impressed. The book, however, is whimsically complex in style and structure, and, with Böll's active collaboration, the story was simplified into a more or less straightforward chronological narrative for the script of the film.[16] The emphasis of the contents was also changed: now the police play a more important role, and in particular the irascible Inspector Beizmenne, who, working hand in glove with the reporter Tötges, is determined to find proof for what he is convinced from the outset is Katharina's unquestionable guilt. Between them, the police and the press manage quickly to mobilize a third group of persecutors against the hapless Katharina: the most frightening persecutors of all, the general public, to whom Katharina has been presented as 'The Murderer's Bride', and who respond with open insults and ostracism, harrying her with threatening letters, pornographic pictures, and obscene telephone calls.

The political themes of THE LOST HONOUR OF KATHARINA BLUM, as if they were not clear enough already, are pushed well and truly home in the film's tailpiece (which has no counterpart in the original book): a deliberately satirical portrait of the lavish funeral of the journalist Werner Tötges, who is described, with unintentional irony, as 'a victim of his profession'. Here, amid a gathering of bloated and smirking worthies, the owner of the *Zeitung* delivers a peroration in which cliché after cliché about 'freedom of opinion', 'pluralism', 'nipping in the bud', and that shibboleth of official acceptability, the 'freedemocraticbasicorder', all come tumbling forth. The speech concludes with the resounding warning: 'Whoever attacks the *Zeitung* attacks us all.' And then comes a final satirical disclaimer: 'Any similarity with certain journalistic practices', reads a concluding title, 'is neither intentional nor coincidental. It is inevitable.'[17]

Many critics of THE LOST HONOUR OF KATHARINA BLUM felt that not just this tailpiece but the whole film had been too polemical, and had sacrificed the subtlety of Böll's original for over-simplistic black-and-white

characterization. All, however, praised the superb conviction with which Angela Winkler played the title role.[18] Simplification may have been a deliberate device to give the film more 'audience appeal', but there were other devices too: the thriller element is played up, intrigue and mystery are major elements, and the brief love affair between Katharina and Ludwig takes on a decidedly sentimental air. At any rate, the film worked, it was an immediate success, attracting not only critical attention, but bigger audiences and more revenue than any other film of the New German Cinema. It was by any standards a remarkable achievement: here was a film that dealt openly and explicitly with the most sensitive issues of contemporary German politics managing to reach an audience of the size that had hitherto seemed accessible only to the blandishments of the very press that it pilloried. In the long run, though, the outcome was more sobering: the problems broached in KATHARINA BLUM did not, of course, disappear as a result of the film; if anything, they became more acute. And then, in September 1976, it was Schlöndorff's turn to be labelled in the Springer press as a 'Baader-Meinhof *Sympathisant*'.[19]

With the money made from THE LOST HONOUR OF KATHARINA BLUM, Schlöndorff went on to make a very different kind of film. COUP DE GRÂCE (DER FANGSCHUSS, 1976), based on the 1936 novel by Marguerite Yourcenar, is his least 'commercial' work, a quiet, sober film, made in black and white, and set in the wintry landscapes and dingy interiors of a Baltic estate after the Russian Revolution, where an old aristocratic family is stubbornly refusing to face up to its own demise. It is a portrait of bitterly restrained characters, filled with locked-up emotions and unspoken sorrows that spring from the social code they have inherited and the historical events that have overtaken them. Of all of Schlöndorff's films, this is the one that reverts most closely to his first work, the YOUNG TÖRLESS he had made over a decade before. Both films were shot in eastern Austria, and in both the settings alternate between the open landscape and the sombre, claustrophobic interiors. In both there is too a sense of febrile decadence, of the imminent breakdown of a once proud aristocratic world, of the end of the unsteady German-speaking colonization of the Slav fringes of Europe.

COUP DE GRÂCE Valeska Gert as the Aunt and Magarethe von Trotta as Sophie von Reval

COUP DE GRÂCE picks up themes from Schlöndorff's intervening films as well. The central figure of the film is a woman, Sophie von Reval, played by Margarethe von Trotta, a complex character, a proud aristocrat who sides with the Reds, and who, at her own insistence, is finally shot by the man she loves. It is through her that the film moves from the untypical world of YOUNG TÖRLESS to enter the mainstream of Schlöndorff's work. Sophie is a woman in the tradition of Elisabeth Junker, of Doris Vogelsang, and Katharina Blum. Indeed, she is a rebel in the tradition of all of Schlöndorff's protagonists, and his description of COUP DE GRÂCE could well apply to all of his work: it is, he says, 'the story of a humiliation that ends with a revolt'.[20]

There had been another woman in the male-dominated world of COUP DE GRÂCE, a cackling, sinister, witch-like old aunt, played by Valeska Gert. Schlöndorff was evidently fascinated by the old cabaret artist he had unsuspectingly engaged for the role, and in January 1977 he visited her little cottage on the Frisian island of Sylt to film an interview with her. This became the sixty-minute portrait JUST FOR FUN, JUST FOR PLAY (NUR ZUM SPASS – NUR ZUM SPIEL. KALEIDOSKOP VALESKA GERT, 1977), in which she comes across as an endearingly naive and highly eccentric old woman. Here, Schlöndorff found, was a living link with the fabulous Berlin of the twenties, a link with the early German cinema (she had played, for instance, with Greta Garbo in THE JOYLESS STREET, and in Pabst's THREEPENNY OPERA), and when, in the spring of 1978 he learnt of her death, he wrote: 'Valeska Gert – barbaric art – German art. Simplicissimus, Breughel, not

Expressionism, but Realism: grotesque and irrational, unfettered by the constraints of Naturalism'.[21]

It was a description that could well be applied to Günter Grass's novel *The Tin Drum*, and Schlöndorff was aware of that, for he was at the time, having completed his contribution to GERMANY IN AUTUMN, in the middle of the hectic preparations for what was to be his – and the German cinema's – biggest film yet. When *The Tin Drum* appeared in 1959 it was immediately hailed as a decisive breakthrough in German post-war literature; today it remains one of the great novels of the twentieth century. It is the story of three decades of German history, but history seen not with the all-encompassing, analytical vision of the historian. Instead Grass presents history from below, history from the thick of things, history as experienced by people rather than by historians. The result is chaotic but vivid, a sensuous kaleidoscope of what life was like for ordinary Germans before, during, and after the Second World War: a history all the more real for its deliberate avoidance of abstractions, even such apparently essential ones as 'National Socialism', 'Anti-Semitism', or 'Nationalism'.

Günter Grass had been approached many times with proposals for a film of *The Tin Drum*. The script offered by the Munich film producer Franz Seitz was the first he found at all acceptable, and this was the one that provided the basis for Schlöndorff's film. There remained a major problem: the hero of Grass's book is a bizarre character called Oskar, a midget with quasi-magical powers, a fanatical beater of toy drums, a rebel from the word go, who at the age of three hurls himself downstairs to prevent himself growing up into that adult world he observes with such devilish perspicacity. Quite by chance Schlöndorff discovered, through a doctor in Munich, that the actor Heinz Bennent, who had played the part of Katharina Blum's lawyer Blorna, had a twelve-year-old son whose physical stature was that of a four-year-old. Schlöndorff had already decided that the part could not be filled by a dwarf: the necessary audience identification would be hard to establish. Günter Grass, moreover, was insistent that Oskar had long been misconceived by *The Tin Drum*'s public: he was not a gnome, but simply a child who had ceased growing. And so it was that young David Bennent – of whom Schlöndorff said it was his eyes, not his

Oskar (David Bennent) as drawn by Günter Grass, complete with drum and eel

size, that made the biggest impression – became the star of Germany's biggest film. (His father too had a role: as Greff the greengrocer.)

The filming of THE TIN DRUM (DIE BLECHTROMMEL) took place in the summer and autumn of 1978. The setting of Grass's novel had been his native Danzig, and many sequences were shot on location there – though, to spare the Poles the cruel indignity of Nazi marches and parades, other sequences were made in Yugoslavia, France, and West Berlin. The result was a mammoth Fellini-esque spectacle of some two and a half hours' duration, made up, true to the episodic structure of the novel, of what Schlöndorff described as 'tableaux' strung together like 'numbers in a variety act'.[22] Oskar's perspective lacks totally the intellectualizing and moralizing sensitivity of the adult's view: he sees, hears, smells, touches, and tastes everything, with no distinction of 'good' and 'bad', 'public' and 'private', 'decent' and 'obscene'. From three feet above the ground in a shabby backstreet of a far-flung corner of Hitler's Reich he experiences the whole of human life, and a traumatic chunk of German history. One thing Schlöndorff did not attempt, however, and that was to film the third part of the book, which sees Oskar at large in the Rhineland of the Occupation and the early Federal Republic:

> The post-war period, Oskar Matzerath in Düsseldorf, that would be a second film, with a different actor. Something for later. Those years I remember myself, the fifties, why not indeed make a film about them, a 'TIN DRUM, PART TWO'?[23]

Just how much Schlöndorff's tongue was in his cheek remains to be seen; at any rate the idea is in keeping with the commercial orientation of his cinematic philosophy. What is most interesting about THE TIN DRUM (Part One?) is the very German-ness of this film that, by the modest standards of the New German Cinema, is little short of a blockbuster. Like Grass's novel, it derives its strength from the concreteness of its historical and social setting, a strength that accrues *because of*, rather than in spite of, the very provinciality of that setting. Schlöndorff's subject matter has always been German, and his favourite theme, the theme of rebellion, has always been examined in distinctively German circumstances.[24] The years in France not only taught him how to make films, but, Schlöndorff says, 'with all those people addressing me with the words "You as a German" . . . I became aware for the first time of my German identity'.[25] Volker Schlöndorff, the most commercial of the new German directors, is at the same time a determinedly German film-maker. He has not forgotten the lesson of MICHAEL KOHLHAAS:

> At the beginning of '77 I made two journeys. One to the West, to California, to Hollywood. The other to the East, via Moscow to Central Asia, to Tashkent. In Hollywood I discussed projects offered to me on the strength of the success of KATHARINA BLUM, so-called international films. In Tashkent I presented and discussed German films. Margarethe von Trotta, Martje and Werner Herzog were there too, as we saw our films with Usbek eyes. After this pendulum swing from West to East I was more determined than ever to stick to my centre – in spite of possibilities elsewhere, in spite of difficulties here. Ever since TÖRLESS I have quite consciously made German films.[26]

THE TIN DRUM Oskar and family: Oskar's mother (Angela Winkler) and his 'Polish father' (Daniel Olbrychski) look on as his 'German father' (Mario Adorf) tries to wrest the precious drum from him; Oskar's response is to emit his first glass-shattering cry

5 WERNER HERZOG

The epithets used to describe the films of Werner Herzog invariably emphasize the critics' feeling that they have been impressed by something that goes beyond rational analysis. Certain adjectives recur time and again: some pick on the sheer intensity of his work and resort to such terms as 'obsessive', 'fanatic', 'titanic', 'apocalyptic', 'holy', 'demonic', or 'awesome'. For others there is a visionary element in Herzog that conjures up notions of the 'mysterious', 'surrealist', 'fantastic', 'dream-like', 'irrational', 'otherworldly', 'bizarre', or the 'eccentric'. One thing they all seem to agree on: Herzog is a poet among film-makers, his films are 'magical', 'haunting', and 'mysterious' – or, quite simply, 'filmic'.

The critics' much-rehearsed epithets are in many cases apt not only for Herzog's films, but equally for the elements out of which they are made: their actors, their landscapes, their music, and the life and personality of Herzog himself. Herzog is indeed something of an 'eccentric' in the New German Cinema in that he has from the very beginning produced every one of his films himself. And the beginning of Herzog's interest in filming lies a long way back: he wrote his first script at the age of 15, and was already trying to make his first film (on penal reform) at 17. From the outset his involvement with film has certainly been nothing short of 'obsessive' and 'fanatic', and it is fitting that a major documentary study of him has as its title his remark 'My films are what I am'.[1] But there is another aspect to the 'eccentricity' and 'fanaticism' of Werner Herzog, and that lies in his life itself, the things he has done, the places he has visited, the people he has met: all experiences that have become inextricably bound up with the films he has made.

Herzog was born in Munich on 5 September 1942; his legal name is in fact Stipetić, after his Yugoslav mother; his father, Herzog says, was 'a sort of *clochard*'. He grew up on a farm in a remote part of Bavaria, a farm behind which there was 'a deep ravine and a mystical waterfall'. He hated school, and set off, at the age of 18, on the first of his many journeys to far-flung corners of the world: in this case to the Sudan, where he was badly bitten by rats whilst lying ill for five days in a deserted barn. Back in Germany he worked nights in a Munich steelworks for two years to save money for film-making. A scholarship took him to Pittsburgh, but he was expelled from the United States, and for a while made a living smuggling arms and television sets across the Mexican border.

Hazardous and strenuous visits to exotic places were to become a hallmark of Herzog's film-making. The stories behind the shooting of his films are every bit as amazing as the films themselves. FATA MORGANA was shot in the Sahara, where Herzog contracted bilharzia, and in Central Africa where he and his crew encountered floods and sandstorms and were repeatedly thrown into crowded, rat-infested jails on suspicion of being mercenaries; in the end they had to abandon their vehicle and equipment when the borders were closed. The short LA SOUFRIÈRE took him to the crater rim of a volcano whose apparently imminent eruption had led to the evacuation of half of the island of Guadeloupe. And, equally in the face of local warnings, for the closing sequence of HEART OF GLASS he took his crew on open boats through stormy seas to the precipitous and barely accessible Skellig Islands off the Atlantic coast of Ireland. Even in the apparently innocuous countryside of Holland, Herzog managed to get himself into a violent and almost fatal confrontation with the locals whilst shooting NOSFERATU. But without doubt the most famous of Herzog's filmmaking exploits came in the shooting of AGUIRRE, WRATH OF GOD, which involved a gruelling trek with all his crew, cast, and equipment – some 500 people in all – into the depths of the Peruvian jungle, an expedition that culminated in a by now almost legendary battle of will between Herzog and the notoriously temperamental star of the film, Klaus Kinski, who was only persuaded not to walk out on the project when Herzog turned a gun on him.

The characters in Herzog's films are always people *in extremis*, people under pressure, people who are in some way 'abnormal' or 'eccentric'; they too are 'visionaries' or 'fanatics'. 'You learn more about the shape of a town from its outskirts than from its centre,' Herzog says. 'Those who people my films are often marginal, not at the centre of things. But they are not freaks. They are aspects of ourselves . . .'[2] People interest him 'when they are on the point of breaking apart, when they become visible at the cracks',[3] an apparently morbid fascination that he justifies with the following analogy:

If you are a scientist and want to find out about the inner structure of some matter you will put it under extreme pressure and under extreme circumstances . . . People under extreme pressure give you much more insight about what we are, about our very innermost being.[4]

The borderline between fact and fiction, between the events behind the films and the films themselves is just as difficult to draw in the case of Herzog's characters as it is in the case of his own life. Herzog has a remarkable capacity for finding extraordinary people, hardly any of them professional actors, to play in his films. People such as Fini Straubinger and the other deaf and blind characters of LAND OF SILENCE AND DARKNESS; the dwarfs of EVEN DWARFS STARTED SMALL; Ahmed the exile Turk in SIGNS OF LIFE (Herzog named his son after him); the ski-jumper Walter Steiner who gambles with death as he explores the furthest reaches of human ability; 'Hombrecito' (he did not know his real name), the Indian flute-player in AGUIRRE, a feeble-minded Peruvian beggar who was at first unwilling to leave the market place in Cuzco, where Herzog found him, for fear that the people would die if he stopped playing – so taken with Hombrecito was Herzog that he dedicated the film to him.

The best-known of Herzog's extraordinary characters is Bruno S., whose role as Kaspar Hauser made him one of the best-known figures in the whole New German Cinema. Bruno S., who later played the lead in STROSZEK, was himself something of a Kaspar Hauser character, having been abandoned by his prostitute mother at the age of three, spending the following twenty-three years in various institutions, mental homes, and correction centres, and eventually being 'discovered' by Herzog working as a lavatory attendant in Berlin. The uneasy suspicion that perhaps these characters are being exploited, that their treatment in Herzog's films is little better than that of freaks in a circus, is something Herzog will not accept: his answer to such criticisms comes in KASPAR HAUSER, where not only is the 'simple' protagonist unambiguously the hero of the piece, but where one sequence actually shows what the circus treatment really means, with Kaspar, Hombrecito, and the 'midget king' Helmut Döring degradingly displayed in a travelling fair.

Herzog's first three films were shorts, shot with a 35mm camera that he 'expropriated' from an institution that refused to lend him one – a camera that he eventually used in AGUIRRE as well. Herzog is often regarded as a singularly earnest film-maker, though in fact there is wit and humour in nearly all his work. In HERAKLES (1962/65), an ironic and sceptical study of 'muscle men', and 'THE UNPARALLELED DEFENCE OF THE FORTRESS OF DEUTSCHKREUZ' (DIE BEISPIELLOSE VERTEIDIGUNG DER FESTUNG DEUTSCHKREUZ, 1966), in which four young men play over-zealous war games, humour is very much to the fore – more so, certainly, than in later feature films such as SIGNS OF LIFE and AGUIRRE which develop further the 'titanism' theme of

HERAKLES and DEUTSCHKREUZ. Between the two came a film, 'PLAYING IN THE SAND' (SPIEL IM SAND, 1964), that Herzog has never released for public viewing, but which, he says, is about 'a chicken in a cardboard box, and children'.

'Chickens,' Herzog added, 'terrify me. I'm the first person to have shown that chickens are cannibalistic and horrifying.'[5] Bizarre little sequences involving chickens certainly crop up in a number of his films, including his first feature, SIGNS OF LIFE (LEBENSZEICHEN, 1967). Shot on Crete and the island of Kos (where Herzog's grandfather had spent many years as an archaeologist), based on Achim von Arnim's early nineteenth-century story *The Mad Invalid of Fort Ratonneau*, SIGNS OF LIFE portrays the 'madness' that befalls a German soldier called Stroszek, sent in 1942 to convalesce with his Greek wife and two other soldiers on an island that lies outside the combat zone. The soldiers are given the task of 'guarding' a useless munitions dump in an old castle overlooking the harbour. Time passes, little happens, the sun beats down, the cicadas hiss and scrape remorselessly, and then one day Stroszek goes beserk. He chases the other three from the castle, fires guns into the air and at the town, where he kills a donkey on the quay. Like the townspeople, the camera retreats, and we see him now only as a tiny figure dashing and clambering frantically to and fro in the castle grounds. Declaring himself commander-in-chief of the Eastern Mediterranean, Stroszek proceeds to use the munition dump to provide the town with awesome firework displays, attempting to 'make the earth shake', and to 'set the sun on fire'. Eventually he is captured and taken away, as he had arrived, on the back of a lorry.

SIGNS OF LIFE already bears many of the hallmarks of Herzog's later work. There is firstly the landscape: as so often in Herzog the landscape seems to dwarf the people who move through it; as in paintings by Van Gogh it threatens and oppresses, driving them to the brink of madness – and beyond. Then there are the characters, who already amply reveal Herzog's penchant for the odd, the bizarre, the outsiders: here in particular those who are in some way separated, like Ahmed the Turk who has lived for ten years on the island away from his family; a gipsy king who wanders Europe in search of his people; a little child in a lonely shepherd's cottage who has no friends and hardly speaks as a result; a little boy whose only remark is, 'Now that I can talk, what shall I say?'. There are the favourite Herzog images, above all images of circularity, which climax here in a stunning wide panning shot of a landscape filled with myriads of identical turning windmills – the vision that causes Stroszek finally to snap. And there is the character of Stroszek himself: like Aguirre, one of Herzog's 'titanic heroes', talked of in sad admiration in Herzog's concluding commentary-over (the quiet, terse commentary itself being a recurring feature of Herzog's earlier work): 'In his rebellion against everything he had begun something titanic, for his adversary was hopelessly stronger. And so he had failed miserably and wretchedly like all of his kind.'

SIGNS OF LIFE was followed by a short film that again made use of the Greek island setting: 'LAST WORDS' (LETZTE WORTE, 1968) investigates the story of a hermit, an old man who for years had lived alone on a deserted island, and who had been fetched back to 'civilization' by two policemen – obviously an attractive subject for Herzog, and one that directly anticipates the story of Kaspar Hauser. 'MEASURES AGAINST FANATICS' (MASSNAHMEN GEGEN FANATIKER, 1968) was a quirky, zany little film of no great consequence (including, incidentally, some footage of the goalkeeper Petar Radenkovic, whose autobiography provided material for Handke's *Goalie's Anxiety at the Penalty Kick* – Herzog himself is a keen football player).

For his next two films Herzog went to Africa. THE FLYING DOCTORS OF EAST AFRICA (DIE FLIEGENDEN ÄRZTE VON OSTAFRIKA, 1969) is a documentary in which Herzog, typically, shows himself fascinated by the clash between the 'science' and 'civilization' of the doctors, and the 'irrational', 'senseless', 'uncooperative' responses of their patients, which Herzog, far from mocking or criticizing, presents with humility and respect. FATA MORGANA (1970) is one of Herzog's – and the New German Cinema's – most remarkable films, a non-narrative documentary poem in which Herzog weaves together sequences shot in Central, West, and East Africa in 1968 and '69. Landscape shots predominate, above all the arid landscapes of the Sahel and the southern Sahara. They are shots deliberately lacking in polish: the pans are often jerky, the cuts abrupt, the focus blurred. Herzog dwells on the patterns, form and feel of the desert and the villages, often using camera movements to create extra effect, as in a particularly beautiful sequence where the travelling camera makes sculpted sand dunes cross and sway like a human body. Many of the landscapes, though, bear the marks of Man's presence: oil wells, decrepit and derelict buildings, shanty towns, dead cattle, hangars, sheds and dumps, wrecks and debris.

FATA MORGANA was originally conceived as a science-fiction film about a doomed planet. It takes place, according to Herzog, 'on the planet Uxmal, which is discovered by creatures from the Andromeda nebula, who make a film report about it'.[6] In its final form it is structured as a three-part myth, with sections entitled 'The Creation', 'Paradise', and 'The Golden Age' respectively. The creation myth that lies behind it comes from the Quiche Indians of Guatemala, and their account of the origins of the world is read in a commentary-over by Lotte Eisner.[7] It is a myth with a sombre ending: the human race is drowned, 'for they had no intelligence'. Certainly the human beings in FATA MORGANA are not very prepossessing examples of the species, and that is particularly true of the white men seen. As the film progresses, Man's presence becomes more intrusive: we see giggling tourists, a frogman holding up a turtle, a zoologist obsessed with lizards, a German woman standing in water teaching African children to recite (in German) 'Blitzkrieg is madness', and, most ridiculously, and most cruelly, of all, an appallingly tuneless singer-cum-drummer accompanied by a determined middle-aged woman pianist on a minute, parsimoniously-festooned stage.

With the progressive intrusion of human beings, the film becomes increasingly self-conscious. The sights, the music, the commentary, and the occasional dialogue, which at first had been knit carefully together, become more unravelled and discrepant. Humour plays a greater role, the commentary becomes more ironic, the characters are held up for almost painfully close and lengthy inspection, but at the same time their awareness of the camera becomes more apparent, and some even begin to play to it. The film's successive stages portray, both in what they show and how they show it, the intrusion of mind into matter, of Man into the primeval landscape. But there is no heroism here,

nothing of the marvelling at the human spirit of WOODCARVER STEINER, LAND OF SILENCE, or KASPAR HAUSER. Man here is, more than anywhere in Herzog, an object of ridicule, a fault in the scheme of things, meaningless like the 'fata morgana' of the title: an indeterminate little object that is seen three times, ill-focussed, floating aimlessly against a shivering horizon.

This bleak view of human pettiness is carried over into EVEN DWARFS STARTED SMALL (AUCH ZWERGE HABEN KLEIN ANGEFANGEN, 1970), whose cynical title is a wicked put-down of human aspiration. This is the story of a rebellion in a penal institution on a barren volcanic island: in fact Lanzarote, shots of which are also used in FATA MORGANA, and whose mingling of the African and the European is reflected in the two striking pieces of music that accompany the film: on the one hand a powerful, wailing Canary Islands folksong (sung by a thirteen-year-old girl whom Herzog recorded in a cave), and on the other hand an African mass from the cathedral of a self-styled Messiah on the Ivory Coast. What gives the film its distinctively unsettling edge is, of course, the fact that all the cast are dwarfs: 'It's a world in which objects have taken on a life of their own and grown monstrous. It's not the dwarfs who are the monsters, but a doorknob or a chair, they've got out of all proportion.'[8]

We know that their rebellion is doomed from the outset, for the film begins with the interrogation that follows its collapse. It is an ugly and aimless rebellion that becomes ever more anarchically destructive and brutal. They destroy crockery and eggs, chop down and burn the director's favourite palm tree, throw food around, burn petrol in plant pots, and hold a mock Christian procession with a monkey held aloft on a cross – a monkey that was the pet of two blind fellow inmates whom they brutally tease. (The blind dwarfs' grotesque welding goggles also appear in FATA MORGANA.) The pointlessness of it all is aptly captured in another of those Herzog images of circularity: in this case an old van that for nearly half the film turns endlessly round and round in the yard, remorselessly demolished and then finally destroyed by the rebel dwarfs. (Herzog uses this same image again at the end of STROSZEK.)

Herzog has often been likened to Buñuel, a comparison he is not too fond of, but one that here more than anywhere else in his work seems inevitable. As Tony Rayns puts it:

> This bunch are low on redeeming social merit. They are mean, petty, vulgar, selfish and destructive, just like Buñuel's recurrent beggars; men and women as confused and undirected as most of the world, trapped in the thought if not the manners of the society that has rejected them as criminals and deviants.[9]

And yet for all the grimness of Herzog's savage little tale, the director's attitude is not critical: the dwarfs as individuals are engaging characters, their antics and their shrieks of delighted laughter hover between the frightening and the infectious. Throughout the film the uneasy Herzogian humour is always at work.

Herzog's next two films were unambiguously humane. 'IMPEDED FUTURE' (BEHINDERTE ZUKUNFT, 1970) and LAND OF SILENCE AND DARKNESS (LAND DES SCHWEIGENS UND DER DUNKELHEIT, 1971) are both documentaries about people who are conventionally termed 'disabled'. 'IMPEDED FUTURE' examines the situation of the physically handicapped in the Federal Republic, whilst LAND OF SILENCE AND DARKNESS is a portrait of 56-year-old Fini Straubinger, who went first blind and then deaf as a child, and was then bedridden for thirty years. Now she helps others in Bavaria who are similarly afflicted to come to terms with their lives. Both films are gentle, patient studies of a whole succession of what the town clerk in KASPAR HAUSER would call 'cases', individuals at worst rejected, at best condescendingly 'treated' by society. As in KASPAR HAUSER, Herzog's message speaks for itself: these people are not 'cripples', they are not inferior; there is an intensity about their lives that asks questions of *us*, the 'normal' ones.

For AGUIRRE, WRATH OF GOD (AGUIRRE, DER ZORN GOTTES, 1972) Herzog returned again to an exotic setting, this time to Peru, to the precipitous Urubamba valley, and the remote Huallaga and Nanay rivers among the jungles of the upper Amazon. Here, in the face of formidable difficulties, he filmed the fictitious story of the rebellion of the conquistador Lope de Aguirre, who, sent out on a reconnaissance expedition, refuses to return to Pizarro's army. Instead, by murder

and intimidation, he gains control of his party, installing the effete Guzman as his puppet 'Emperor of Eldorado', and declaring himself the all-conquering 'wrath of God'. Battered at first by rapids, later becalmed, Aguirre and his cowed cohort drift downstream on a raft. Steadily a collective madness of despair grips them all; disease, starvation, and the poisoned arrows of the forest Indians take their toll, until at the end the crazed Aguirre remains alone on his raft with a dream of marrying his now dead daughter, and founding the purest dynasty there ever was to rule the whole of New Spain.

AGUIRRE was conceived from the outset as a more commercial film than any Herzog had made before. It was to be a film with more 'action', a film with more 'surface', with more audience appeal. In the event it has indeed turned out to be one of his most popular films, and the explanation may well lie in the way Herzog has pushed his fascination with landscape and the character of his 'titanic' hero to new extremes. Visually it is magnificent, often beautiful, sometimes overwhelmingly so. The opening sequence is breathtaking, as, to the ethereal music of Popol Vuh, the heavily-laden expedition is seen, at first in extreme long-shot, later in close-up, painfully threading its way down a precipitous mountain path, from the misty heights above to the steamy jungle far below. The closing shot is equally famous, as the camera closes in on and then circles round and round the demented Aguirre, standing defiant on his becalmed raft, now invaded – in ultimate mockery of his imperial pretensions – by hundreds of little death's-head monkeys. In between these two sequences, the sights and sounds of the tropical river, from the terrifying roar of the rapids to the sinister utter silence of the lower reaches, broken only by the sudden mocking cries of animals and birds, are conveyed as incident after incident draws the hapless expedition to its doom.

Pitted against the relentless majesty of the primeval landscape is the equally relentless will of Aguirre himself. With his fierce, contemptuous face, his glaring maniac eyes, and his demonic swagger, he is the real

AGUIRRE, WRATH OF GOD Aguirre (Klaus Kinski) and his dying daughter Flores (Cecilia Rivera)

titan among Herzog's heroes, a rebel obsessed with the idea of betrayal, a visionary adventurer adrift on a *bâteau ivre*. But the sheer grandiosity of Aguirre's madness is too dangerously close to the ludicrous to be presented in dead earnest. In fact Herzog avoids a potentially ruinous tumble from the sublime to the ridiculous by injecting unambiguous humour into the film: he deflates the tragedy of death with quirky last words such as 'Long arrows are becoming fashionable', uttered by a man killed by the Indians, and such wilful grotesqueries as a head that carries on counting after it has been chopped off. But underlying the whole film is a much more significant humour that stems from, and points up, the discrepancy between the painfully preserved trappings of European civilization (above all the two elegantly robed women – Aguirre's daughter, and the mistress of Ursúa, the deposed leader) and the brute, vulgar realities of life in the jungle. It is a discrepancy that runs through all of Herzog's work, here specifically an implicit critique of the vanity of imperialist 'conquest', everywhere a quizzical vision of the glory and the folly of human aspiration.

With THE GREAT ECSTASY OF WOODCARVER STEINER (DIE GROSSE EKSTASE DES BILDSCHNITZERS STEINER, 1974) Herzog presents for the first time a real-life figure in the tradition of the soldier Stroszek and the conquistador Aguirre – but now without laughter (unless it be in the figure of Herzog himself, who appears as a breathless, excited reporter, leading one critic to suggest 'The Great Ecstasy of Steiner-fan Herzog' as a more suitable title[10]). Prepared for a television series called 'Frontier Posts', this 45-minute documentary must be one of the most beautiful pieces of sports reporting ever made. It is a study of the world ski-jump champion Walter Steiner, by profession a Swiss woodcarver. Concentrating on a competition in the Yugoslav resort of Planica, Herzog (who himself once had ambitions as a ski-jumper) shows Steiner before, during, and after his jumps, in public and in private, both in training and in the competition. The much-vaunted slow-motion and stop-motion shots, rendered all the more unworldly by the strains of Popol Vuh, capture the superb grace of the ski-jumpers' 'flight', as well as the desperate agony of their falls. Steiner is very much a man *in extremis*, alone with his ambitions, his fears, his dreams, pushing forward the frontiers of his achievement – and of human experience – in an ever re-negotiated private gamble with injury and death.

The story of Kaspar Hauser has long exercised a fascination over German writers that has led to its exploitation in various novels, poems, and plays – most recently in Peter Handke's *Kaspar* of 1968. It is a compelling tale, both at the level of simple mystery as well as for the intriguing social, psychological, and philosophical issues it raises. Kaspar Hauser was a foundling, but one, it seemed, who had been kept apart from all human contact, knowing no language and none of the conventions of inter-personal relations. He was left one day in 1828 in the middle of the main square at Nürnberg, a prayer-book in one hand, a letter addressed to the local regimental riding-master in the other. He was given shelter, and taught to speak and behave like 'normal' human beings. But then a number of mysterious attempts were made on his life, and in 1833 he received a stab-wound in the chest from which he died. Many rumours and hypotheses sprang up about him, but none has ever satisfactorily explained the mystery of his identity, his origins, and his death.

The story's potential appeal for Herzog is clear. Whereas Truffaut's L'ENFANT SAUVAGE tackles the 'wild boy' of the Aveyron from the perspective of French rationalism, adopting the viewpoint of his educator, Herzog's THE ENIGMA OF KASPAR HAUSER (JEDER FÜR SICH UND GOTT GEGEN ALLE, 1974) is steeped in German Romanticism, with its respect for the virtues of the 'natural', the 'wild', for the irreducible mysteries at the dark heart of life. Kaspar's release from his dungeon, where he has been shackled for his first seventeen years, is a release into the beauties of the world, and Herzog at his most lyrical presents us with exquisitely painterly shots of the lush countryside around the old Franconian town of Dinkelsbühl that open our eyes to that freshness of vision that Kaspar himself experiences. But his release from jail is equally his initiation into the society of men, exchanging a physical imprisonment for the 'taming' of his mind and senses. The world Kaspar enters is beautiful, but flawed by Man. An opening sequence, to music of Orlando di Lasso, lingers on a field of young corn that surges and billows in the wind. Superimposed is an amended quotation from Büchner's *Lenz* – itself the

THE ENIGMA OF KASPAR HAUSER Kaspar (Bruno S.) is questioned by the Professor of Logic (Alfred Edel); Daumer's housekeeper Käthe (Brigitte Mira) looks on

story of a man whose tragic otherness is complemented by an ecstatic intensity of perception: 'But can you not hear the dreadful screaming all around that people usually call silence?'.

Kaspar can certainly hear it, and once he has learnt to speak he expresses the horror of the world in phrases of Lutheran simplicity and force: 'Mother, I am set aside from everything'; 'People are to me as wolves'; 'I feel as if my appearance on this earth has been a hard fall'. The outside world, it seems, is harder for Kaspar to bear than the womb-like dungeon he has left behind. It is a world where, in the bleak words of the film's German title, it is a matter of 'every man for himself and God against all'. There is in fact much of the Christ figure about Kaspar Hauser – his mysterious origins,

his saintly innocence, the failure of the world to appreciate him, his cruel death – and Herzog points this up in an untypically heavy-handed shot early in the film where the camera takes a meaningful look at a crucifix and a caged bird – a bullfinch, in fact, whose German name 'Gimpel' colloquially means a 'dunce' or 'simpleton'!

Herzog is careful to distinguish the attitudes of the people Kaspar encounters. The town officials are anxious to *classify* him for the sake of civic order; the pastors want to save his soul; the showman wants him as a freak for his travelling fair, just as the effete Lord Stanhope wants a pet that will make an ideal conversation piece and provide endless fun at parties. Others are better intentioned, like the simple family he first lives with, who patiently and affectionately teach him rudimentary manners, or Herr Daumer, his final tutor and guardian. Daumer is kindly and well-intentioned, but even he has but the merest inkling that perhaps there is something precious in Kaspar that must not be 'civilized' away.

Like AGUIRRE, THE ENIGMA OF KASPAR HAUSER gains much of its force – and it is a most remarkable film – from the strength of personality of the central character, and from the beauty of its images and music. But there are important differences between the two films. Bruno S. in his consummate, and virtually autobiographical, rendering of Kaspar is not the mad titan that Kinski played as Aguirre. Instead he is an heir to the figures from earlier documentaries: like the Africans in THE FLYING DOCTORS, or Fini Straubinger and her friends in LAND OF SILENCE AND DARKNESS, he is the living evidence of potentials for experience and perception that we can scarcely conceive of. And as in the documentaries, there is in KASPAR HAUSER a warm humanity that is far more assured than the uneasy irony of DWARFS and AGUIRRE. Humour there certainly is, but it involves laughter *with* Kaspar at the 'civilized' world that is so determined to win him over. It is a humour that comes over more than anywhere in Kaspar's encounter with the professor of logic, a determined pedant who cannot accept Kaspar's blindingly simple answer to his fatuous conundrum: a sequence that reveals most clearly where the film's sympathies lie, for it never fails to delight audiences, who regularly break into gleeful applause at Kaspar's 'victory'.

Landscape too has a different function in KASPAR HAUSER. Aguirre had come to civilize the wilderness, and in SIGNS OF LIFE as well the hero's rebellion had been inspired as much as anything by the maddening hostility of the landscape. Kaspar, one senses, is on the side of the nature around him. He has visions of landscape, of the Caucasus, of nomads in the Sahara, of Irish pilgrims struggling up the mist-girt Croagh Patrick (though Kaspar, to the pastors' dismay, is no Christian: 'At the top, there was Death,' he says). And Herzog complements these flickering, grainy, silent visions with other, clear and lucid shots that have a musical accompaniment, as in the opening sequence of trees, a boat, a lake, a washerwoman kneeling on the bank and the music of Tamino's aria from *The Magic Flute*: 'Is this feeling love?'. The aria comes again at the end of the film, as the hunch-backed, limping town clerk walks up the road after the post mortem on

Kaspar, delighted that the 'abnormalities' it has uncovered mean he can, after all, be dismissed as a 'freak', a mere medical 'case'. Civilization can breathe again. Tamino has the last, mocking word: 'Yes, it is nothing but love,' he sings.

The three documentaries with which Herzog followed the Kaspar Hauser film were all completed in 1976. The third, 'NO ONE WILL PLAY WITH ME' (MIT MIR WILL KEINER SPIELEN) is a fourteen-minute short about children in Munich. The other two are more substantial, and each in its way is a classic example of Herzog's approach to film-making: on the one hand a film that observes some bizarre people who, like figures in some of Herzog's earlier work, hover on the verge of making fools of themselves, on the other hand the most apocalyptic of Herzog's grandiose landscapes, a volcano in the fury of imminent eruption.

HOW MUCH WOOD WOULD A WOODCHUCK CHUCK?, subtitled 'Observations on a new language', looks at the 13th International World Livestock Auctioneering Championships, held in Amish County, Pennsylvania. The – to the uninitiated ear – incomprehensible gabble of the livestock auctioneers, their posturing and mannerisms, their fanatical devotion to their way of life, represent exactly the sort of quirky slice of life one might expect Herzog to uncover. But there is more to it than that. Like Upton Sinclair and Bertolt Brecht before him, Herzog sees in the American livestock markets the epitome of capitalism, and in the language of the auctioneers he perceives an extreme kind of lyric whose relationship to the economic system he compares with that of the liturgy to the Church. This 'new language' is the ultimate voice of capitalism, and Herzog finds it, he says, at one and the same time (and here too there are echoes of the early Brecht) both 'fascinating' and 'horrifying'. Herzog found a further significance in this outwardly trivial occasion, and that stemmed from its fortuitous location among the pious Amish, whose whole pre-capitalist way of life was so totally counter to all that the Championships stood for. (Their Pennsylvania Dutch, he points out, doesn't even have a word for 'championships'.) The contrast between the gaudy, raucous hurly-burly of the livestock ring and the shy, gentle Amish who come to watch is clear and stark. Herzog's sympathies are with the Amish, whose existence, he stresses, poses none of the threats to the environment that have ravaged so much of the United States. The horrified fascination with modern America was to surface again in STROSZEK, whilst the romantic respect for innocence, simplicity, and natural dignity remains a dominant note in Herzog's work.

FATA MORGANA and AGUIRRE had been films where the story of their making was as compelling as the final product. LA SOUFRIÈRE is a film in that tradition, but it goes even further, consciously deriving much of its impact from its matter-of-fact documentation of its own extraordinary genesis. La Soufrière is a volcano on Guadeloupe, and when Herzog heard that it was about to erupt with a force equivalent to that of five atom bombs, he went straight, with a team of two, to the evacuated southern part of the island. The film he brought back shows the streets of the incongruously French-looking town of Basse Terre, now deserted except for scores of stray dogs, some of which had died, leaving a foul stench in the already sulphur-laden air. The traffic lights – which the departing townsfolk had, in their haste, forgotten to turn off – were changing methodically, absurdly, and sinisterly from red to green and back in the silent streets. In the morning Herzog and his companions awoke to find the sea full of thousands of drowned snakes that, disturbed by the tremors, had fled the mountainside in the night. Driving across country the team reached the crater, and then, on the slopes of La Soufrière itself, they found an old man who had refused to leave, and who lay there waiting for the death he felt God had preordained. Later they found two more equally fatalistic farmers, who had stayed to guard their animals. Scientists had declared that the eruption of La Soufrière was inevitable; in the event, it did not take place, and Herzog returned with his film. In its portrait of men *in extremis*, men confronted with apparently certain death, men threatened by a landscape of apocalyptic beauty, in its comment on the unsteady and transitory status of human civilization, LA SOUFRIÈRE is already quintessential Herzog. Its real fascination, however, derives from the fact that these men now quite explicitly include the film-makers themselves: the film itself participates in the elemental drama it portrays.

There were noteworthy peculiarities in the making of HEART OF GLASS (HERZ AUS GLAS, 1976) as well, for this was the film in which Herzog, at the start of each day's shooting, put the cast into a hypnotic trance in order to achieve an effect of collective hysteria, of a community sleepwalking to its downfall. The community in question is a village in the Bavarian Forest in the early nineteenth century. Its downfall is occasioned by the death of the last man at the local glass factory to hold the secret of making the fabulous ruby glass. Hias, a young shepherd gifted with prophetic powers, is unable to help, and nothing comes of the sacrifice of a servant-girl either. In the end Hias has a vision of long-forgotten hermits setting off in a tiny boat across the open sea from their rocky island to see if there really is an abyss at the end of the world.

HEART OF GLASS is Herzog's least successful film, redeemed only by the beauty of its visuals. There are haunting genre scenes, sombre brown shots of the peasants' daily life; but above all there are landscape shots as compelling as any Herzog has made: apocalyptic visions of clouds streaming like a great waterfall across the forest; volcanic terrain, hot streams and lava humps; burnt forests; ravines and chasms and mountainsides; the grey and green of the Irish Atlantic coast, with flocks of gannets swirling, to the cries of the kittiwakes, like wisps of mist in the air above the sea. The film fails, however, in Herzog's attempt to make the dialogue, the action, and the story match the intensity of these shots. The millenarian central thesis of the film – that one day factories may be as obsolete as castles are today – is intriguing, but it is lost in the inconsequential, pretentious, and frequently preposterous jumble of pronouncements and events that makes up the 'story'. The experiment of hypnotizing the actors has not paid off: the film lacks pace; what was intended as mystery and madness actually comes across as torpor and monotony. The acting loses rather than gains from the actors' hypnotic trance: all seem reduced to the level of somnambulistic zombies.[11]

Herzog's next film, STROSZEK (1977), is about as far removed from the dark mysteries of HEART OF GLASS as anything he has made. This is the second film that stars Bruno S., and, as in KASPAR HAUSER, it is a quasi-autobiographical study of a man released from prison into a world that turns out to be even more constricting and hostile than the cell he has left behind. That world this time is contemporary, and no longer just Germany, but above all America, for Bruno, together with his little old neighbour Herr Scheitz (the town clerk of KASPAR HAUSER), and the prostitute Eva, set off from Berlin for Wisconsin to escape the violence of her gangster pimps. There, in an unprepossessing, God-forsaken spot called Railroad Flats the three innocents abroad install themselves in a seventy-foot mobile home parked on land belonging to Scheitz's motor-mechanic nephew. The American Dream quickly turns sour: Eva gets a job as a waitress at a nearby truck-stop, but soon she is back to whoring again, and finally takes off with two truckers en route for Vancouver. Unable to keep up their payments, Bruno and Scheitz watch incomprehendingly as their home is auctioned off (by an auctioneer straight out of HOW MUCH WOOD WOULD A WOODCHUCK CHUCK?). They hold up a barber – a ludicrous raid, that nets them 22 dollars, which they immediately spend on a frozen turkey in the shop across the road, after which Scheitz is arrested. Bruno escapes in the nephew's tow-truck to an Indian reservation in North Carolina, an out-of-season tourist trap, where we last see him going endlessly up and down on the deserted chair-lift.

'Bruno is going into freedom,' the hero proclaims on his release from prison, and he blows his precious rail-wayman's signal horn in celebration. He blows the horn again on arrival in America, from the top of the Empire State Building, in fact. But he had made another remark at the beginning: 'It all goes round in circles', and that is the one that turns out to have been the more prophetic. There is no freedom for those such as Bruno, and the film ends in an orgy of Herzog's favourite images – dominating them all the image of pointless cricularity. As his abandoned and burning truck turns ceaselessly below, Bruno rides round and round on the chairlift, clutching his gun and his frozen turkey; meanwhile in the amusement arcade at the foot of the lift, chickens dance and play the piano, a rabbit drives a fire-engine, and a duck beats the drums.

It is a zany, chaotic climax, in which all hell is let loose, the hell of modern America that Herzog had glimpsed in the auctioneers' liturgy of HOW MUCH WOOD WOULD A WOODCHUCK CHUCK? It is a sequence that brims over with symbols and meaningful images, like the sticker on the till in the Cherokee diner that says 'No Pets' – a gruesome request in view of the per-

STROSZEK Cold turkey: Stroszek in America

Stroszek in Germany: Stroszek (Bruno S.), Herr Scheitz (Clemens Scheitz), and Eva (Eva Mattes) plan the journey to Wisconsin

forming animals over the road, and of the Indians themselves who are only there for display. A reminder too of the way Bruno's pet mynah bird had been confiscated on arrival in New York, replaced now in his befuddled affections by the all-American pre-packed turkey. 'Thank you, please come again,' (circularity again!) chants the waitress, in the obligatory formula of plastic politeness, echoing the imprecation to 'Have a good day, sir' of the smooth young bank clerk after he had repossessed the trailer home. Across the way a sign reads 'Please Do Not Litter': it refers to the gaudy chair-lift, an eyesore that scars the wooded hillside.

And on the back of Bruno's seat is another sign: 'Is this really me!'. America, Herzog seems to be saying, is a place where people all too easily lose their identity. Bruno had set off from New York full of hope, to the accompaniment even of a snatch of road-music, but, like the Indians, in his lumber jacket and broad-brimmed hat he has only adapted outwardly; inwardly he has simply lost whatever real self he ever had.

After the obscurantism of HEART OF GLASS Herzog made with STROSZEK his most conventionally narrative film, a 'ballad', as he calls it, a film that inevitably stimulated critics at home and abroad to reach for the

epithet 'accessible'. Its themes are unprecedentedly explicit, its dialogue direct and no longer mediated so much through imagery. The early sequence in a Berlin hospital where a doctor lovingly shows Bruno a premature child, marvelling at the wonders of human potential, is even unaccustomedly facile and uncomfortably sentimental, and slips into bathos at the doctor's remark that this child may one day be Federal Chancellor. 'It began with the homes they put me in,' Bruno tells Eva, and then proceeds to develop his thesis of America as a vast prison more subtle and deceptive than the honest-to-goodness four walls he knew in Berlin. 'Herzog for the first time becomes a decorator of themes, an annotator of his own pursuits and obsessions,' as Richard Combs puts it.[12] But like KASPAR HAUSER the film derives its real strength from the figure of Bruno S. Here too the audience cannot help but warm to him from the outset, and again a cheer goes up when, after having given the fatuous prison governor his 'great Hungarian word of honour' that he will henceforth avoid the temptations of drink, Bruno's first act on leaving prison is to slip smartly into the nearest bar.

'Who would dare to re-do *Hamlet* after Shakespeare? I would!'[13] So Herzog is reported to have commented on his decision to film a new version of one of the classics of German silent cinema, Murnau's NOSFERATU of 1922, which he considers 'the most important film ever made in Germany'.[14] Despite the unabated popularity of vampire films, no directors have followed Murnau's first cinematic exploitation of the subject with such fidelity to detail as Herzog. More than one critic has spoken of Herzog's NOSFERATU THE VAMPYRE (NOSFERATU – PHANTOM DER NACHT, 1978) as essentially Murnau plus sound and colour. The story of the vampire Count Dracula, who journeys from his native Transsylvania to wreak havoc on a quiet North German port, finally to be defeated by the self-sacrifice of a woman pure in heart, is a well-known variant of the Beauty-and-the-Beast legend, and Herzog adheres closely to it both in outline and detail, as well as observing the major conventions of the vampire genre as a whole.

WOYZECK Klaus Kinski in the title role

However, NOSFERATU THE VAMPYRE is still distinctively a Herzog film. There are once more the astounding stories about the film-making itself: the story, for instance, of the eleven thousand rats that Herzog surreptitiously released into the streets of Delft for the closing sequence (white rats, by the way, but Herzog wanted grey rats, so he painted them). There are once more the Herzogian landscapes, from the mountains of Czechoslovakia (representing Transsylvania) to the canals, streets, and old Dutch houses of Delft (representing not Murnau's Bremen, but the nearby port of Wismar, today in the GDR). There are shots that are again unmistakably Herzog, like the glimpse of Dracula's raft swirling down a torrential river that is so obviously an echo of AGUIRRE; the Transsylvanian inn that immediately brings HEART OF GLASS to mind, as do the images of a civilization breaking down in hysteria as the plague takes its grip on Wismar; the grotesque mummified corpses (which Herzog found in Mexico), with which the film opens; the racing clouds over Dracula's castle and above the blowing sand on the seemingly infinite beach with which it closes.[15]

Thematically there are obvious links as well with Herzog's earlier work: the invasion of a sleepy bourgeois community by something it can neither understand nor cope with had been explored in KASPAR HAUSER, and the titan-motif, here in a peculiarly demonic form, apocalyptic even, had long been a favourite of Herzog's. To compare the reptilian vampire Dracula with the gentle and innocent Kaspar may seem distasteful, not to say far-fetched, but in fact it is precisely the way that he has rendered the ghoulish Count uncomfortably sympathetic that is Herzog's principal innovation in his treatment of the story. Or perhaps one should say Klaus Kinski's innovation, for he, just as he had done in AGUIRRE, and just as Bruno S. did in KASPAR HAUSER, manages by the sheer intensity and conviction of his acting to give NOSFERATU its focal strength. With his great claws, his fangs, his bloodshot eyes, domed head, and whitened face (his traditional Japanese make-up took up to five hours each day to put on) he is not just a figure of horror, but also of pity. Cursed with eternal life (nosferatu is Romanian for 'undead'), like Frankenstein's monster and King Kong before him, he yearns for affection and understanding – and here he is very much in that Herzog tradition of characters, both real and fictitious, whom the world rejects because they are different.

But even Kinski's magnificent performance does not redeem the film of its inherent weaknesses, indeed in part it even contributes to them. They are essentially weaknesses of style: much of the film is funny, but one constantly gets the feeling that the humour is, for once, unintentional. Herzog seems too fond of his by now familiar mannerisms – above all the insistent beauty of the visuals – to have noticed the sheer over-the-top ludicrousness of much that happens here and of the way the characters react to events. But then perhaps one is meant to laugh at the manic, cackling figure of Renfield, perhaps even Dracula is meant to be both tragic *and* comic. Certainly 20th Century Fox, the film's distributors, seemed uncertain, for they initially withdrew the English version, which had elicited gales of laughter from the first audiences, and substituted a subtitled one.

That a major American distributor is handling NOSFERATU is a sign of the times. Like other West German directors, Herzog is set for a breakthrough to the international market – and not just the art-house circuits. The tale of Dracula is well-known, and already much exploited, and NOSFERATU is the first film (with the partial exception of KASPAR HAUSER) in which Herzog's subject matter is not a private discovery, but a long-familiar component of popular mythology. Herzog has talked of his films as showing 'things that no one has seen or known of before',[16] of himself as seeing 'something on the horizon that most people have not yet seen', of seeking 'planets that do not exist and landscapes that have only been dreamed'.[17] By tackling the well-worn subject matter of NOSFERATU he has forfeited something of that revelatory impulse.

Yet the mystery remains. The tale of NOSFERATU is superbly anti-rational: the eruption of the plague of rats (already made a potent symbol by Camus) that brings a smugly comfortable bourgeois world tumbling to the ground is a further element in Herzog's continuing fascination with the fragility of a self-deluding 'civilization'. For Herzog, not only are the irreducible mysteries of existence a fact of life, but the cinema is the supreme medium for conveying this fact. The cinema itself, he insists, is essentially an irrational medium, deriving its strength not from the world of 'reality', but from the world of dreams. Time and again Herzog has expressed his aversion to modern rationalism, an aversion that is directed particularly forcefully against any over-academic approach to the cinema:

> People should look straight at a film. . . . That's the only way to see one. Film is not the art of scholars, but of illiterates. And film culture is not analysis, it is agitation of the mind. Movies come from the country fair and circus, not from art and academicism.[18]

Herzog's work is a repeated plea for recognition of the validity and beauty of the visions of those who, by force of character or circumstances, move beyond the carefully circumscribed bounds of 'normality', 'reason', and 'civilization'. His heroes are outcasts (that he has followed NOSFERATU with a version of Büchner's *Woyzeck* is further evidence of this fascination[19]), or self-willed exiles from the world of 'moderation'. For the latter he reserves a certain irony, derived from the awareness that the celebration of human potential can easily tip into ridicule at its fatuousness. His outcasts, however, are presented with warmth and a wondering sympathy. It is the strength and freshness of their vision that his films seek to capture.

And Herzog himself? 'My heart,' he says, 'is very close to the late Middle Ages.'[20] But his films – which, he insists, he makes as an 'artisan' rather than an artist – are rooted in the contemporary world, even though only future generations may be able to see this. Likening himself to Kafka, Kleist, Büchner, and Hölderlin, whose 'centrality' was appreciated only after their death, he dismisses today's pop stars and mass entertainers as the ones that history will finally recognize to have been the real 'eccentrics' of the age.[21] He is quite certain of his own position: 'I think rather that it's the others who are the outsiders.'[22]

6 RAINER WERNER FASSBINDER

i Background and Beginnings

Fassbinder is without doubt the best-known of the new German directors. Although he is the youngest of the 'big seven', he is by far the most prolific and versatile German director. The range of his work in the cinema is wider than that of any of his contemporaries, and he has experience in all major aspects of cinema and theatre activity. As an actor he has played in many of his own films and plays, as well as in stage plays by other authors and films by other directors. He has written the scripts of nearly all his own films, as well as plays for television, radio, and the theatre, and his other activities have included producing and editing films, and composing and songwriting. By the mid seventies Fassbinder had made close on thirty feature films in a whole variety of genres: gangster films, political satire, screwball comedy, adaptations of classical literature, science fiction, a Western, and a host of uncomfortably self-conscious domestic melodramas that have for many become the epitome of his work.

Indeed, for many, Fassbinder has become the epitome of the whole New German Cinema, as the sheer volume of his production and the relative popularity of his appeal have ensured him a wider audience than his fellow directors have found, both at home and abroad, and both in the cinema and on television. It was Fassbinder who, with FEAR EATS THE SOUL, in 1973 made what was arguably the best-known German film of the mid seventies, and the one that first brought the New German Cinema to the attention of a wider public outside West Germany itself.

Fassbinder was born on 31 May 1946 in the small spa of Bad Wörishofen in south-western Bavaria. His father, Hellmuth, was a doctor, and his mother, Liselotte, a translator (of, amongst other things, the works of Truman Capote). Fassbinder remembers the household as 'rather chaotic', quite lacking in the usual 'rules and regulations' of middle-class life. The house contained 'nothing but literature and art'; his parents gave him a volume of Dürer reproductions when he was five, and the little boy's rare contacts with his father seem to have been typified for him in the occasion when the two of them together made a tape-recording of Goethe's *Faust*. All in all it was a lonely childhood. The parents divorced in 1951, and Fassbinder stayed with his mother. He was left very much to his own devices, and his mother regularly sent him off to the cinema so that she could get on with her work in peace. Later Fassbinder was to cast his mother – under the names of 'Lilo Pempeit' and 'Liselotte Eder' – in various more or less minor roles in a number of his films.

Fassbinder's childhood clearly left its mark on him and on his films: the cold, lonely lives of his characters and their desperate longing for love and affection are a reflection of his own early experience – no more so than in his first feature with its telling title LOVE IS COLDER THAN DEATH, and in the 1976 film with the most pro-

grammatic title of all, I ONLY WANT YOU TO LOVE ME. The days spent in the cinema at his mother's behest were influential too. From around the age of seven he claims to have spent every day of his childhood at the cinema, sometimes going to two or even three performances; here, at an early and impressionable age, he became familiar with the products of Hollywood, the cinema that in his later career as a film-maker he was to seek to emulate.

Fassbinder was educated at a Rudolf Steiner school, and then at secondary schools in Augsburg and Munich. He left school in 1964, and took on a number of different jobs, including office work, decorating, and a post in the archives of the *Süddeutsche Zeitung*. It was during this time that he began attending a private drama school. In the summer of 1967 he joined one of Munich's fringe theatre groups, the *action-theater*. Here he first acted in, then directed, then wrote adaptations of various plays. (A priceless record of these early months of Fassbinder's career in Jean Marie Straub's short film THE BRIDEGROOM, THE COMEDIENNE AND THE PIMP, which shows the *action-theater* troupe, including Fassbinder, in Straub's production of Ferdinand Bruckner's *Sickness of Youth*.) Fassbinder's first original play, *Katzelmacher*, later to be made into his second feature film, was premiered at the *action-theater* in April 1968. This was the heyday of the student movement, a troubled and exciting period in politics and the arts, two fields that now in any case had become inseparable. The *action-theater* was very much of its time, anarchic, subversive, and critical, reflecting and reacting to the events of the day. The authorities were uneasy about the little troupe in the Müllerstrasse, and on 21 May 1968 (the same day as a Munich newspaper reported that Fassbinder had been arrested during the disturbances in Paris) the *action-theater* was served with an official warning that its electricity cables were unsafe. The 'faulty' cables had been isolated, and were due to be repaired when police closed the theatre on 6 June. Shortly before, the *action-theater* had been threatened with suspension of its licence because it had entered the realm of 'political cabaret', contrary to the 'predominantly artistic' activities stipulated in its permit.

The following month ten members of the original group, including Fassbinder himself, Rudolf Waldemar Brem, Kurt Raab, Peer Raben, and Hanna Schygulla, resurfaced as the 'anti-teater', playing Peter Weiss's *Mockinpott* at the Munich Academy of Fine Arts. Eventually, in the autumn of 1968, the *anti-teater* found a home in the 'Witwe Bolte', a bar in Schwabing, the 'bohemian' quarter of Munich. Here the traditions of the *action-theater* found a new lease of life, and Fassbinder's second play *Preparadise sorry now* (the title was in English) was performed – a piece about 'fascistoid attitudes in daily life' involving the 'moors murderers', Ian Brady and Myra Hindley. At the end of 1969 the *anti-teater* too lost its backroom home in the Schwabing bar, and, at the same time, its 'underground' existence. In November 1969 Fassbinder's work made its first appearance on the stage of an 'establishment' theatre, when the Bremer Theater put on his cabaret *Anarchy in Bavaria*, and his version of Goldoni's *Coffee House*. But more significant in retrospect was the fact that the Bremer Theater showed two films to accompany the *anti-teater* plays: LOVE IS COLDER THAN DEATH, and KATZELMACHER.

Fassbinder's experience of film-making actually predated his involvement with the *action-theater*. He had already applied for admission to the West Berlin Film and Television Academy in 1965, but failed the entrance examination. In the same year he scripted and directed his first film: a ten-minute short called THE CITY TRAMP (DER STADTSTREICHER), and in 1966 he made another short, THE LITTLE CHAOS (DAS KLEINE CHAOS). Fassbinder acted in both of these, as did his financial backer Christoph Roser, and, in THE LITTLE CHAOS, Fassbinder's mother (under her assumed name 'Lilo Pempeit').

THE CITY TRAMP was, according to Fassbinder, inspired by his favourite film of the time, Eric Rohmer's LE SIGNE DU LION. Rohmer's *clochard* stumbles ever deeper into decrepitude in the almost deserted Paris of the *grandes vacances*, only to become the beneficiary of an unexpected inheritance at the end. Fassbinder's tramp is shown in an autumnal Munich, where he finds a pistol. He attempts to get rid of the gun, but two men who have been observing him for some time take it from him. The film ends with a game, almost a dance, of 'piggy in the middle' in the Englischer Garten as the two men throw the gun from one to the other and the tramp tries to catch it – most ironi-cally, considering that his whole object had been to get rid of it. There is a certain development in the ten minutes of this first Fassbinder film from the serious opening (the alcoholic and homeless tramp), through the humour of his vain attempts to get rid of the gun, to the ritualistic levity of the closing sequence; but of greater significance for Fassbinder's later work is the mood engendered by the physical and social setting. Here already are major ingredients of LOVE IS COLDER THAN DEATH and many subsequent feature films: uncommunicative outsiders, guns, a hint of petty gangsterism, and a bleak and hostile Munich.

In THE LITTLE CHAOS three young people selling magazine subscriptions successfully rob a woman in her home. Here the gangster theme comes to the fore, but these are self-conscious, would-be gangsters. Their movements and gestures are studied echoes of Hollywood models: the first of the many wry references to the American cinema and the transposition into a German milieu of the lifestyle it portrays that are such a typical feature of Fassbinder's films. Typical too is the ironic, parodistic element in the American reference: in Fassbinder's film a Hollywood convention is broken – the 'villains' get away with it.

ii Echoes of Hollywood: The Gangster Trilogy

THE CITY TRAMP and THE LITTLE CHAOS were followed by Fassbinder's involvement with the *action-theater*. Then in 1969 he and the *anti-teater* troupe began to make films. It was a portent of things to come that in the first year alone they made three full-length features under Fassbinder's direction. All three were set in Munich, and two of them – LOVE IS COLDER THAN DEATH (LIEBE IST KÄLTER ALS DER TOD) and GODS OF THE PLAGUE (GÖTTER DER PEST) – took up the gangster theme again. In the first film Fassbinder himself plays the leading part of Franz, a small-time pimp who is torn between his mistress Joanna (Hanna Schygulla) and the gangster Bruno (Ulli Lommel), who is sent after Franz by the syndicate that he has refused to join. Joanna informs the police of a bank robbery the two men have planned; in the shoot-out Bruno is killed, but Franz and Joanna escape. (The film is dedicated to 'Claude Chabrol, Eric Rohmer, Jean-Marie Straub, Lino and Cuncho': a night-time sequence on the

Landsberger Strasse, a decrepit main road leading out of Munich and a favourite beat for prostitutes, was provided by Straub, who had used another take of this in THE BRIDEGROOM, THE COMEDIENNE AND THE PIMP.)

Now that Fassbinder had graduated from shorts to the feature film he was able to study human relationships and establish in this sphere themes that were to remain present throughout his subsequent work: loneliness, the longing for companionship and love (both homo- and heterosexual), and the fear and reality of betrayal. This is a low-key film, with muted tones, long, quiet sequences, and little dialogue, for Fassbinder's characters are essentially inarticulate, with a life style that is a false and inadequate expression of what they are and what they feel, for it is adopted from the alien clichés of popular culture – the clichés of Hollywood crime films.

There are curious comic interludes amid the brooding sadness of LOVE IS COLDER THAN DEATH. By cruelly but wittily confusing a sales assistant the three protagonists manage to steal three pairs of sunglasses in a department store; another sequence has a shot motorcycle policeman exclaiming (in English), 'Oh, Boy!', for no apparent reason as, clutching his stomach in the approved manner, he falls dying to the ground. And in the most distinctive interlude of all Bruno and Joanna, stealing food in a supermarket, are followed by the camera in a series of dance-like surges and retreats to the accompaniment of an electronic version of the *Rosenkavalier*: an edgy, threatening sequence shot in eery faded tones.[1]

The other 1969 gangster film, GODS OF THE PLAGUE, is, even by Fassbinder standards, unremittingly bleak and sad. The settings are drab, dingy, seedy, and, above all, dark. The characters are again lost and lonely, silent and locked up within themselves, beaten by a largely undefined but oppressive world outside. The hero is again called Franz, Fassbinder's favourite name for his downtrodden protagonists, and one that he himself adopted in this and other films that he edited under the pseudonym 'Franz Walsch'. (In the 1978 film DESPAIR there is even a glimpse of a book ostensibly by one Franz Walsch.) Not by chance 'Franz' is a name that in modern German literature epitomizes the downtrodden little man on the fringes of the underworld of the big city, for this was the name of the hero

of Alfred Döblin's 1929 novel *Berlin Alexanderplatz*, *the* novel of the Berlin of the Weimar Republic, and one that for years Fassbinder has wanted to film. (He first came across Döblin's novel when he was fourteen, an event that, he claims, made him want to be an artist, adding that he 'adopted' Franz from that point on.) Fassbinder's Franz in GODS OF THE PLAGUE, when asked his name by a suspicious hotel clerk, replies 'Franz Biberkopf', the very name that Döblin gave *his* hero, and that Fassbinder was later to adopt in the central role that he played in FOX.

There are other little jokes in GODS OF THE PLAGUE. Franz's friend Günther has adopted the alias 'Schlöndorff' (Margarethe von Trotta, who plays Franz's second girlfriend, is married to Volker Schlöndorff); and like the motorcycle policeman in LOVE IS COLDER THAN DEATH both Franz and Günther utter bizarre quotations before they drop dead. 'Cobbler, stick to your last' gasps Franz, whilst Günther's dying words come out in English: 'Life is very precious, even right now.' Throughout the film Günther speaks German. He is, he asserts when challenged at one point, a Bavarian. But Günther, whose nickname is 'Gorilla', is a half-caste, one of that generation of 'Occupation Bavarians' fathered by black GI's in the post-war years who had to grow up in the all-white world of provincial southern Germany. Although his race actually plays only a minor role in this film, he belongs to that group of 'outsiders' – the blacks, the immigrant workers, the homosexuals – whose peculiar exclusion from society is used by Fassbinder time and again to give exemplary exaggeration to general human problems.

Günther is Franz's best friend, even though he has shot Franz's informant brother. Franz, released from prison, drifts straight back into the petty underworld, where he meets Joanna, who wants to help him. But he flees her possessive love, and ends up with Margarethe. (As so often in these early Fassbinder films, the names, when they have no other significance, are simply those of the players, in this case Margarethe von Trotta; Franz's anonymous mother in the film is in fact Fassbinder's mother, here again appearing under the pseudonym of 'Lilo Pempeit'.) Joanna betrays Franz's and Günther's plan to raid a supermarket to the police, and as a result Franz is shot by a crooked and singularly vindictive inspector in one of those explosions of repressed violence that become a recurrent motif in many subsequent Fassbinder films. Günther, also shot, manages to make his way to, and shoot, the pornography pedlar Carla, who had tipped off Joanna, before he himself dies. The film finishes with Franz's desolate funeral, attended by Joanna, Margarethe, and his mother.

Within this morbidly depressing tale there are brief moments of release, of transient happiness and even declared affection. The one moment of real spontaneous positive emotion from Franz occurs when he first meets Günther again, and he exclaims 'Crazy!' as they embrace one another. Similarly, one whole sequence stands out from the rest, when Franz, Günther, and Margarethe drive out into the country to visit the farm of an old gangster called Joe. Here, for once, there is a sense of release and escape from the dark claustrophobia of the city as Günther's sports car speeds through the Bavarian countryside. During the drive Franz even confesses his love for Günther, whereupon the camera cuts exultantly to a helicopter shot from far above showing, of all things, a wide and open sunlit landscape. Later Franz again mentions love: the three of them, he says, have no need of money as long as they love each other, and together they dream of an island paradise. But the dream, as always in Fassbinder, is all too brief, reality all too insistently cruel. The final glimpse of paradise is a mockery of the innocent but futile visions that had gone before: Franz leaves his dark underworld for the last time to enter a clean and well-lighted place, the consumer paradise of the supermarket he has come to rob (an echo of the supermarket sequence in LOVE IS COLDER THAN DEATH). He dies among the gleaming ranks of canned and packaged goods, after he and Günther have been taken on a guided tour of the closed store by its proud young manager, a former acquaintance who has made it in the 'straight' world. He too dies in the final shoot-out.

A year later Fassbinder was to make another gangster film, stressing the link with LOVE IS COLDER THAN DEATH and GODS OF THE PLAGUE by returning, after four intervening colour films, to black and white stock (thereby also echoing more accurately the classic Hollywood cinema). THE AMERICAN SOLDIER (DER AMERIKANISCHE SOLDAT) of 1970 is an episodic pastiche not only of Fassbinder's first two gangster movies, but of the Hollywood gangster genre as a whole. There had been moments of stylized wit in LOVE IS COLDER THAN DEATH and GODS OF THE PLAGUE, but the sheer exuberance of Fassbinder's handling of the genre in this last part of his gangster trilogy is a remarkable symptom of the speed at which his talent for parody had developed in his first two years of feature-film making.

The 'American soldier' of the title is a professional killer by the name of Ricky who returns from Vietnam to his native Munich, where he is hired by three policemen to do away with a number of 'undesirables'. Eventually he ends up killing the girlfriend of one of the policemen, and is gunned down by the policemen in a corner of the main station together with his friend Franz Walsch (i.e. Fassbinder, using his favourite pseudonym again). This showdown is the crowning moment of the film, and one of Fassbinder's most memorable sequences. The two friends in their death throes strut and stagger and finally collapse in an outrageously stylized parody of the archetypal Hollywood 'B' movie. But then Fassbinder does something quite unexpected. Ricky's brother, hitherto cold and distant, comes dashing down the steps and hurls himself on Ricky's body, and, in a desperate declaration of the love he has repressed and withheld for so long, he embraces his brother, caressing him, flailing and thrashing, indeed almost dancing with the body on the station floor. This last shot is shown in slow motion, and is held for such a long time that it moves from surprise through embarrassing insistence to a lyrical tenderness that is underlined by the accompanying music, the English lyrics of 'So much tenderness', the song that Fassbinder wrote for the film, and that is sung by Günther Kaufmann, the 'Gorilla' of GODS OF THE PLAGUE.

The sudden and frenzied outburst of hitherto repressed passion, the revelation of love and a need for love that has been thwarted and now comes too late: these central and recurrent motifs in Fassbinder are perfectly exemplified in this closing sequence of THE AMERICAN SOLDIER. As this raw nerve is touched, the film shifts for its final moments with disturbing suddenness from parody into stylized earnestness. But the essence of THE AMERICAN SOLDIER is allusion and quotation: Fassbinder here reflects not only on the Hollywood of Howard Hawks and Samuel Fuller, but also on his own films of only a year before.

THE AMERICAN SOLDIER The showdown: Fassbinder as Franz and Karl Scheydt as Ricky, the American Soldier; in the background Ricky's brother (Kurt Raab) and his mother (Eva Ingeborg Scholz)

The three gangster films of 1969–70 were not made in immediate succession. THE AMERICAN SOLDIER was separated by four other films from GODS OF THE PLAGUE (and followed by two more before the year was out – 1970 saw the production of no fewer than six films by Fassbinder and his *anti-teater* colleagues). GODS OF THE PLAGUE was in its turn separated from LOVE IS COLDER THAN DEATH by Fassbinder's second feature film, KATZELMACHER.

iii Stylization and Realism

GODS OF THE PLAGUE was a winter film in mood and setting, its dark sequences set largely indoors and often at night. KATZELMACHER by contrast is a summer film, a predominantly outdoor and daytime film, its tones over-exposed and bright, with a soundtrack that – again in distinct opposition to GODS OF THE PLAGUE – carries much extraneous noise, the chirping of sparrows and the rumble of traffic. But Fassbinder's summer is no less oppressive than his winter. The cold of GODS OF THE PLAGUE is here matched by an equally uncomfortable heat. In GODS OF THE PLAGUE the characters had muffled and wrapped themselves against the winter and the dark; in KATZELMACHER the summer and the sun seem to irritate and enervate, the characters flop and sprawl or listlessly stroll in their white and dusty yard.

'Katzelmacher' is a Bavarian term of abuse directed at immigrant workers from the Mediterranean countries that equates their sex-lives with that of tom-cats. By the late sixties some two million foreign workers had been drawn from their homelands to help keep the wheels of the German Economic Miracle turning. They were by then officially known as '*Gastarbeiter*', 'guest workers', but many Germans still used the 1950s designation '*Fremdarbeiter*', 'foreign workers', a term that had overtones of the slave labourers of the Nazi years. Their exploitation and lack of integration had attracted Fassbinder's attention for some time, and in his second film he himself played the role of Jorgos the Greek. *Gastarbeiter* crop up in a number of later films as well (in WILD GAME one of them is actually addressed as a '*Katzelmacher*'), and in FEAR EATS THE SOUL German attitudes to immigrants were to be explored in some detail.

KATZELMACHER portrays a group of rootless and bored young couples, whose relationships Fassbinder describes as follows: 'Marie belongs to Erich, Paul sleeps with Helga, Peter lives off Elisabeth, Rosy does it for money with Franz' (and, one might add, with the others too). Much of their time is spent exchanging petty-bourgeois clichés, idle chatter, and empty boasts; drinking, playing cards, intriguing, or simply sitting around. The arrival of the *Gastarbeiter* Jorgos leads to a growing curiosity on the part of the women, and in turn to envy and antagonism among the men. Violence now becomes more manifest, often in the form of a sudden cruel slap delivered to a woman by 'her' man – a frequent motif in many later Fassbinder films. Such incidents increase towards the end as irritability mounts until, in what many German critics saw as an outburst symptomatic of the fascist tendencies still latent in West German society, the men finally round on the innocent Greek and beat him up.

KATZELMACHER was originally written as a short stage play (the *anti-teater* performed it in twenty minutes). Fassbinder prefaced it with a note explaining that it should have been a play about older people, but all the actors at the *anti-teater* were young – a point that is not without relevance for all his early films where nearly all the parts were played of necessity by actors in their early to mid twenties. The stage version focussed on a village square, and had the *Gastarbeiter* Jorgos present from the outset. In the film the setting has been transposed to an anonymous suburban block of flats (in reality on the edge of Munich), and it is not until well into the one and a half hours running time that the Greek arrives: an alteration that enables the relationships and attitudes of the characters to be established first before the 'action' begins. In fact, by holding back the arrival of Jorgos, Fassbinder has placed the film, as opposed to the play, clearly into that most fundamental dramatic (not to mention mythic and religious) tradition in which an outsider sets the cat among the pigeons by descending upon a community and straining to breaking point and beyond its hidden tensions and unresolved contradictions. That such outsiders, like all 'alien' minorities, often then become scapegoats (most notoriously in recent German history) is a basic fact of social psychology that is not lost on Fassbinder. Indeed, given that the life of Christ is *the* archetypal scapegoat legend of Western culture, it is not inappropriate that Jorgos's 'chosen one' is the girl called Marie – the only character in Fassbinder's first half dozen or so films played by Hanna Schygulla with a name other than 'Joanna' or 'Hanna'.

It would be wrong, however, to see KATZELMACHER as a film about the '*Gastarbeiter* Problem'. It is in the first instance a film about Germans, and if it makes anything clear it is that the tensions and conflicts associated with the arrival of immigrants have in fact been latent in the host society all the time. The *Gastarbeiter* acts as a catalyst, unleashing the pent-up jealousies, rivalries, antagonisms and frustrations of the milieu into which he enters. He then becomes a scapegoat, blamed and punished for problems he has not caused but merely made manifest. Both KATZELMACHER and FEAR EATS THE SOUL make it clear that the '*Gastarbeiter* Problem' is really a 'German Problem'.

KATZELMACHER is one of Fassbinder's most stylized films: stylized in its characterization, its dialogue, its locations, and its camera work. Its overall structure and the movements of the actors are virtually choreographed. Sequences and actions are, like the dialogue itself, sparse and spare, and the general effect is deliberately anti-naturalistic. Few of the film's 104 sequences last longer than a minute, and all simply play on variations of a strictly limited number of groupings and settings: the characters as a group leaning or sitting on the railings outside the block of flats; the couples together alone; or various pairs from the group exchanging platitudes or simply staring vacuously ahead. Most stylized of all is a variant of this third category that regularly punctuates the film in which – to the accompaniment of piano music and a dubbed dialogue uniquely free of background – a couple (two women, or a woman and a man) walk across the yard towards the camera, which pulls back before them. (The music is Schubert's 'Sehnsuchtswalzer', an appropriate ironic counterpoint to the kitschy and often absurd yearnings with which these characters react to the circumscription of their stunted lives.)

Anti-naturalistic stylization was soon to be recognized as one of the hallmarks of Fassbinder's work. In these early films it cannot be dissociated from the exigencies of film-making with limited resources, but it is clear that Fassbinder's stylization is not merely anti-naturalism *faute de mieux*. It is rather a deliberate form of alienation, of that 'Verfremdung' in the Brechtian tradition that in the post-war years had swept all before it in the German theatre. In the cinema Fassbinder was aware of associated developments in particular in the work of Straub and Godard. So quickly and so totally did he himself adopt a frequently rough-and-ready stylization that he was, almost within a matter of months of his debut as a director, able in succeeding films to indulge in ironic and parodistic references to his own mannerisms. In KATZELMACHER the repetitive round of settings and groupings, the sparsely-furnished rooms and the empty courtyard are not only part of Fassbinder's stylization, but a reflection of the monotony and emptiness of the characters' lives. The dialogue too is 'alienated'. In form it is a stylized Bavarian dialect; in content it circles barely articulately round a handful of petty bourgeois clichés about love, order, and, above all, money, for money comes into most of the conversations and all the relationships, with a monetary value being placed on every aspect of life. Like so many of Fassbinder's characters, the protagonists in KATZELMACHER are simply unable to talk beyond the ritual rehearsal of the stereotyped phrases that have trapped their minds and their lives.

KATZELMACHER was filmed in nine days in August 1969, and was followed in the autumn by the filming of GODS OF THE PLAGUE. Fassbinder concluded his first year as a feature-film maker with his first colour film, WHY DOES HERR R. RUN AMOK? (WARUM LÄUFT HERR R. AMOK?), shot in two weeks in December 1969. The film was co-directed by Michael Fengler, and Fassbinder has in fact since asserted that it is really Fengler's work rather than his. Be that as it may, even if WHY DOES HERR R. RUN AMOK? was a new departure at the time for Fassbinder, it can in retrospect be seen as forming an integral part of his work, the beginning of that major group of films about ordinary people, their frustrations, problems, and tragedies, set in realistically sketched milieux, for which Fassbinder has now become famous.

The feature that most sharply distinguishes WHY DOES HERR R. RUN AMOK? from the first three 1969 films is its realism. Here it contrasts most strongly with the rituals of KATZELMACHER. Indeed, the two films stand at the beginning of two traditions that work themselves out – sometimes separately, more often mingled together – in all of Fassbinder's following work, for stylization and realism are not just the two poles of his work, but in combination they give it its peculiarly uncomfortable distinctive touch. WHY DOES HERR R. RUN AMOK? lacks all stylization in camera technique, cutting, and dialogue. Only the outlines of the scenes were sketched by Fassbinder and Fengler, and the cast then very convincingly improvized the dialogue. Some of them indeed were 'real' people rather than members of the *anti-teater* team, which succeeded in adding still more to the naturalism of the acting.

The film portrays the all-too-'normal' daily life of Herr Raab (played by Kurt Raab: here again is an example of the Fassbinder habit of simply adopting the actors' names for the characters they play). Herr Raab is a technical draughtsman, married, with a small son. We see him at home, at work, in the car, in the street, in a shop, at a parents' evening, and at the doctor's; he mixes with colleagues, neighbours, friends, and relatives. Many of the locations occur only once – another major distinction from KATZELMACHER and its ilk – though a few do recur, Herr R.'s office, for instance.

Some sequences are so well observed as to be painfully true to life: the occasion, for instance, when Herr R. goes to buy a record for his wife, a record he has heard on the radio, but whose title he cannot remember; he cannot even remember the sex of the singer, and tries in vain to sing it to the giggling shop assistants. Equally memorable is a sequence in which his parents come to visit, a visit that degenerates into an argument between his wife and mother as they all go for a walk in the snow and temporarily lose their son. The proprieties of daily social life again begin to crumble at the office Christmas dinner-dance, where Herr R. stands up to make a slow, laboured, and drunken speech ending with a proposal that they all 'drink brotherhood' with one another, the embarrassing German ritual that precedes the adoption of the familiar 'thou' form of address. Unfortunately the boss is not prepared for such familiarity; he makes an excuse and leaves, together with his wife and sister.

The pressures of middle-class life are invisibly taking their toll, exacerbated by the tension between Herr R.'s petty-bourgeois background and his wife's somewhat 'better' origins. Money and status again play a major role. One day some neighbours, three women and a man, pay a social call on Frau R. Again the mood and mannerisms of such occasions are captured perfectly. In their trendily miniscule skirts (if anything dates the early Fassbinder films, it must be the mini-skirts of the female players) the women counter any awkwardness with a very German determinedly casual friendliness. The conversation revolves around money and status, though in the 'nicest of possible ways'. The neighbours betray an almost prurient curiosity in the R.s' financial state, Herr R.'s promotion prospects, and the son's problems at school.

A visit by a woman neighbour occasions the incident that gives the film its title. One evening Herr R. is trying to watch television – but with some difficulty, for the set is not working properly and needs constant adjustment, and the neighbour is talking incessantly to his wife about a skiing holiday. Herr R. lights a candle-stick, with which he then fells the neighbour with a blow on the head. He then proceeds to kill his wife in the same way, and goes to their sleeping son's bedroom and kills him too. Next morning the police come to his office and inform his colleagues of what has happened.

Herr R. is shortly afterwards found hanged in the lavatory. As the film ends the words 'Why does Herr R. run amok?' again appear on the screen, their function now changed from that of a title to a question posed to the audience.

Why indeed does Herr R. run amok? Notwithstanding its macabre ending this is for much of the time a funny, even hilarious film (a point about many Fassbinder films that is all too often missed by German critics). Its comedy is a comedy of manners, and it is these manners, the attitudes and values, the sheer comfortless emptiness behind the comfortable façade of petty-bourgeois and middle-class life in modern West Germany, that finally drive Herr R. to triple murder and suicide. The sudden eruption of brute violence is a familiar motif in Fassbinder; here it is particularly startling as it is not defused by stylization. Herr R., like so many of Fassbinder's protagonists, suffers from lovelessness. The world he lives in is a harsh, competitive, and jealous one. It has replaced love and caring with a superficial bonhomie and the niceties of social convention. Even the protagonist's name in the form it appears in the title – 'Herr R.' – has been depersonalized and placed at a 'polite' distance. After the murders Herr R. switches off the troublesome television set, but we just have time to catch the opening words of a song: the song is 'Stand by me', the words are 'When the night is cold'. As with other American pop songs in Fassbinder, there is no evidence that the protagonist hears, let alone understands the words. They are a signal to the audience, an appropriate and ironic reflection of what is happening in the characters' minds. Herr R. has not enjoyed the love he needed; he is about to enter the coldest night, the night of his guilt and death. Other Fassbinder titles come to mind: 'Love is colder than death', and, echoing the now hopeless plea 'Stand by me', the film 'I only want you to love me'. Herr R. is one of the first of that long line of Fassbinder's quiet, sad characters whose desperate need for love is forever thwarted in an unfeeling world: Hans Epp in THE MERCHANT OF THE FOUR SEASONS, Franz in WILD GAME, Effi Briest, Franz Biberkopf in FOX, Xaver Bolwieser, and, of course, Peter in I ONLY WANT YOU TO LOVE ME.

iv The Year of Experiment

Nineteen seventy was, in quantitative terms, Fassbinder's most productive year, a year in which he made no fewer than six full-length films. They represent an odd and patchy assortment of genres, moods, styles, themes, and settings. One, RIO DAS MORTES, was a whimsical comedy. WHITY was a rumbustuous mixture of Euro-Western and steamy Southern melodrama. In THE NIKLAUSHAUSEN JOURNEY (DIE NIKLASHAUSER FART) Fassbinder tried his hand at the cinematic variants of Brechtian alienation effects practised by Straub and Jean-Luc Godard, and in THE AMERICAN SOLDIER he produced the resounding epitaph to his own earlier gangster films. BEWARE OF A HOLY WHORE (WARNUNG VOR EINER HEILIGEN NUTTE) was a film about filming, the film in question being in fact WHITY, and the whore in question being the cinema itself. The year closed on an unpromising note with Fassbinder's most disappointing film, PIONEERS IN INGOLSTADT (PIONIERE IN INGOLSTADT).

What in fact seems to have been happening in 1970 was that Fassbinder was casting around for a new beginning, for subjects and styles adequate to his only vaguely realized intentions. Hence the emphasis on pre-existing filmic forms (the Western genre, his own – and Hollywood's – gangster movies, or the mannerisms of Godard); hence too the obsession with the process of filming in BEWARE OF A HOLY WHORE. This was a year of experiment for Fassbinder; there was thus much that was shaky, and a number of the films were 'one-off' efforts, with neither major precedents or progeny in his œuvre. THE AMERICAN SOLDIER was the self-conscious culmination of a brief but formative tradition in his career; PIONEERS IN INGOLSTADT neither completes nor begins a tradition, and the same can be said of RIO DAS MORTES. Fassbinder made no more 'Westerns' after WHITY, and no more films about films after BEWARE OF A HOLY WHORE. The overt and 'alienated' didacticising of Godard evident in THE NIKLASHAUSEN JOURNEY is also without obvious parallels elsewhere in Fassbinder's work.

In RIO DAS MORTES two friends, Michel and Günther, try to raise money to realize their dream of searching for gold in Peru on the Rio das Mortes. Michel's girlfriend Hanna does not want them to go, but eventually they find a patroness to finance their trip. At the airport Hanna draws a gun on them as they walk to the plane, but she does not fire. Their plane takes off, followed up into the sky by the camera – a moment of release and relief after the indoor sequences that dominate the rest of the film.

The overall effect of RIO DAS MORTES is of an uncharacteristic blandness, its general mood one of mild humour arising from the discrepancy between the boys' naive visions and the constraints of mundane reality. RIO DAS MORTES is hardly in the mainstream of Fassbinder's work: it contains such untypical elements as a sequence where a group of women interweave before graffitti of a canon-like penis and the letters USSA exchanging remarks about women's liberation; it contains an interview in which the boys ask Carl Amery about the politics of underdevelopment and the role of the Church in South America. Certainly it also contains the familiar Fassbinder themes of frustration and lack of fulfilment, problems that are given an unambiguous social and political context: Hanna is studying educational science, and finds that her textbooks are simply guides to the suppression of children, handbooks on 'adjustment' and 'integration'; Michel is a tile-layer, but gets only a fraction of the money clients pay for his work; Günther (played by Günther Kaufmann) wants to prove to the world that, although he is black, he is still a 'real' German. But the frustrations of the characters do not develop the tension, the violence and melodrama that one is accustomed to in Fassbinder. The film's insipidness shows just how important these elements can be to make his work succeed.

Melodrama returns with a vengeance in WHITY. In a rambling Faulkneresque Southern-style mansion live the landowner Ben Nicholson, his nymphomaniac second wife Kate, and the two sons from his first marriage, the homosexual Frank and the half-wit Davy. Their obsequious servant is Ben's third son, the illegitimate half-caste Whity, who is asked by various members of the family to shoot various others. Eventually he shoots the lot, and dances off into the desert with Hanna, a prostitute and singer from the local saloon bar.

WHITY was another of the new departures that Fassbinder made in 1970. Like the others it was a departure that led nowhere in particular. This was Fassbinder's first film shot abroad – it was made at Almeria in Spain. It was his first wide-screen film, and with its Hollywood-style titles and its crystal-clear soundtrack awash with plangent music it has an immediate effect very different from that of any preceding Fassbinder production. The contents are incongruous, to say the least. The Nicholson family in their palm-girt mansion belong to one tradition; the desert township with its saloon bar, its jail, and its cowboys belongs to another, and the incongruity is further compounded by the songs sung by Hanna to the cowboys in the bar (one of whom is played by Fassbinder himself) – love-songs from a modern German tradition, songs in the manner of Kurt Weill, in fact.

WHITY is an outrageous film. And for that reason an enjoyable one: so blatant is its disregard for the distinctions between the genres it purports to adopt, and so exuberant is its melodrama that it has much of the charm of the tongue-in-cheek spoof that attaches to THE AMERICAN SOLDIER. In commercial terms, however, WHITY was a singularly unsuccessful film: the critics disapproved of Fassbinder's apparent abandonment of the familiar West German milieu, it failed to find a distributor, the television corporations were not interested, and the general public never got to see it.

THE NIKLAUSHAUSEN JOURNEY was more fortunate, being commissioned and broadcast by the *Westdeutscher Rundfunk*. Such official sponsorship seems improbable today in the more cautious climate of the early eighties, for THE NIKLAUSHAUSEN JOURNEY is revolutionary in form and content – or perhaps one should say *post*-revolutionary, for formally it is derivative of the innovations of such directors as Godard, and in content it reflects the reassessment of the potential for change that the Left was forced to make after the German student rebellion and the May events of 1968 in France.[2]

THE NIKLAUSHAUSEN JOURNEY is based on the appearance in 1476 of a shepherd called Hans Böhm in the Franconian village of Niklashausen. Böhm claimed to have been visited by the Virgin Mary, and preached revolution: the abolition of property and the just distribution of goods. He attracted many thousands of followers, but was burnt at the stake in Würzburg on the orders of the bishop after only four months. Out of this historical event Fassbinder decided to make a film that speaks to a modern audience, a film that shows 'how and why a revolution fails'.

To this end the medieval and modern in character and setting are mingled in a totally unconstrained manner. Böhm, for instance, is accompanied both by a hooded monk and by a second character known as 'The Black Monk', played by Fassbinder in a black leather jacket. Declamatory speeches are made about the revolution, about exploitation and oppression, and the settings include a pop concert, a quarry, and a camp site where Böhm is arrested by two German policemen and two black American military policemen, who proceed to massacre all and sundry. Böhm and two friends are finally crucified and burnt in a car-wrecker's yard. An uprising breaks out, and the film closes with the words of the Black Monk: 'But he and his comrades had learnt from their mistakes. They took to the mountains; two years later the revolution succeeded.'

THE NIKLASHAUSEN JOURNEY was shot in May 1970. In August came THE AMERICAN SOLDIER, and then in September Fassbinder made the fifth of his six films of that year, BEWARE OF A HOLY WHORE. Under the motto 'Pride comes before a fall' this is a humorous look at the business of film-making. At least three films are involved. Firstly the fictitious PATRIA O MUERTE, a film 'against state-sanctioned violence' that the team we watch are ostensibly making on location in Spain; secondly WHITY, the filming of which provided the original idea; and thirdly, as Fassbinder himself has pointed out, this is also a film that observes *itself* being made – thus no attempt is made to disguise the fact that what we see is not happening in Spain but on the Italian coast near Sorrento: Italian number-plates, Italian advertisements, and even a passenger helicopter marked 'Ischia Sorrento' are soon allowed to give the game away.

The making of WHITY had been a traumatic experience for the *anti-teater* team, which nearly broke apart over the film that some saw as a disastrous failure. BEWARE OF A HOLY WHORE represents Fassbinder's attempt to come to terms with that experience in a typically dramatic act of confession and self-analysis. In it we see the actors and technicians of a German film crew who have descended on a Spanish hotel and are now waiting for their director, their star, their government subsidy, and even the film stock itself. The focal setting is the lobby-cum-bar of the hotel where we observe the characters' comings and goings, their erotic relationships – homosexual, heterosexual, and bisexual – that are formed and undone almost by the hour, their intrigues, jealousies, and outbursts. The director is not in fact played by Fassbinder, but by Lou Castel wearing Fassbinder's famous black leather jacket. When he arrives he attempts to impose some order on the chaos that greets him; the team constantly thwarts him with acts of petty rebellion, and eventually he is beaten up. In the end, however, filming actually gets under way.

Clearly the image and role of the director are Fassbinder's main concern here. He cajoles and rants, broods and bosses, and all the time is painfully set apart from 'his' team. The relationship between director and crew is presented in all its awkward contradictions, its mutual dependencies and antagonisms, a relationship all the more problematic in a group like the *anti-teater* who liked to regard themselves as a 'collective': 'BEWARE OF A HOLY WHORE,' Fassbinder said, 'is specifically about the situation of trying to live and work as a group.' Indeed, the role of the director is seen as symptomatic of the role of the artist in general, and Fassbinder closes the film with a quotation from one of the classic documents in German literature of the artist's plight, Thomas Mann's *Tonio Kröger*: 'I tell you, I am often tired to death of portraying humanity without sharing in it.'

There is in German literature a long tradition of soul-searching by artist-heroes. Indeed the mainstream of German fiction has been quite obsessed with the dilemmas of the sensitive outsider and his relationship to the world of 'normality'. Perhaps this is why critics have tended to take BEWARE OF A HOLY WHORE too seriously. It may be a searingly frank confession, a revealing insight into Fassbinder's most personal problems, and a treasure house of arcane allusions for adepts of the *anti-teater*, but it is above all very *funny*. The sheer chaos and hysteria, the utter shambles of it all are in themselves inevitably outrageous. As the film progresses, drunkenness and violence increase, with everybody – except the whisky-drinking star Eddie Constantine – repeatedly ordering 'Cuba libre' at the bar. To this basic slapstick mixture Fassbinder adds such zany trappings as the sight one evening of the hotel manager slumped, for no apparent reason, across the reception desk, or the spectacle late one night of the remnants of the evening's gathering at the bar being persuaded to sing a hymn by Fred (Kurt Raab). All things Spanish are treated with ill-concealed contempt (ironically, in view of the film they are supposed to be making), and even the unfortunate waiter, a chirpy drudge who cheerfully clears up smashed glasses and accepts German mockery without demur, becomes an unhappy figure of fun when at the end he suddenly refuses to serve another Cuba libre and is beaten up for his insolence. The humour is cruel and crude, laughter at ineptness, disaster, and discomfiture, and it adds a further uncomfortable dimension to a film that touches many raw nerves.

Fassbinder had dedicated his film KATZELMACHER to Marieluise Fleisser, whose plays and stories about the poor and the oppressed in the Bavarian provinces were 'rediscovered' in the 1960s, and were much admired by the *anti-teater* team. Her classic 'comedy' *Pioneers in Ingolstadt* was first written in 1927. It shows what happens to two girls when the young soldiers are stationed in their sleepy little town. One of them, Alma, flits from one to another; Berta, on the other hand, falls in love, only to be abandoned. If Fassbinder's film was intended as a homage to the grand old lady of Bavarian popular drama (the filming took place in November 1970, the month of her sixty-ninth birthday), it was a sorry and most unfortunate flop. The production was singularly inauspicious. The Second German Television Service commissioned the film, but was unwilling to accede fully to Fassbinder's wish to set the play in the present, as this might offend the West German Army, the *Bundeswehr*. As a ludicrous compromise, within a basically contemporary setting some of the soldiers wear uniforms with Nazi emblems. Fassbinder was later to admit that he simply lost all interest while the film was being shot. This is all too apparent: Fleisser's tight and bitter-sweet original is soon dissolved into tedium and irrelevance.

v The Breakthrough to the German Public

PIONEERS IN INGOLSTADT was not only the last of the six films Fassbinder made in 1970, it was also the last production of the *anti-teater* in its original form. The tensions and dissensions that had surfaced in the making of WHITY, problems that were reflected in BEWARE OF A HOLY WHORE, and that undoubtedly contributed to the failure of PIONEERS IN INGOLSTADT, led finally to the winding up of the 'collective', and the founding of Fassbinder's own production company, 'Tango-Film'. The hectic year of experiment behind him, Fassbinder now settled down to a – by his standards – comparatively leisurely style of film-making, and entered a new, more mature phase of his career. Nineteen seventy-one in fact brought only one new film, THE MERCHANT OF THE FOUR SEASONS (DER HÄNDLER DER VIER JAHRESZEITEN), which Fassbinder shot in eleven days in August.

Where PIONEERS IN INGOLSTADT had been something of a disaster, THE MERCHANT OF THE FOUR SEASONS was one of the crowning successes of Fassbinder's career. The critics were almost unanimous in their enthusiasm. Wilfried Wiegand, for instance, described it in the *Frankfurter Allgemeine Zeitung* as 'one of the most important German films for years', and in the *Süddeutsche Zeitung* Günther Pflaum went so far as to describe THE MERCHANT OF THE FOUR SEASONS as 'the best German film since the war'. Fassbinder, it

THE MERCHANT OF THE FOUR SEASONS Hans Epp (Hans Hirschmüller) unwittingly employs his wife's lover Anzell (Karl Scheydt)

seemed, had finally found a more assured style that was adequate to his subject matter and his talent.

THE MERCHANT OF THE FOUR SEASONS is the story of another of Fassbinder's unfortunate unloved ones. Hans Epp meets only with misunderstanding, antagonism, indifference, or betrayal from the people – and in particular the women – who might have brought meaning and warmth into his life. To escape his ambitious mother he flees to the Foreign Legion. On returning he is soon dismissed from his job as a policeman because a prostitute has seduced him at the police station. He becomes a costermonger (hence the title, a literal translation from the French '*marchand des quatre saisons*', which is no more used in German than it is in English), as a result of which his class-conscious 'great love' refuses to marry him. The woman he does eventually marry is also cold and distant, treating him with scorn and disdain. While he is in hospital convalescing after a heart attack she is unfaithful to him. When Hans comes home he is unable to carry on his work; unknowingly (and coincidentally) he signs on the wife's lover as an assistant, until the wife engineers a ruse that gets the man dismissed. The next assistant is more sympathetic: Harry, an old friend from Hans's Foreign Legion days. But Harry gradually takes over Hans's place in the family, the household, and the business. Hans withdraws from the world, no one seems to need him or notice him. Then one day he goes and takes his leave of his relatives, and in his local bar simply drinks himself to death. After his funeral his widow leaves with Harry.

One of the most impressive aspects of THE MERCHANT OF THE FOUR SEASONS is the performance of the protagonist, played by Hans Hirschmüller, who manages to convey perfectly the downtrodden little man, without pathos, and with a sad humour that never becomes too comic. Hans, in fact, becomes a figure not unlike Goretta's 'lace maker', but Fassbinder's 'gentle creature' is, typically, a male character. All the usual Fassbinder tensions and emotions are present here, but the keynote is delicacy and a convincing authenticity. The story is simple, the situations are trite: the material is that of any number of Hollywood melodramas. But the parody, the exaggeration, the stylization with which Fassbinder had previously tackled potential triviality are here replaced with the revelation of the human reality behind the routines of melodrama, the truth behind the clichés.

Nineteen seventy-two saw the production by Fassbinder of two feature films and a television series. The two films were both based on plays: THE BITTER TEARS OF PETRA VON KANT (DIE BITTEREN TRÄNEN DER PETRA VON KANT) was a version of Fassbinder's own stage play of the same name, and WILD GAME (WILDWECHSEL) was derived from the play by Franz Xaver Kroetz. Outwardly the two films have little in common. PETRA VON KANT, subtitled 'A Case of Illness', is one of Fassbinder's most stylized, theatrical, and wordy films. It runs for over two hours, during which the camera never leaves the opulent studio-apartment of the dress-designer heroine – the 'stage' on which the small cast of actresses (there are no men in the film) work out their various relationships with Petra. WILD GAME, on the other hand, takes place in a working-class milieu, its characters are semi-articulate, its settings are varied and frequently located out of doors.

Petra von Kant, once widowed, once divorced, with a daughter at boarding school, lives and works in a sumptuously decadent pleasure-dome of an apartment, slavishly attended by her assistant-cum-secretary Marlene. Petra's friend Sidonie von Grasenabb introduces her to the vaguely sluttish Karin, whom Petra wants to employ as a mannequin, and with whom she soon falls possessively and jealously in love. One morning Karin casually tells Petra of a brief affair with a black man. The relationship changes: Petra at first insults Karin, then begs her to stay. Karin nonetheless leaves to rejoin her husband who has just returned from Australia. Petra is visited on her birthday by her daughter Gaby, her mother, and Sidonie; drunk and in furious despair she stamps on her delicate china tea-set and tells them all to go to hell. Alone with Marlene she slowly realizes that her sin has been tyranny and possessiveness: 'I didn't love Karin at all, I just wanted to own her.' Too late she tries to make amends, to 'give' Marlene her freedom. Marlene's answer (she never speaks a word in the whole film) is to put an appropriate record on the hi-fi: 'The Great Pretender'. Then she packs her case and leaves.

The figure of Marlene is the strongest link between this film and its predecessor, THE MERCHANT OF THE FOUR SEASONS. She is another variant of the Hans Epp character, used and abused, unloved, permanently on the periphery of other people's lives. Throughout the film she is present in the background of the action, working on a design, typing, always silently watching. Her importance for Fassbinder is attested by the fact that although the stage play is dedicated to Margit Carstensen, who plays the part of Petra, the film is dedicated 'to the one who here became Marlene'. Marlene realizes that to accept Petra's offer of 'freedom' would merely confirm her bondage still further: it would not only be conceding Petra's right to rule over her life, but it would also simply perpetuate the role she plays of the means to another person's ends – the means here of assuaging Petra's conscience. Unlike other similar characters in Fassbinder, Marlene commits neither suicide nor murder (though she briefly toys with a pistol before dropping it into her case at the end). Instead she, who for so long had seemed utterly broken and helpless, rebels, taking the freedom that only she can give herself.

THE BITTER TEARS OF PETRA VON KANT was filmed at Worpswede, the artists' village near Bremen (Bremen airport is mentioned when Karin arranges to meet her husband). With WILD GAME Fassbinder returned to Bavaria, to the petty-bourgeois and working-class milieu that characterizes the bulk of his films. Franz Xaver Kroetz, the Bavarian author of the play, was, like Fassbinder, born in 1946. His work is partly in the tradition of the popular peasant theatre of Anzengruber and Thoma, partly in that of the Naturalism of Gerhart Hauptmann. But more than anything, he has come to be regarded as a latter-day exponent of the *Volkstheater* of Marieluise Fleisser and Ödön von Horváth. Like them he is concerned with that segment of the working and lower middle class that has no clear roots, no clear identity, traditions, or culture, and above all no real language. For Kroetz language, or rather the lack of language, is a central issue: his underprivileged protagonists remain trapped in their social deprivation because they do not have the language to analyse their problems, let alone to communicate them to others. They resort to the clichés and sententious stereotypes of the class above them: reactionary attitudes that only betray their own interests. Inarticulacy affects their personal life too: their feelings and emotions are ill-served by their restricted capacity for verbal expression, they talk in approximations and broken phrases, or remain silent. Armed only with the clichés of popular romance and melodrama they struggle to confront the depth and complexity of their own emotions, adopting the handed-down jargon of a debased and debasing commercialized 'culture'. And when all else fails, their frustration vents itself in sudden outbursts of 'mindless violence' which, reported but never analysed, are then fed back into their world in the sensational stories of the mass press.

Such themes, characters, and settings are of course familiar Fassbinder territory, and it is no surprise that he should have produced a version of a play by his contemporary and fellow-Bavarian. WILD GAME is about many of Fassbinder's favourite themes: the oppressive constraints and hypocrisies of provincial petty-bourgeois attitudes; the frustrations of inarticulacy; the violence that can erupt from such constricted circumstances; and, above all, the tragedy of lovelessness

again, of love betrayed, of feelings unshared – a tragedy here conditioned by specific social, political, psychological, and even historical circumstances.

WILD GAME tells a story of teenage love: here once more the immensely trite and hackneyed subject is taken by the horns as Fassbinder looks for the truth behind the falsehoods and superficialities of a thousand sentimental songs. Hanni, a fourteen year-old schoolgirl, meets and sleeps with a nineteen year-old boy called Franz, who works in a ghastly chicken slaughterhouse. (In this case the favourite Fassbinder forename was actually already there in Kroetz's play.) A jealous friend reports him, and he is sent to prison for seducing a minor. After his release Franz continues to meet Hanni in secret. Hanni becomes pregnant, and persuades Franz to kill her father, as he is the main obstacle to their relationship. Franz is again arrested, this time for murder. The final scene takes place outside the courtroom. Hanni now seems a little girl again as she nonchalantly plays hopscotch on the shadows of the corridor floor; she informs Franz that their child was deformed and died two minutes after birth, and then

WILD GAME Harry Baer as Franz and Eva Mattes as Hanni

goes on to proclaim that their relationship was never real love, only a physical affair. Franz professes agreement, then asks what name she would have given the child. 'Michael,' she replies. By now Franz's face is wet with tears: 'Michael,' he concludes, 'that would have been nice.'

Throughout the film Franz's emotions – his deeper and deeper love for Hanni – clash with the image he has been conditioned to project. Harry Baer, who plays the part, manages magnificently to convey the disjunction between Franz's genuine feelings and the hollow clichés with which he has to express them or, with tough-guy crudity, 'manfully' belittle them. With his motorbike and his rocker garb,[3] Franz is not allowed, by social convention, to admit to such emotions as love, and so, when he first awkwardly introduces Hanni to his cronies in the café, he is obliged to adopt a façade of bravura, professing contempt for her as soon as she is out of earshot. So it is throughout the film, right through to the final sequence in the courthouse. So often it is Franz's soulful eyes that have given him away, pleading for some recognition and reciprocation of his love; now it is his tears that finally belie the cool, casual, indifferent façade.[4]

Franz, who incriminates himself out of love for Hanni, teased, egged on, and then betrayed, is one of a long line of similar Fassbinder characters, and undoubtedly in the film Franz's role is the central one. This is, however, in both theme and characterization, a very rich film, and it would be a misrepresentation to dismiss the other characters as 'secondary'. The film is 'about' a specific society, it is 'about' all of these people, and, with the exception of two most improbable Hollywood-style detectives who have stepped straight out of Fassbinder's earlier films, all of the characters convince. WILD GAME is an extraordinarily compassionate film, a film without villains, for the actions of all the characters are shown, in true naturalistic fashion, to be conditioned by their environment. The characters are of course unaware of this conditioning: Franz resorts to accusing 'Fate' – the ultimate key to all events for the resigned and bewildered – as the explanation for what has happened. ('You are my destiny' proclaims one of the three Paul Anka songs that ironically punctuate the action.) But as the settings and speeches indicate, their tragedy is in fact caused by political and economic conditions, by history and society, and more specifically by the peculiarly *German* experience of history and a peculiarly Bavarian petty-bourgeois Catholic society. (Hanni's house is generously adorned with crucifixes and religious pictures, including a large madonna and child to which the camera moves and lingers at the end of one sequence in her pregnancy; Franz too wears a crucifix; and across the river behind the opening titles a church can be seen: it is there again during a riverside sequence towards the middle of the film, at the end of which the camera zooms briefly towards its twin towers.)

Thus even the father, the most obvious candidate for villain of the piece, is treated with understanding. He yearns for the order and discipline of the Nazi years, when such 'degenerates' as Franz would have been sent to a concentration camp. The solution is castration, he proclaims, and adds, 'It's because we haven't got a regime any more but a government.' His wife's views are less extreme: 'The Nazis made their mistakes too,' she observes, to which the father agrees that it was 'not right' to gas the Jews; but then his personal indignation overrides his glimmerings of better judgement, and he concludes, 'I'd rather we gassed a hundred thousand Jews than have my child done wrong to by some swine like that.' Such disastrous and offensive sentiments do not however turn the father into a villain. His youth, we learn, like that of so many of his generation, was lost to Hitler, fighting and suffering on the Eastern Front; he grew up in a different world, believing in discipline, order, propriety. The modern world with its social and sexual permissiveness is to him an aberration, a threat to the wholesomeness that he believes his daughter should enjoy. 'In five years' time,' he says, 'she'll blame us for letting her wreck her prospects of a normal future,' and thus discipline is what she needs, for her own good. The parents' bigotry is thus shown as a function of their incomprehension and fear of the world around them, a result even of the quite genuine love they have for one another as well as for their daughter.[5]

In portraying the father as a man who is incapable of following through the logic of his arguments because his fund of clichés does not extend that far, Fassbinder is sticking very close to Kroetz's original. Indeed, throughout the film, the text of the play is followed very carefully. It is thus perhaps surprising that the film WILD GAME led to accusations by Kroetz that Fassbinder's attitude to the characters was 'obscene', that the film as a whole was 'pornographic'. Admittedly Fassbinder had added a couple of brief sequences that, after a legal case brought by Kroetz, were later removed. In one of them Hanni propositions a *Gastarbeiter* when Franz is in jail, and in another the father makes sexual advances to the (consenting) daughter. Even the hint of incestuous sexuality that the film in its cut version still retains (a shot of the father looking lasciviously at Hanni, who smiles as he walks away) by no means undermines the basic compassion with which Fassbinder approaches all these figures. Kroetz's complaints are wide of the mark: Fassbinder's film is if anything even more indulgent than the original play.

In the summer of 1972, after a year of research and preparation, Fassbinder's biggest-ever project was produced, the television series EIGHT HOURS DON'T MAKE A DAY (ACHT STUNDEN SIND KEIN TAG), consisting of five parts of roughly one and a half hours each. The series was commissioned by the WDR – the *Westdeutscher Rundfunk*, the biggest and one of the most progressive of the nine regional broadcasting corporations that provide the programmes for the first television channel in West Germany, and the corporation that has most often been associated with Fassbinder's work. Fassbinder was to make a popular 'family series', a series about working people in Cologne, the WDR's home city. It turned out to be one of the most remarkable events that West German television had ever seen, for within the constraints of one of the most stereotyped of popular genres Fassbinder created a didactic portrait of three generations of a working-class family finding their way through to a greater awareness of – and thus potentially mastery over – the economic, political, social, and psychological mechanisms that frustrate them in their daily lives at home and at work: a far cry from the pessimistic image of the benighted Bavarian lower classes in WILD GAME. EIGHT HOURS DON'T MAKE A DAY was followed with interest by a large audience, and was widely discussed in the media. Most right-wing critics not surprisingly disapproved of it, but so did some on the left, who complained of a lack of 'realism' – a sorry misapprehension of Fassbinder's technique of presenting a series of popularizing 'exemplary tales' rather than radical documentary. EIGHT HOURS was originally intended to run for eight episodes; in the event only five were made. No convincing official explanation has ever been given for this truncation: such prevarication leads inevitably to the suspicion that the implications of the series were simply becoming too radical for the WDR hierarchy to sanction. Somewhat less evasive statements by Fassbinder himself seem to confirm the suspicion that the WDR had suddenly been stricken with that all too familiar allergy of broadcasting corporations: an attack of cold feet brought on by something too hot to handle. Problems in the characters' private lives that went beyond the confines of the original image of a (more or less) happy family met with objections, according to Fassbinder, as did an increasingly radical critique of the activities of the trade unions planned for later episodes.

Each of the five episodes of EIGHT HOURS DON'T MAKE A DAY has as its title the names of two characters whose relationship plays a major role in it, a device that immediately points up the 'human interest' angle from which Fassbinder tackles his subject matter. Episode One, entitled 'Jochen and Marion', makes use of the very traditional pretext of a family gathering to introduce us to the characters: here, the grandmother's sixtieth-birthday party. Her grandson Jochen, a focal figure in the series as a whole, goes out to buy some drink, and returns with Marion, whom he has met by chance by the vending machines that they were both using. Later another relationship is cemented when the ebullient Grandma (the other focal figure of the whole series) picks up the charming but shy elderly Gregor in a park – a park where she manifests her characteristic humane rebelliousness by hoodwinking a park-keeper, through an appeal to his very German respect for official proclamations and bureaucratic jargon, into allowing children to play on the grass. As in all the episodes a balance is struck between sequences at home and sequences at work. (The title of the series reflects its concern with the role the workplace plays in people's lives: most 'family series' prefer to ignore it and concentrate almost exclusively on home and social life.) Although we see something of Marion's work in the small-ads department of a local newspaper, the principal workplace in the series is the factory where Jochen and his colleagues are employed as toolmakers (the factory sequences were actually shot on location in the Mannesmann works). Here a dispute arises over the firm's withdrawal of a productivity bonus after an improvement suggested by Jochen has, according to the management, made it 'superfluous'. The episode closes with the unexpected death of the much-liked foreman, a result, it seems, of the stress caused by the dispute.

Episode One carefully sets the scene for the events that are to follow. Three basic settings are established: home, workplace, and place of entertainment (in this case a bar). So too are personalities and relationships. And finally, the first glimmerings of a new political awareness are hinted at in the grandmother's rebellion against the petty park regulations, and in the discussions between the workers, who finally win back their bonus by a pointed campaign of 'accidental' minor sabotage. Above all, the first episode establishes a basic theme of the whole series: that work and home life cannot be separated. The problems of the one spill over into the other; both are integral parts of the lives of these people, and not the mutually exclusive spheres that so many television series, plays, and films would have us believe.

Episode Two, 'Grandma and Gregor', shows the old couple vainly in search of a flat. Grandma, shocked by the astronomical rents, determines to set up an accommodation bureau for old people, but then decides instead to get a Kindergarten set up in an abandoned library. With the help of Jochen and his colleagues the nursery is made ready, only to be closed by the police. Demonstrations and protests finally lead to its reopening under a trained nursery teacher. At work, Franz Miltenberger, one of Jochen's older colleagues, applies for the vacant foremanship, but is turned down by the management.

Episode Three, 'Franz and Ernst', is the weakest of the series, lacking the vigour and authenticity of the others. It is concerned in particular with the appointment of a new foreman. Ernst, the management's choice, is an outsider, and is given the cold shoulder by the workers who had wanted Franz to get the job. It turns out that Ernst would in fact rather be employed elsewhere in the factory in any case, and he willingly helps Franz prepare for his examination.

In Episodes Four and Five personal relationships come to play a major role, whilst at the same time – particularly in Episode Five – the characters' political insight grows by leaps and bounds (too fast, it seems, for the WDR, for this is where the series was stopped). Episode Four is called 'Harald and Monika', and revolves around the making and undoing of two marriages. Monika is Jochen's sister, unhappily married to the offensive little tyrant Harald. Jochen and Marion, meanwhile, decide to marry, and at their wedding Harald and Monika agree to separate. While all this is going on, Jochen's best friend Manfred is falling in love with Monika. . . . Episode Five, 'Irmgard and Rolf', brings in another love story, the Irmgard in question being a very prim and proper colleague of Marion's. Her reserve and snobbery are at last broken down by her affection for Rolf, another of Jochen's colleagues, whom she met at Jochen's wedding. Yet another love relationship is cemented at the end of the episode when, through the cunning agency of Grandma, Monika and Manfred are able to declare their love to one another.

So much sentimental romance sounds on the surface singularly out of place in a would-be didactic, radical, and emancipatory series. Yet its presence and the way it is handled typifies Fassbinder's technique in this as in his other works: the ostensible sentimentality is part of the deliberate mass appeal of EIGHT HOURS DON'T MAKE A DAY. On closer inspection it turns out not to be so trite after all. Fassbinder uses it as a vehicle for 'smuggling in' all sorts of radical messages. Thus the relationship between Grandma and Gregor presents them not in the debasing stereotype of old people as doddery half-wits, but as a couple who are actually having an affair, and thoroughly enjoying the raised eyebrows this causes. Monika's marriage to Harald comes to grief because of Harald's authoritarian attitudes, not only towards Monika herself, whose proper place he insists lies in the home, but also to their little daughter, who, he feels, should be 'trained' rather than educated, 'slotted in' to her role in society – an echo of the attitudes that had distressed Hanna in RIO DAS MORTES. And then, in addition to questioning stereotyped images of old people, women, and education, most of the 'sentimental' relationships in the series also confront attitudes to the working class, as in Marion's mother's initial reservations about her daughter's choice of a worker, reservations that are soon overcome when she discovers Jochen is also a person, someone, in fact, with whom she develops a close and warm friendship. Similar inhibitions are overcome by Irmgard when she falls in love with Rolf; and Monika, after a brief affair with a slick swindler, also frees herself from the unpleasant bourgeois Harald by finding happiness with the pleasant factory worker Manfred.

Episode Five, however, is more concerned with the politics of the shop floor than with those of marriage. It begins with the news that the management is planning to move the toolshop to an inconveniently distant suburb of the city. As a response to this the workers draw up a list of demands which, to their surprise, meet with broad approval. Amongst other things they obtain permission to determine both the division of labour among themselves and their working speed. Most of the factory sequences so far have shown them talking, scheming, or arguing; now in a sequence of almost lyrical shots we see them working, and working with zeal and enthusiasm. They achieve a saving of many hours on their first project under the new scheme, for which they receive a bonus. The subsequent celebration, however, becomes somewhat muted when their Italian colleague Giuseppe raises doubts that have not occurred to the others: they have, he points out, saved the company a given amount of money by working more efficiently, but have themselves been given only half that amount for their pains. In a later sequence they return to the topic, and Marion suddenly quite spontaneously thinks her way through to the theory of surplus value: 'I see now that when you work you only work partly for yourself.' 'Giuseppe said something like that too,' someone else muses. Giuseppe has in fact raised earlier the issue of workers' control too. In the canteen he had read a letter from a colleague in Italy about a strike in which the workers had occupied their factory; tired of doing nothing, they started up the production lines, and soon discovered that now they were running things themselves they were producing more. (Yet another radical ideal is 'smuggled in' here in Giuseppe's importation of activist Italian attitudes: the ideal of 'proletarian internationalism'.)

The implications of this train of events and ideas are far more radical than the sort of thing television corporations normally think fit for popular 'entertainment', if indeed they will countenance them at all. The factory boss has already indicated that it is in the *management's* interest to let the workers determine their own working arrangements; it is already dawning on the group that they have been hoodwinked into producing yet more profit for their employers under the pretext of generous 'concessions'. They have now realized two things: worker control increases production and the enjoyment of their work, but the more they produce the more the company takes in the way of profits. The sharing of profits, and full self-determination – the elimination, in other words, of the owners and bosses from the company hierarchy – is the obvious next step, a natural topic for the next episode. But the next episode was never made.

The role of Giuseppe in Episode Five is typical of the philosophy behind the whole series: those whose role in society is traditionally regarded as passive, and who are thus traditionally the most exploited and least privileged members of society – *Gastarbeiter*, women, old people, and ultimately the whole working class itself – are here shown in an active role, analysing, questioning, and generally taking the initiative. The process of self-emancipation is shown as the result of having the courage to *think*. It is also made clear that people can be won over by the example and the enthusiasm of the activist. The changing of attitudes is shown to begin unpromisingly with a recital of conservative, pessimistic, resignatory platitudes, pouring cold water on the activist's proposals. Then comes something more positive: though still somewhat sceptical, people begin to become intrigued, and then decide to 'give it a try' after all. The final stage comes when, flushed with the experience of actually having done something with their lives they take spontaneous action, and have now become activists themselves.

In EIGHT HOURS DON'T MAKE A DAY it is Grandma who is *the* guiding force behind the characters' growing political emancipation, with her constant injunctions to *think*, and then act. This comes over particularly clearly in the exemplary Kindergarten sequences of Episode Two. The project begins when Grandma and Gregor find that a small street-corner public library is being stripped out. The librarian informs her that the people in the area are too lazy to read, to which Grandma replies that they are perhaps too busy working. In the street outside children are forced to play among the parked and moving cars. Grandma has an idea. In order to realize it she must first spread her enthusiasm to others. Gregor is soon won over, as are Jochen and his colleagues, who spend the night decorating and fitting out the abandoned library as a Kindergarten. Half way through the night it dawns on them that this most sensible, logical, and decent of activities is in fact illegal, a realization that soon fills them with a spirit of delighted adventurousness at the sheer rebellious naughtiness of it all. Next Grandma must woo the children: after initial hesitation they come flooding in. The mothers are more wary: a sequence in a supermarket even shows them exchanging horror stories of children being lured into such dubious premises and then chopped up and eaten. But they too gain confidence and enthusiasm, and eventually take part with their children in a 'paint-in' at the city hall, a demonstration that forces the city authorities to back down and adopt – albeit with ill-grace – the Kindergarten project.

The Kindergarten episode is a nice example of what the whole series is trying to do: to show ordinary people confronting the injustices and the unnecessary deprivations that frustrate them. It shows the mechanisms, the processes of analysis and action, by which people can gain more insight into, and control over, their daily lives. This was particularly important in West Germany where the ideals and activities of the Left have never managed to win over the bulk of the working class, let alone the population as a whole. By clothing his subversive messages in the garb of a popular television genre Fassbinder was trying to break down the popular image of radical activity as the exclusive province of freaks, deviants, and terrorists. Here again the Kindergarten episode is exemplary: under the watchword of 'anti-authoritarian education' the late sixties and early seventies saw the opening in many West German cities of so-called 'child shops' ('Kinderläden') – self-help day-care nurseries set up in abandoned commercial premises. For all too many people these were simply another left-wing aberration: Fassbinder's achievement is to show ordinary people setting up their own *Kinderladen*, inspired by everyone's image of the warm-hearted, mischievous granny.

There are, however, two important areas in which

EIGHT HOURS DON'T MAKE A DAY fails to live up to its premisses. The first of these is its portrayal of women. Grandma is admittedly nothing short of a feminist, and Marion is a relatively liberated young woman, whilst in Monika we are presented with the plight of the mentally and physically battered wife. But these are the exceptions: most of the women in this series are shown as housewives who unquestioningly look after their menfolk, waiting on them at table, sewing, and ironing (this is especially true of Franz's wife and Jochen's mother). Perhaps by simply showing women in this situation Fassbinder is intending to question it, but such a coy approach has not been his technique with the other issues raised.

The other questionable point concerns the role of television in the characters' lives, or rather its apparent lack of any role. When asked what their main leisure activity is, most West Germans, like other Europeans, put television at the top of the list. In most families, several hours each day are devoted to watching television. There is in EIGHT HOURS a brief mention of television when, in Episode Two, Grandma mentions that she has watched a programme about old people's homes. At this Harald's hackles rise: 'On television!' he exclaims, 'they're always manipulating people so much.' This is a richly witty little incident, complemented by a sudden camera zoom to Peter Märthelsheimer, the producer of the series, who is an extra in this scene. (The device of zooming in to the face of someone reacting to a remark is a frequent device in this series.) 'Manipulation by the mass media' had been a major talking point among the radical Left of the late sixties. Harald, a die-hard reactionary, has picked up this phrase and adopted it for his own suspicions of *left*-wing bias in the media. In the shape of Harald, Fassbinder is partly anticipating criticisms of EIGHT HOURS, but at the same time he is making a valid, though by now decidedly hackneyed, point of his own. Television does 'manipulate': it is perhaps the most important medium for the consolidation of the ideology from which these people are beginning to distance themselves. EIGHT HOURS is itself television, a challenge to the traditional role of the medium, and evidence that it can serve a different function. It is thus odd that this awareness does not translate itself from the form of the series to its content, and show us the characters themselves confronting the television set as they must do in real life. Or perhaps it is not so odd: one can well imagine that a critique of television *on* television might be felt too subversive by even the most liberal-minded of broadcasting organizations. Perhaps we should after all be thankful that EIGHT HOURS even got as far as Episode Five.

After EIGHT HOURS DON'T MAKE A DAY Fassbinder began shooting EFFI BRIEST in the autumn of 1972. This film was, however, shot in two stages, and was not completed until the autumn of the following year. In the meantime 1973 saw the completion of three other films: WORLD ON A WIRE (WELT AM DRAHT), FEAR EATS THE SOUL (ANGST ESSEN SEELE AUF), and MARTHA. Having tried his hand at the crime film, the Western, and the family series, Fassbinder turned with WORLD ON A WIRE to another popular genre, science fiction. The complicated and action-packed story, based on a novel by Daniel F. Galouye and made in two parts for television, revolves around Fred Stiller, the head of a cybernetic research institute who is determined to get to the bottom of the mysterious 'suicide' of his friend and predecessor Vollmer. He is helped by Vollmer's daughter Eva, who falls in love with him, and who confirms what Fred is beginning to suspect: that their world is not real, but merely a computer projection. Such knowledge is dangerous: Stiller is hunted and shot by the police, but Eva 'saves' him by transferring his consciousness to another world.

Part One of WORLD ON A WIRE is shot largely indoors in opulent, sleek, futuristic offices and houses to the accompaniment of almost constant muzak. Part Two destroys some of the futuristic impression with its more seedy settings, including shots of the streets and traffic of contemporary suburban Paris (a location that emphasizes the many overtones in this film of Godard's ALPHAVILLE), and there is some uneasy cutting from French to German locales. Nonetheless, Part Two still has plenty of the space-age interiors that had dominated in Part One, and with its eery electronic sounds, its sinister sudden disappearances and mysterious metamorphoses WORLD ON A WIRE seems on the surface to have little connection with the rest of Fassbinder's work.

Yet there are links that lead both backwards and forwards to other films. As in EIGHT HOURS DON'T MAKE A DAY Fassbinder here smuggles overt political implications into a genre that normally studiously avoids them. The film contains, for instance, the shady Hartmann steel concern that puts pressure on Stiller and his institute, whilst militant solidarity is exemplified in the strike called by the institute's workers to have Fred reinstated. Fred, in fact, is a rebel, a revolutionary even, for he knows too much, he knows they are being used by someone else, and is determined to escape this alienated role. It is worth bearing in mind that WORLD ON A WIRE was made at a time when the search for terrorists in West Germany was degenerating into a hysterical witch-hunt against radicals in general, for Fred is outlawed, declared insane, accused of murder, and hunted and hounded by the police and people, when in reality his dissatisfaction with the way things are stems from the fact that he is the one person who knows the truth about this society. But Fred is not just a political rebel, there is something of the existential hero about him too, for he knows they are shadows, that their existence is absurd, and the old question is raised again whether this knowledge which brings such pain and panic is really desirable: he could live so much more happily in ignorance of the truth.

Betrayal by love had been a recurrent theme in earlier Fassbinder films. Here there is a happy ending, for Fred enjoys salvation by love: the love that breaks down class barriers (as in EIGHT HOURS) or the boundaries of race and culture (as in FEAR EATS THE SOUL) here becomes a love that, with almost religious overtones, transcends the levels of reality, as Fred is 'saved' and 'elevated' to a more authentic existence by Eva. Yet a doubt must remain at the end: are the levels of reality perhaps infinite? Has Eva not simply pulled Fred one rung up a ladder that stretches upwards from one computer projection to the next? Fred was, after all, himself working on computer simulations of yet another possible world. The puzzle, worthy of Juan Luis Borges, is reflected in a device that was soon to become a new hallmark of Fassbinder's work: the use of mirrors. The film opens to the music of Bach, the 'Art of Fugue', interweaving sequence upon sequence in an echo of the multiple layers of reality that seem to reflect one another in an infinite wilderness of mirrors – and there are mirrors a-plenty in this film, where the motif of the interchangeability of existence already anticipates one of Fassbinder's ultimate mirror-pieces, DESPAIR.

vi The International Breakthrough

Up to 1973 Fassbinder's work was known only to a limited circle of cineastes outside West Germany. Then FEAR EATS THE SOUL, made in September 1973, won the International Critics' Prize at the 1974 Cannes Festival. This was the film that brought a breakthrough to a much wider audience through cinema and television showings in many countries, and finally established not only Fassbinder's reputation as a talent to be reckoned with, but also confirmed for many foreign critics that the 'New German Cinema' was more than just an empty catch-phrase. The material for FEAR EATS THE SOUL had been anticipated in THE AMERICAN SOLDIER in a bizarre sequence where, as the ex-soldier Ricky and the porn-dealer Magdalena lie embracing naked on a hotel bed, the frustrated chamber-maid Margarethe sits between them and the camera and tells the true story of Emmi, the charwoman, who one rainy evening went into a bar frequented by *Gastarbeiter* and danced with Ali the Turk, whom she later married. But one day Emmi is found strangled, on her neck the marks of a signet ring bearing the letter 'A'. The police are unable to find the killer – so many Turks are called 'Ali'.[6]

Here, in essence, is the story of FEAR EATS THE SOUL, but it undergoes some changes. Hamburg, the location of the original, has become Munich, and the *Gastarbeiter* is no longer a Turk but a Moroccan, not least to enable the actor El Hedi ben Salem to fit the part (he had already played a *Gastarbeiter* in WILD GAME and in EIGHT HOURS DON'T MAKE A DAY). More fundamental, however, is the change that the ending undergoes: now Emmi is not murdered.

In FEAR EATS THE SOUL Fassbinder examines two sets of reactions to this unlikely marriage between the dumpy German widow and the tall young Arab: firstly those of other people, and then those of the couple themselves. Ali's and Emmi's marriage brings out all the latent prejudice against *Gastarbeiter* in Emmi's family (she has three married children), among her neighbours (particularly the local grocer, who simply turns her out of his shop), and among the women she works with, who refuse to talk to her. At this level the film is not saying anything remarkable or original: we know that racial prejudice exists, and that in West Germany it manifests itself in particular as prejudice against *Gastarbeiter*. Fassbinder has shown this before, notably in KATZELMACHER, and, as in that film, he is not concerned here so much with the problems faced by the *Gastarbeiter* themselves, as with the problems of West German society that their presence brings to the surface. In KATZELMACHER, however, he had shown how a crypto-fascist mentality is caused to erupt when something not particularly remarkable happens: a *Gastarbeiter* forms a relationship with a nubile young German girl. The shocking thing about FEAR EATS THE SOUL as far as the secondary characters, and for that matter the audience, is concerned are the untrite twists that Fassbinder has given to a very trite situation. The relationship now is not just sexual, but very much an emotional one; the couple do not just become lovers, but they actually marry. But of course Fassbinder's most important innovation is the age difference between the couple: Emmi is quite literally old enough to be Ali's mother. It is this as much as anything that arouses not only the indignation, but also the sheer incredulity of the world outside. Emmi is, as far as they are concerned, not only behaving like a whore, but is mad to boot.

By showing the relationship between Ali and Emmi as something perfectly natural (an achievement attributable in large measure to the conviction with which Brigitta Mira plays Emmi), FEAR EATS THE SOUL becomes not only a statement about the artificiality of racial prejudice, but also an assertion of the neglected needs and rights of old people, on a par with that made through the Grandma and Gregor episodes of EIGHT HOURS DON'T MAKE A DAY.

It has often been remarked that FEAR EATS THE SOUL is in this respect remarkably close to Douglas Sirk's 1955 film ALL THAT HEAVEN ALLOWS, in which a wealthy widow incurs the contempt of her friends and relations when she falls in love with a young gardener. (Fassbinder, interestingly enough, did not know Sirk's film at the time of the maid's monologue in THE AMERICAN SOLDIER, but he had seen it by the time he made FEAR EATS THE SOUL.) The melodrama of Sirk's films has become an important point of reference for Fassbinder in his attempts to make German films in the Hollywood manner. Fassbinder's analysis of the social and psychological roots of prejudice goes further, however, than Sirk's portrait of small-town American life in the 1950s. In the middle of FEAR EATS THE SOUL Ali and Emmi go away on a holiday. When they return attitudes have changed: neighbours, relations, colleagues, the shopkeeper, all seem to have become more friendly – on the surface, at least, for it is made clear that their outward attitudes are governed by self-interest: they all need in various ways to exploit the couple they had initially ostracized. But now that the external pressures on Ali and Emmi are diminished, cracks begin to show in their own relationship. It becomes clear that Emmi herself is not entirely free of the prejudices of her fellow Germans. She begins to treat Ali less as a person and more as an object. Ali in turn visits an old girl friend; the marriage suddenly seems in trouble. But then, in an echo of the opening sequence, Emmi and Ali are dancing again in the *Gastarbeiter* bar, when Ali suddenly collapses in agony. In the hospital a perforated stomach ulcer is diagnosed, a common result of the stress that *Gastarbeiter* are placed under, says the doctor. Ali will need much care and attention if a recurrence of the complaint is to be avoided. In a sentimental but appropriately bleak 'happy ending' Emmi resolves to look after him.

vii Four Married Women

FEAR EATS THE SOUL was followed by a trio of works that deal with marriage from the woman's viewpoint, all three of which were premiered in the first half of 1974: NORA HELMER, MARTHA, and EFFI BRIEST. A year later, a fourth film was added to the group in the shape of FEAR OF FEAR.

NORA HELMER (which is the usual German title for the Ibsen play that is known in England as *A Doll's House*) was a video production for television made in May 1973. It was badly received by the critics, who found it excessively mannered. Fassbinder, in trying to capture the claustrophobia of the Helmer household, had plastered the set with mirrors, glass partitions, doors, and filigree drapes, around which, and through which, the cameras waltzed and swirled and peered. Fassbinder had attempted a 'reinterpretation' of Ibsen

which, apart from making up the unfortunate Mrs Linde (played improbably by the traditionally sexy Barbara Valentin) with what looked very much like flour, also turned Nora herself into a much more self-possessed character from the outset. This had the effect of taking much of the force out of the final confrontation between Nora and Torvald, which no longer comes with the shock of pent-up tension released. But it was not this that bothered the critics so much as the visual tricks: Fassbinder had seriously over-indulged his growing delight in mirror images, framed shots, and camera movements. The visual gimmickry that comes to the fore in WORLD ON A WIRE, and becomes a feature of nearly all subsequent films, is at its most obtrusive in NORA HELMER.

MARTHA was much better received. Fassbinder took the idea for the film from the American thriller-writer Cornell Woolrich-Hopley, whose novels *The Bride Wore Black* and *Waltz into Darkness* had been adapted for the cinema by François Truffaut. Shortly after her father's unexpected death during their holiday in Rome, Martha Hyer meets and marries an impeccably suave and wealthy engineer by the name of Helmut Salomon. Marriage rapidly becomes a prison for the highly-strung Martha, in which she is subjected to Helmut's increasingly sadistic 'educational measures', which involve leaving her isolated in their vast and gloomy mansion while he goes off on his regular business trips. Martha secretly meets Kaiser, a former colleague from the library where she once worked. One day in his car she is stricken by panic at the thought that they are being followed. The car crashes, and Kaiser is killed; Martha is crippled for life. Helmut collects her from hospital in her wheelchair: 'Now you are mine forever,' he says.

This grim little tale hovers between the black humour of Buñuel, the melodrama of Sirk, and the edginess of Hitchcock. But in its subject matter it lies in the tradition of Ibsen, and the links with *A Doll's House* are obvious. In MARTHA Fassbinder succeeded where in NORA HELMER many felt he had failed. MARTHA too has its visual mannerisms, but here they are well integrated, they concentrate rather than distract the attention. MARTHA in fact is one of the most tightly-controlled and well-paced of Fassbinder's films, where a compelling nervousness that matches

EFFI BRIEST Hanna Schygulla as Effi, Wolfgang Schenk as her husband von Instetten, and Karlheinz Böhm as the family friend Wüllersdorf the heroine's barely-suppressed hysteria is achieved in the tension between the cool presentation and the explosive contents.

MARTHA was both preceded and followed by EFFI BRIEST (FONTANE EFFI BRIEST), for although the actual shooting time of this film was only fifty-eight days (which was nonetheless more than Fassbinder had devoted to any other work), the male lead, Wolfgang Schenk, fell ill, and it was a year before filming could be resumed in the autumn of 1973. Theodor Fontane was perhaps the only nineteenth-century German novelist whose work bears comparison with the realist classics of French, Russian, or English literature. A lifetime of experience and observation went into his work – quite literally, for he was in his fifties when he first began writing novels. The first draft of his major work *Effi Briest* was written in 1890, stimulated by news of a real event, and appeared in its final form in 1895, by which time Fontane was seventy-six. (He died in 1898.)

The setting of the story both in time and place are important: Fontane places it in his own time in his native Prussia, and it reflects the social codes of a still intact but slightly uneasy landed aristocracy. At seventeen Effi (played in the film by Hanna Schygulla in the best of her many major roles for Fassbinder) is married at her parents' instigation to Baron von Instetten, a contemporary of her mother's. Her husband shows affection, but no real love. He is a man of principles and ambition, and, left alone while he goes off in the furtherance of his career, Effi feels isolated in the cold and snobbish privincial world of the little Baltic Sea town where they live. A friend of her husband's, Major Crampas, himself unhappily married, and something of a rake, gives her the attention and understanding that she lacks, and she has a brief affair with him. Instetten and Effi move to Berlin. The Crampas affair is long forgotten when one day Instetten finds some incriminating letters. Although six years have elapsed, as a matter of principle rather than out of any sense of jealousy or vindictiveness Instetten challenges Crampas to a duel, and kills him. For similar reasons he then sends Effi away from home, keeping custody of their little daughter whom he turns against her mother. Effi eventually returns to her parents; her spirit crushed, her will to live broken, she dies a year later.

It would be easy to see this story as an indictment of a rigid and heartless, outmoded morality; an assertion of the rights of the free spirit, of passion over stifling conventions. Comparisons with such other nineteenth-century heroines as Anna Karenina, Emma Bovary, or Nora Helmer come to mind. And yet that is not how Fontane paints things: 'Marriage is order', was his comment on Ibsen's *Doll's House*. Fontane's manner is restrained, sceptical even, and in *Effi Briest* it is Effi's father who has the last word with his resigned sigh, 'Such things are beyond us.' Effi's attitude is similar; she has internalized the attitudes of her society, and accepts as just the retribution she suffers for her innocent transgression.

Fassbinder's film keeps very close to Fontane in all respects, and accordingly restraint is the keynote throughout its 141 minutes' running time. As a token of this, EFFI BRIEST was made in black and white, using a slow and beautifully modulated film stock. The fervid, explosive tension of MARTHA has been replaced with a calm and gentle melancholy. The exaggerated mannerisms of NORA HELMER give way to sober precision, although Fassbinder's determination to find every excuse to frame images in mirrors does still run away with him at times. EFFI BRIEST shows Fassbinder at his most modest. This is 'the film of the book' in the best sense, a film instinct with respect and understanding for its source. The German title, 'FONTANE EFFI BRIEST', makes clear the homage to the author that is intended. Contrary to common practice in filmic 'adaptations' of books, Fassbinder's film does everything to proclaim its origins as a novel. *Effi Briest* is divided with classical symmetry into five sections. The film too is made up of a series of distinct episodes marked off by the unusual technique of fading out the picture to a blank white screen at the end of an episode, and fading in from white at the beginning of each new one. Quotations from the novel appear as intertitles, summarizing intervening events or the coming episode, or pointing up a moral. In a voice-over narrative Fassbinder himself, in a tentative, almost wondering tone, reads passages from the novel.

The commentary is never angry, just as the sequences are never overtly emotional, with all scenes of violence being carefully avoided. It is precisely by this very restraint that EFFI BRIEST makes its impact: it is a far cry from the melodrama so often associated with Fassbinder, but its message is nonetheless clear. Its formal restraint mirrors the restraint that has been the deadener of these people's lives, the represser of their emotions and feelings. Nature and convention are reflected in Effi's father and mother (not to mention Instetten) respectively. But nature is also there literally in the fields and woods, the lakesides and the beach – scenes that alternate with numbingly cultured wealthy interiors. The landscapes are beautiful, but not wild; they are nature 'tamed', the estates of the Prussian aristocracy. So too Effi's father, kindly, tolerant, gentle, is no romantic rebel: he too, in his melancholy resignation, ultimately accepts the all-pervasive social code. In the manner of the earliest novelists, Fassbinder has appended a subtitle to his film. In full it reads: 'FON-TANE EFFI BRIEST or Many who have an inkling of their possibilities and needs and yet still accept the prevailing order in their heads in the way they act and thereby consolidate and confirm it absolutely' – a motto that could serve for all of Fassbinder's films, but which here serves as the only thematic emphasis in a most unemphatic work.

In the spring of 1975 Fassbinder made FEAR OF FEAR (ANGST VOR DER ANGST), which, in its portrayal of the tribulations of a married woman, is a pendant to the NORA HELMER / MARTHA / EFFI BRIEST trilogy. The film is based on the semi-autobiographical account written by Asta Scheib, a young Schweinfurt housewife. Margot, a young married woman, suffers from debilitating attacks of anxiety. She gets little help from others: her husband, kindly enough in his way, is at work all day and revising for exams in his free time; her mother-in-law and her sister-in-law who live on the next floor of their apartment block are ashamed of her 'illness', and react with contemptuous hostility; the chemist over the road provides her with prescription-free supplies of valium, only in order to have a superficial affair with her; her doctor is simply bewildered; and a psychiatrist wrongly diagnoses schizophrenia. Only two people seem to offer any contact or sympathy: there is firstly her next-door neighbour who himself has serious psychiatric problems – but she rejects his desperate appeals for company because he is 'mad'; and secondly there is her little daughter Bibi, her closest and most beloved companion – but Bibi is too young to discuss things. Finally Margot goes to a clinic for treatment. She returns nominally 'cured', only to discover that the 'mad' neighbour has killed himself. It seems a new attack of her old anxiety is coming on again – the closing credits begin to 'swim', a crude and questionable device used throughout the film to signify Margot's 'Angst'.

FEAR OF FEAR takes up once more the theme of lovelessness, of the need for warmth and companionship in an indifferent or even hostile society. But unlike Fassbinder's many other films on this theme, FEAR OF FEAR operates in something of a vacuum. The perspective is that of Margot herself (hence the recurrent 'swimmy' sequences); the social context in which she lives is not elaborated, and her own inability to define what is wrong leaves the audience with the task of piecing things together to an extent that is rare in Fassbinder's work. As the title indicates, Margot is trapped in a vicious circle of anxiety: at one point she tells her husband 'I am afraid of . . .', but is unable to complete the sentence. Lore, the acerbic sister-in-law, simply pronounces Margot to be 'mad' after the (false) schizophrenia diagnosis. Her mother-in-law finds Margot's affection for Bibi is unnatural: 'All that kissing and cuddling, that's not normal,' she declares, to which Lore triumphantly proclaims '*We*'re the normal ones.' The dismissal of human warmth, love, and affection as 'abnormal' is a symptom of something wrong in society, and not of any 'illness' in Margot. If anything, her problem is that she has human needs in a world that makes little provision for their satisfaction. Margot simply needs someone she can talk to, no one seems able to prescribe the one cure she needs, which is *company*. It is an ultimate irony that in the expensive clinic to which she finally resorts her room-mate at any one time is either undergoing sleep-treatment, or sitting bolt upright in bed in a dream-like trance.

At two points the wider world intrudes into this claustrophobically hermetic film. One of these brings in the theme of education. Margot one day goes to collect Bibi from Kindergarten, and is outraged to find the children sitting in silence as a punishment for being 'wicked'. 'Can a four-year-old be wicked?' she asks her husband. 'Of course,' he replies, and goes on, like Harald in EIGHT HOURS DON'T MAKE A DAY, to talk of education as a preparation for the harsh realities of life.

Margot would like to take Bibi out of the Kindergarten and have her at home with her; her husband quietly but firmly rejects the idea. Bibi, when given the choice, is uncertain, but says she cannot do it tomorrow, because tomorrow they have to make their Chinese lanterns, and she cannot do it the day after tomorrow, because the day after tomorrow they have to. . . . It is frighteningly clear that the little girl, simply by being sent from this 'abnormal' mother to a 'normal' Kindergarten is already being conditioned for the programmed adult world of commitments that get in the way of human relationships – being prepared, that is, for the 'harsh realities of life'.

The other intrusion of the outside world is brief and uncommented, but memorable because of its apparent gratuitousness. Several times in the film the camera looks down from Margot's window through the crown of a chestnut tree to the street below. Normally these shots show people meeting or passing, but once, quite unexpectedly, a police armoured car passes noisily across. This incident is surely not as fortuitous as it may at first seem: it reminds one with a shock that is all the greater for its uniqueness of the wider political reality of West Germany in 1975. It brings a glimpse of the wider anxiety gripping this whole society, of the repression needed to bottle in the frustrations it has created. The armoured car is the political equivalent of Margot's valium: an attempt to quell the symptoms by those who are too shortsighted to cure the illness.

viii Outcasts

Before the completion of EFFI BRIEST Fassbinder had been involved in 1973 with a very different film, this time not as director, but as producer. The film in question was TENDERNESS OF THE WOLVES (DIE ZÄRTLICHKEIT DER WÖLFE), a film 'from the Fassbinder stable' in that its director, Ulli Lommel, and most of the leading players (including Fassbinder himself) were members of the Fassbinder team. TENDERNESS OF THE WOLVES was a new version of Fritz Lang's 1931 film M, based on the case of the Düsseldorf child murderer Fritz Haarmann. Joseph Losey had directed a remake of the story in an American setting in 1951; Ulli Lommel's version is set in Germany in the black-market period after World War Two. In it the bald Fritz Haarmann, a black-marketeer in meat of dubious provenance, patrols a station for the police, where he picks up his victims. Eventually he is found out and taken away.

Haarmann in TENDERNESS OF THE WOLVES is presented as a pathetic, and even a likeable character, a petty thief and a roguish confidence trickster who, disguised as a priest, sanctimoniously begs for clothes on behalf of a well-known charity. His furtive flashing eyes and jerky movements when he is finally hunted and trapped are a direct reminiscence of Peter Lorre's famous performance in the Fritz Lang original. Indeed, the general purport of Lommel's film – the rendering sympathetic of an outcast 'monster' – is close to the original too, and inasmuch as TENDERNESS OF THE WOLVES lacks much of the gripping tension and pace that Lang created, it is no real advance on M.

Where Lommel does differ fundamentally from Lang is in his concentration on the figure of Haarmann. In Lang's film the murderer comes only slowly to the fore; the viewpoint initially is that of the police and populace. (The mysterious murders, incidentally, engender a public mood of suspicion, hysteria, and denunciation that is uncannily like the state of 1970s West Germany that was to be portrayed in GERMANY IN AUTUMN.) Lommel's Haarmann is in the foreground from the outset, and so are his crimes. Lang had shown nothing of M's murders; Lommel shows all. It was this tongue-in-cheek explicitness, the nudity, the macabre and bloody vampirism, and the homosexuality (for the victims here are boys, and no longer M's little girls) that brought public objections, censorship, and then the inevitable *succès de scandale* to TENDERNESS OF THE WOLVES.

If there is a common denominator in the films Fassbinder made between 1974 and 1976 it lies in what could broadly be described as the figure of the outcast. Clearly Haarmann in TENDERNESS OF THE WOLVES is one such figure. In following films homosexuals, old people, disillusioned radicals, and unloved children are portrayed, whilst the 1976 film SHADOWS OF THE ANGELS, which Fassbinder scripted and acted in, deals with prostitutes, racketeers, and homosexuals again, as well as raising the sensitive issue of the role played in West Germany by the country's Jewish community.

The homosexual motif has always been present in

Fassbinder's films, implicitly in the early detective films, explicitly in such works as PETRA VON KANT.[7] In FOX (FAUSTRECHT DER FREIHEIT), made after EFFI BRIEST in the spring and summer of 1974, it plays a major role. It would be wrong, however, to see FOX as a film *about* homosexuality. This is no more a central theme than it was in PETRA VON KANT, or than racial prejudice was in KATZELMACHER or FEAR EATS THE SOUL. FOX operates within a totally homosexual milieu, a world of gay bars, shops, and offices, but apart from occasional digs at homosexual self-consciousness, it presents this world as an uncommented norm. The result is twofold: in the first place it makes FOX, for all its artifice and fictionality, a unique portrait of part of the gay scene in West Germany; and secondly a kind of alienation-effect is achieved, which Fassbinder has himself noted:

I think it's incidental that the story happens among gays. It could have worked just as well in another milieu. But I rather think that people look back at it more carefully precisely because of its setting.
. . . through a moment of positive shock, the whole story also looks different.[8]

The story is the old Fassbinder one of trust betrayed; the little man in need of help who is exploited instead. Love and class are the basic ingredients in another unashamedly sentimental melodrama. Fassbinder, in his biggest-ever film role, plays 'Fox, the talking head', a fairground attraction who finds himself out of a job when his boss and lover is arrested for tax offences. Fox, whose real name is Franz Biberkopf (Döblin's hero again), is picked up by Max, an antique-dealer, and introduced to his friend Eugen. Fox, the leather-jacketed proletarian, has both curiosity value and sex appeal for the wealthy and refined Munich circles into which he has now moved, but more to the point is the fact that he has just won half a million marks in a lottery. Eugen uses the money to purchase and furnish a new apartment for them both, as well as rehabilitating his father's foundering printing business, and going on a holiday to Morocco with Franz (a sequence shot in Marrakesh). When it becomes clear that Franz will never learn the manners of the 'better' classes, and when the money begins to run out, he becomes an

embarrassment and a burden to Eugen, who simply returns to his former lover, Philipp. Franz, broken-hearted, takes an overdose of valium, and dies in the shiny, deserted concourse of the new Marienplatz underground station. His body is robbed by two small boys; Max and his former fairground employer are seen passing quickly by on the other side.

The destruction of the unfortunate Franz divides FOX into two distinct parts. Initially he is a resilient character, cocky, cheeky in the face of the sybaritic finery of his new acquaintances. Eugen's attempts to 'educate' him, however (an echo of the 'education' suffered by Martha and Effi Briest) undermine his self-confidence. Fox becomes a pathetic figure, too pathetic perhaps, for his guilelessness and passivity as he is systematically exploited by all around him are only just made credible by the insecurity caused by his humiliation, and by his desperate love for Eugen. Like that other Franz in WILD GAME his love and dependence seem to grow in inverse relation to the possibility of fulfilment.

The final sequence in the underground station closes with a seemingly endless shot in which the two small boys, having looted Fox's pockets and taken his watch, now remove his denim jacket. The symbolism is blatant: even in death Fox is a victim – falling now to the scavengers – to be exploited to the full. The significance of his name is emphasized in the fact that the denim jacket, now seen in close-up, bears the inscription 'FOX' in studs on the back: the film has shown us the wealthy classes on one of their 'fox hunts'. His name may have other implications, though, for 'Fox' in German means a fox terrier: like Franz Kafka's Josef K., Fassbinder's Franz Biberkopf dies 'like a dog'.[9] The location of his death, in its gleaming but cold and soulless modernity, is a symbol of the affluent society that has brought him to this end. On the wall is a cigarette advertisement proclaiming 'Enjoyment in the Style of the New Age'. FOX is a film about the ruthlessness of this wealthy, exploitative society. Its German title, FAUSTRECHT DER FREIHEIT, literally 'Fist-law of Freedom', is a nonce construction that is roughly the equivalent of the English phrase 'law of the jungle', or 'law of the gun' – though the mention of 'freedom' points to the ideal that West Germany likes to see enshrined in its liberal, capitalist order.

FOX Karlheinz Böhm as Max, Fassbinder as Franz, and Peter Chatel as Eugen

FOX was the only film Fassbinder made in 1974. By the latter part of the year he was busy with a new job as dramatic director of one of West Germany's best-known theatres, the *Theater am Turm* in Frankfurt. Many of the old *anti-teater* team were involved with him in a project to reinvigorate the 'TAT', but in the event little was achieved. Promised productions failed to materialize, there were financial problems, rows, and eventually a scandal eagerly promoted by the media. As with the *anti-teater*, the tensions and temperamental clashes portrayed in BEWARE OF A HOLY WHORE led to the disintegration of another attempt at 'co-determination' in the Fassbinder troupe. After just one year in his new job, Fassbinder left the 'TAT' in August 1975.

The previous month Fassbinder had been involved in another scandal when MOTHER KÜSTERS' TRIP TO HEAVEN (MUTTER KÜSTERS' FAHRT ZUM HIMMEL), filmed in Frankfurt in the spring of 1975, was turned down by the Berlin Film Festival for fear of political reprisals. An unofficial screening in Berlin seemed to vindicate the Festival's timidity: the film did indeed arouse protests and threats – but they came not from the Right, as had traditionally been the case with Fassbinder's work, but from the Left.

The film's title is partly an echo of the German term for the religious feast of the Ascension – '*Himmelfahrt*' – but more pertinently it is taken from one of the classic radical films of the Weimar period, MOTHER KRAUSE'S TRIP TO HAPPINESS, directed in 1929 by Piel Jutzi, who two years later made a version of Döblin's *Berlin Alexanderplatz*. Jutzi's film is about the political and personal events leading up to the suicide of an old working-class woman; despite the tragedy of her death, the film concludes with an optimistic shot of workers marching to right the wrongs that have crushed the heroine.

There is no such revolutionary optimism in Fassbinder's film. His Mother Küsters (played by Brigitta Mira, the female lead in FEAR EATS THE SOUL) is suddenly widowed when her husband, threatened with redundancy, commits suicide after killing one of the bosses in the tyre factory where he has worked for twenty years. Her son and his wife desert her, and her daughter makes use of the scandal to further her career as a cabaret singer. Mother Küsters is harrassed by reporters, who are making a lot of running out of her personal tragedy. In her desolation, she finds understanding and quiet sympathy from a wealthy couple, the Tillmanns, who turn out to be communists. They also find her case worthy of publicity as well for its exemplary propaganda value. Mother Küsters is finally approached by a young anarchist, who inveigles her into visiting the offices of a magazine that has given sensational coverage to her story. Once there, the anarchist and his colleagues produce weapons, proclaiming themselves the 'Küsters Command', and demanding the release of all political prisoners in West Germany. The film in its original version closes at this sequence with rolling titles over a still of Mother Küsters' benumbed and dismayed face, telling us that she and the anarchist were killed shortly afterwards in a shootout with the police. In November 1975 Fassbinder added a new conclusion, an absurdly fortuitous and ironic 'happy ending', in which Mother Küsters finds consolation with an equally lonely nightwatchman.

MOTHER KÜSTERS' TRIP TO HEAVEN is another Fassbinder melodrama about the exploitation of someone's distress and vulnerability, and the betrayal of their goodness and credulity. Everyone seems determined to make something out of Mother Küsters' tragedy: the mass press, her daughter Corinne, the communists, the anarchists, and even the factory, which uses the murder her husband committed as an excuse not to pay her widow's benefits or compensation (even though their action triggered off the whole train of events). The portrayal of the activities of the sensationalist mass press against a background of terrorism is particularly interesting in view of the fact that 1975 was also the year in which Volker Schlöndorff and Margarethe von Trotta made their famous film on precisely this topic, THE LOST HONOUR OF KATHARINA BLUM. In the earlier parts of MOTHER KÜSTERS the press theme is especially prominent, as reporters invade the Küsters' flat. One reporter in particular, Niemeyer, manages to win Mother Küsters' trust, but probes for scurrilous details, and takes picture after picture of her daily life, culminating in a series of shots of the distraught widow weeping over a photograph of her husband. His story, like those of Tötges in KATHARINA BLUM, is a travesty, presenting the dead husband as a violent man and a drunkard, who beat his children and made life a misery for his wife and family. Niemeyer soon becomes the lover of Corinne, in a relationship where each exploits the other in the furtherance of their careers, she providing him with information, and he helping her to get a job in a friend's nightclub, where she is billed as the 'Daughter of the Factory Killer'.[10]

Niemeyer is, however, a more complex character than the Schlöndorffs' and Böll's Tötges. Niemeyer, like Tötges, drives a flashy car, but unlike the studiously elegant lady-killer of KATHARINA BLUM, he wears jeans and a leather jacket, and is in general much quieter and more introspective than Tötges. He describes the minute, book-lined room in which he lives as 'the last remnant of the Revolution'. It soon becomes clear, in fact, that Niemeyer is one of the many disillusioned radicals of the 1960s who, in the 1970s, have 'sold out to the system'. (The opposite course was taken by those who turned to terrorism: in the closing sequence it appears that Niemeyer and the anarchists know one another from former days.) He is a man whose conscience about his despicable work is not entirely clear; Tötges, on the other hand, suffers no such qualms.

The other major characters also represent reactions to the failure of the ideals of '68. The anarchists are desperados, for whom violence is now the only answer. The Tillmanns, on the other hand, are a quiet, melancholy couple. They are certainly not the villainous cynics that caused many to reject this film outright for its allegedly travestied portrait of the Left. Clearly Fassbinder is poking fun at what he sees as the other side of the coin from terrorism: the 'embourgeoisement' of the official Communist Party. The Tillmanns (their name is an echo of 'Thälmann', one of the great communist leaders of the 1920s – indeed some accounts of the film seem to get the two names confused) live in an elegant house that Mrs Tillmann has inherited, a house where they entertain their comrades to a glass of wine, while for a Party meeting, held in an art gallery full of old masters, Tillmann carefully exchanges his usual fashionable tweed for a leather jacket.

There are, however, no signs that their communism is 'radical chic'. (The magazine office, on the other hand, is adorned with a poster about the 1848 Revolution.) Their lives seem to bring them little fulfilment, their house is dead, with no children and no signs of daily life. They are gentle, pensive people, bewildered and saddened; one senses their frustration at the virtual impossibility of realizing the ideals to which they have sincerely devoted themselves. They are, it seems, genuinely concerned with Mother Küsters as a person; they often exchange glances in her presence, but they never smirk. Mother Küsters is of potential use to them politically, but they do not force this role on her. The article Tillmann writes meets with Mother Küsters' spontaneous approval as a correct statement of the facts, although, like Katharina Blum when shown objective reports of her case, Mother Küsters asks what use this is when nearly everyone reads only the sensationalist mass press.[11] Like Fassbinder's other protagonists, Mother Küsters is certainly exploited, but not by the Tillmanns: they come off much better – thanks in particular to the carefully controlled acting of Karlheinz Böhm and Margit Carstensen – than the film's detractors hastily assumed.

During the early part of 1976 Fassbinder became involved in another scandal, a scandal that, like the *Theater am Turm* affair, again involved Frankfurt, and one that, like the criticisms of MOTHER KÜSTERS, brought surprising accusations, accusations this time of anti-semitism. Frankfurt has the reputation of being the hardest and least hospitable of West German cities, a place whose dedication to its role as the country's financial capital has led to the destruction of much of the inner city and its replacement with a passing imitation of the Manhattan skyline; a place, moreover, where prostitution, drug addiction, and violent crime are more rife than practically anywhere else in Europe. This was the image that lay behind Gerhard Zwerenz's 1973 novel *The Earth is as Uninhabitable as the Moon*, which pictures Frankfurt as the epitome of all that is worst in capitalism. In 1975 Fassbinder wrote a play based on Zwerenz's novel, *The Garbage, the City, and Death*, a play that was to have been performed by his troupe at the 'TAT' had they stayed on there. Fassbinder then decided to make a film based on the play, but this project too had to be abandoned when the Film Promotion Office refused him a grant. The Office was unhappy about what it saw as the potentially anti-semitic implications of *The Garbage, the City, and Death*, which, in a milieu of pimps and prostitutes, features a wealthy Jewish property speculator, as well as a Nazi. Meanwhile, Fassbinder's publishers, the Suhr-kamp Verlag, hastily withdrew the text of the play. In the end, the film was made, not by Fassbinder, but by the Swiss director Daniel Schmid, with Fassbinder playing one of the central roles.

SHADOWS OF THE ANGELS (SCHATTEN DER ENGEL) – a title that seems to refer to the 'Angels' in Rilke's *Duino Elegies*, for at one point the cycle's bleak opening plea, 'To whom shall I cry for help?' is quoted – is a more highly stylized film than anything Fassbinder himself has directed, with a carefully choreographed scenario, and formal, rhetorical, philosophical dialogues that at times break into verse. It traces the life and death of Lily, the most beautiful and least successful of a group of prostitutes who solicit beneath one of Frankfurt's bridges. Lily, whose father is a Nazi drag artist with a crippled wife, is picked up by an immensely wealthy Jewish property speculator in a big black car. He adopts her as his companion, but she wants to die, so he strangles her on some wasteland outside the city. The corrupt police chief has her pimp – played by Fassbinder – brought in and thrown out of the window.

SHADOWS OF THE ANGELS is above all a film about corruption, and a film about Frankfurt, the city that personifies the monetary principle at its worst. It portrays the corruption of morals, the corruption of love, the corruption of politics and of society by and for money. Its characters are on the whole, to draw a fine but vital distinction, corrupted rather than corrupt. None of them are really wicked, for they are victims of something that has gone wrong in the world around them. This is no more true than of the Jewish property magnate: in rebutting the accusations of 'left-wing fascism' and 'racialism', Schmid claimed that it was not gratuitous bad taste to make the speculator Jewish. His financial success was a reflection as much as anything of Germany's bad conscience, which meant that a blind eye was turned to his shady activities. Certainly the film shows the property speculator as almost a victim himself of the society from which he profits: cruising silently around in his big black car he is a sad and lonely figure like everyone else in the film. His wealth has isolated him still further from his fellow beings: the money flows in, he says, he cannot stop it, it is all so easy in this society.

It had long become a popular cliché to apostrophize Fassbinder as the '*enfant terrible*' of the German cinema. The Berlin Film Festival had helped this reputation on its way when they turned down MOTHER KÜSTERS in 1975. In 1976 they did it again, rejecting his new film SATAN'S BREW. SATAN'S BREW (SATANSBRATEN) is Fassbinder's most chaotic and offensive film. Its central character is a failed poet left over from the revolution of 1968, Walter Kranz, who is working on a magnum opus provisionally entitled 'A Cloacal Epic of Humiliation'. Kranz decides to adopt the persona of the poet Stefan George, who died in 1933, but this turns out to be expensive, so he tries for a while to earn money as a pimp in order to pay for a circle of young acolytes to attend his Thursday-afternoon readings (an earlier attempt to pick up a young man in the station lavatory having been unsuccessful), as well as paying for his tailor-made Stefan George suit, and generally running his household. This latter includes his half-witted brother who is erotically obsessed with dead flies, offering specimens from his collection to any girl who takes his fancy, and a woman admirer of his works with a warty face, goofy teeth, and goggle-like spectacles.

SATAN'S BREW is a hysterical exercise in bad taste, redeemed only by its vitality and zany humour, in which all restraint is thrown to the wind as the scenes, characters, and situations that Fassbinder had worked with for years are allowed to explode into near meaninglessness. I ONLY WANT YOU TO LOVE ME (ICH WILL DOCH NUR, DASS IHR MICH LIEBT) is by contrast a quiet, controlled, sad film. Here the motif of the outcast and the theme of lovelessness come together in the central character, a prisoner whose crime was an uncontrollable reaction to the unfeeling world in which he has grown up. The film is based on a true account taken from *For Life*, a book of interviews edited by Klaus Antes and Christiane Erhardt. (Erika Runge, well-known for her own interview-based documentary accounts of ordinary people's lives, plays the part of an interviewer in the film.) The story is punctuated with flashbacks and flashforwards, but the main narrative is chronological, tracing the life of the protagonist, Peter, from his childhood through to his imprisonment for manslaughter in early adulthood. Peter grows up in a little town in the Bavarian Forest where his father has a small bar in which Peter helps out. In his spare time he builds his parents a fine new house, but they are cold, embittered, and distant; they merely use their son, and show no trace of love. Peter marries his childhood sweetheart, a shop assistant, and the couple move to Munich, where Peter gets a job on a building site. Money now becomes a major problem: money to furnish their flat, money to feed and clothe their baby. Peter's father meanwhile has got himself a comfortable job as a commercial traveller, but Peter cannot bring himself to go begging to him. Instead he turns to his wife's lonely old grandmother. Beneath her flat is a bar with a landlord just like his father; Peter is drinking there one day when the man's son comes in, only to be coldly rejected. Peter, who had just been going to call his own father, kills the landlord with the telephone. He is sentenced to ten years in prison.

The title I ONLY WANT YOU TO LOVE ME occurs twice in the film: once with the 'you' in the singular, when Peter makes this request of his wife, and then again in the closing sequence as the interviewer asks him whether he likes his life: Peter is unable to answer, but then the title appears – this time with the 'you' in the plural – and makes his answer for him. The central theme of Fassbinder's œuvre is here given a stark and unambiguously simple treatment. Love is needed, love is denied, and a cold and tragic life is the result. The film touches on such earlier aspects of the love theme as love between old people (an elderly couple sitting snuggled together in a bar are turned out because 'it's not nice at their age') – an echo of both EIGHT HOURS and FEAR EATS THE SOUL, whilst the loneliness of old people is reflected in the figure of the grandmother. Equally, the theme of 'education for the harsh realities of life' lies behind Peter's childhood experiences, though the foregrounding of the motif of loveless childhood (with, one suspects, autobiographical overtones) is new in Fassbinder. It is Peter's parents who have broken him in a way that can never be made good. In later life he finds a wife who does love him, a grandmother-in-law with whom he shares sympathy, affection, and companionship; even the contractor and the foreman at the Munich building site are genuinely concerned for his well-being and do their best to help him. But it is too late: Peter is simply not equipped to live in this world.

The earliest flashback concerns an incident in Peter's childhood when he gives a bunch of flowers to his mother, but the flowers were stolen from a neighbour's garden and Peter's hapless advances are rewarded with a brutal beating from his mother. Denied spontaneous love, Peter tries to buy it, and throughout the film we see him time and again giving bunches of flowers – above all to his wife, but also to her grandmother, and to his own mother. In a world where a monetary value is placed on everything he desperately tries to retain his wife's affection with presents. He wants to give her 'a decent standard of living', and becomes entangled with impossible hire-purchase commitments. Yet still he showers her with presents, a dress, a gold bracelet, a knitting machine, and still more pot plants and bunches of flowers. He has to work longer and longer overtime, sees less and less of his wife, while financial worries bring greater and greater tension to their marriage. The cruel ethos implanted in his childhood and reflected in the world outside has trapped him in a vicious circle, a circle all the more vicious for its absurdity, for his wife loves him, and would love him just as much without all these presents. But so insatiable is Peter's need for love, so desperate his fear of losing it, and so unprepared is he for recognizing freely-given love when he meets it, that he blunders helplessly forward into deeper and deeper trouble.

CHINESE ROULETTE Ulli Lommel as Kolbe and Alexander Allerson as Gerhard Christ

ix The New Fassbinder: Finish and Finesse

The motif of the unloved child is taken up again at a more sophisticated level in CHINESE ROULETTE (CHINESISCHES ROULETTE, 1976). With this film Fassbinder returns to an upper-class milieu, and, as in those other Strindbergian chamber-pieces PETRA VON KANT and MARTHA, he here studies destructive relationships between a limited number of people in a limited setting. But whereas the earlier films had drawn much of their strength from their concentration on the tensions between a pair of people, in CHINESE ROULETTE, without any loss of concentration, the field is broadened into a complex pattern that plays off individuals, pairs (both separate and interlocking), larger groups, and ultimately the whole cast against one another in ever-shifting perspectives.

The main action of CHINESE ROULETTE takes place in an elegant old mansion, the country retreat of a wealthy businessman, Gerhard Christ. Gerhard, having told his wife he has to go to Oslo on business, collects his French mistress from the airport and takes her to the mansion, only to find his wife Ariane already there with *her* lover, Gerhard's secretary Kolbe. It transpires that their meeting has been engineered by Angela, the Christs' crippled daughter, who soon also turns up with her mute governess, Traunitz. The scene is now set for a classic melodramatic confrontation, but Fassbinder twists the tension still higher by adding two further characters, the surly housekeeper Kast and her sinister son Gabriel, and then lets the whole volatile combination culminate in the game that gives the film its title. Chinese roulette – like the original meeting the game is played at Angela's instigation – involves splitting the characters into two teams, with one team secretly selecting a person from the other team, this second team then having to elicit by means of a series of questions which person from among their number is 'it'. The questions are often cruelly personal, the answers are even more savage, culminating in Angela's reply to her mother's question as to what the person chosen would have been in the Third Reich: the commandant of the concentration camp at Bergen-Belsen, she says. For a moment they think Kast must be intended, but then Angela in fiendish glee declares it is her mother. Thus far uneasy and exaggerated laughter has enabled the characters to remain in control of the tension beneath the surface, but the 'game' has been in deadly earnest, laughter can no longer provide the safety-valve: Ariane takes a pistol, points it at Angela, but then turns and shoots Traunitz in the neck. The film closes with a view from outside the mansion: it is night, and what looks like a religious procession passes in front of the building to the sung words, 'Mary help us in this valley of tears, Kyrie eleison'; a shot rings out, and the picture freezes. (Some versions add to this already dense and cryptic cluster of visual and auditory impressions the superposed written text: 'Are you willing to enter into marriage and remain faithful to one another until death you do part?'.)

CHINESE ROULETTE was technically Fassbinder's most sophisticated film – until DESPAIR, that is, with which it has much in common, and with which, in retrospect, it can be seen to introduce a new phase in his work. Its sophistication lies most obviously in the camera work, for it is through the ceaseless movements and stylized positioning of the camera that the shifting relationships between the characters are traced, and it is these relationships rather than the characters themselves that the film is about. It is a film about the gaps between people, gaps that the camera transforms into perfect spatial metaphors of the unfolding drama as it traces the interwoven lines of attraction and repulsion,

love, lust, hatred, and jealousy. Only once is a hint of psychological motivation introduced when Angela tells Gabriel that her father's affair dates back to the beginning of the illness that crippled her, whilst her mother took a lover when the doctors declared her case to be hopeless.

This explanation of the Christs' infidelity is in fact dismissed as nonsense by Kast when Gabriel mentions it to her, and one is simply thrown back again into the formalistic ritual. The pattern of relationships at the core of the film is self-contained and self-sufficient, but Fassbinder has chosen to add a host of subsidiary hints and allusions with which he teases the viewer into vain quests for meaning – quests that are constantly thwarted by the tangential and inadequate nature of these apparent 'leads'. There are, for instance, suggestions of an intriguing wider background to what is going on here, as when Gerhard, on learning that Angela has organized this traumatic weekend, remarks darkly to Kast, 'Ali ben Basset was murdered in Paris last week. Now we two are the last.' Gabriel later asks his mother who this ben Basset is, and is snappily informed it is no business of his. Kast and Gabriel are in any case a most mysterious and sinister couple. In one heavily Bergmanesque sequence Gabriel stops at a filling station where, apparently apropos of nothing, he asks the attendant if he has ever been in hell: the man nods his affirmation.[12] On another occasion it is Kast who gives alms to a beggar at the door, whereupon the 'blind' man removes his dark glasses and drives off in his Mercedes. There is even a suggestion, again never elaborated, that the dumb governess Traunitz, who finally becomes the vicarious victim of Ariane's hatred for her daughter, is the last, dispossessed scion of an old family whose ancestral seat is this very mansion in which she is now shot. Certainly at one point Angela reminds Traunitz of a lost battle way back in her family history, and then, after the shooting, as Kast phones for an ambulance she gives the address as 'Schloss Traunitz', the first and only mention of the mansion's name.

Such an abundance of wantonly cryptic references is something new in Fassbinder, and part of the generally playful way in which he handles CHINESE ROULETTE – playful, that is, in the sense of the magisterial formalism with which he arranges and rearranges his characters' lives, the way in which his camera sweeps, glides, and circles around them, surging and retreating, catching them in studied poses, framed in doorways and windows, reflected in mirrors, and glimpsed through the glass cases and the cage of twittering birds that adorn the mansion's main room. Fassbinder plays games with his characters, arranging them like chessmen on a board; he plays games with the audience, dazzling, bewildering, and intriguing them; and the games culminate in the deadly Chinese roulette that the characters play with each other.

With PIONEERS IN INGOLSTADT Fassbinder had made a contribution to the rediscovery of Marieluise Fleisser; with BOLWIESER (1977) he paid homage to another long neglected Bavarian writer. The novelist Oskar Maria Graf was born in 1894 in a village to the south of Munich. Like Fleisser he was a realist, a close observer of the mores of provincial Bavaria, a left-wing pacifist who became a persona non grata during the Third Reich. In exile from 1933 onwards, he fled in 1938 to the USA, where he remained until his death in 1967. The first version of *Bolwieser* appeared in 1930 with the subtitle '*Novel of a husband*', and was based on a true event that Graf had learnt of when he visited Wasserburg am Inn on a cycling holiday. Fassbinder's 1977 film was originally made in two 100-minute parts for television, and is one of his most immaculate works, a visually sumptuous period piece that evokes perfectly the atmosphere of provincial life in pre-war Bavaria.

Xaver Bolwieser (played by Kurt Raab) is a station master in a sleepy little town, whose life is taken up with his public office and his private passion for his wife Hanni. Hanni has an affair with the butcher Merkl, whose business has been aided with a loan from her generous dowry. The love-lorn Xaver is constantly taunted by other men for his dependence on and obedience to Hanni. Merkl instigates legal proceedings to stop the gossip that his affair with Hanni has engendered. Xaver perjures himself in testifying to Hanni's innocence. Eventually he is arrested for this, while Hanni in the meantime has begun an affair with the local hairdresser. Xaver is divorced in prison, and on his release he wanders the countryside, ending up working for an old ferryman. When the old man dies, Xaver buries him, and takes on his work. The film's closing credits appear over a long drawn-out shot of great beauty that shows Xaver ferrying two people across the partly frozen river, snow on the land around.

Like CHINESE ROULETTE, BOLWIESER portrays passions constrained by rules, and rules being broken by passions. Xaver's and Hanni's marriage is based on obsessive sensuality, and it is this destructive power of sensuality that here seems to outweigh the love that was the undoing of so many earlier Fassbinder characters. The theme is taken up by men in the film who note the dangerous temptations of Woman, and by the recluse-like old ferryman, who warns against Desire. Xaver's passion is opposed by his job: he has to don his uniform at regular intervals throughout the day for the arrivals and departures of the trains that interrupt the attentions he lavishes on his wife. His passion is further opposed by the hypocritical morality of the little town in which he lives. It is opposed too by the law that he foolishly transgresses. And ultimately it is opposed by the passion of others, the sensuality of his wife and that of her lovers. And so, after the bitter experience of deception and the awful years in prison, Xaver finally withdraws from the wordly life of the passions to the monastic seclusion of the ferryman's hut.

The closing sequence is the culmination of a general pattern that informs the whole film in which the quietness and calm of natural landscape are repeatedly contrasted with the drama acted out indoors. Unlike in CHINESE ROULETTE, however, the tension between violence and order, passion and peace, does not exist in a vacuum in BOLWIESER. There is a clear social, geographical, and historical context that provides the parameters of these events: the context of provincial Bavaria in the late twenties. The violent abandon of Bolwieser's emotional life is contrasted with his public office – a hierarchical world where rank and position are of the essence, a Prussianized world in which there is much standing to attention and barking of brusque commands. Already there are signs of what all this is leading to: the odd Hitler salute, the odd swastika, and then the appearance of one of Bolwieser's underlings in full Nazi uniform are tokens not only of a sickness in this little society, but reminders of a wider world outside.

In CHINESE ROULETTE Fassbinder had for the first time introduced major foreign players – Anna Karina and Macha Méril – as guests among his more familiar cast. In BOLWIESER he had painted a portrait of Germany in the years before the Nazi seizure of power. In DESPAIR he takes both these innovations several steps further to create a film that is one of the major 'international' productions of the New German Cinema, and one that attests to the continuing fascination that the Weimar years have held for filmmakers in the 1970s. DESPAIR (EINE REISE INS LICHT (DESPAIR), 1977), which was to be Fassbinder's most lavish and expensive production to date, is a far cry from the low-budget, deliberately simplistic, and plodding melodramas of his earlier work. The list of credits is impressive: the film is based on a novel by Nabokov, the script was written by Tom Stoppard, the leading role was played by Dirk Bogarde. The critics were duly impressed. The Germans in particular, flattered no doubt at making what looked like a major international breakthrough, were dazzled by the film's technical brilliance and apparent thematic complexity. Siegfried Schober, writing in *Der Spiegel*, was, for instance, quite rapturous in his praises:

Fassbinder's film is many things, a sardonic comedy about marriage, a complex psychological thriller, a jig-saw puzzle of a study about the disintegration of a personality and a world. It is also and above all else a fascinating visual tour de force: new and daring in a way that no other commercial film of recent years is, full of dissonances, stylistic leaps, contradictions, and audacity. Just as Stravinski's 'Rite of Spring' revolutionized music, so Fassbinder's DESPAIR now revolutionizes the cinema: Fassbinder's chef d'œuvre, a work that puts paid to a dominant artistic idealism and at the same time ushers in a new bewitching aesthetic.[13]

Fassbinder had been working on the idea of filming *Despair* for some five years – in fact ever since he picked up a copy for 50 pfennigs in a second-hand bookshop. When Nabokov first wrote the novel (in 1932 in Russian) the setting was more or less contemporary: Berlin in the last years of the Weimar Republic. The historical and political context was, however, of little significance for Nabokov. In the film the context is given more prominence, and it is implied that what happens to the hero is to a large extent occasioned by, and a reflection of, what is happening in the world around him. Hermann Hermann is a wealthy Russian émigré in Berlin, a chocolate manufacturer, married to the voluptuous Lydia, who is having an affair with her cousin, the artist Ardalion. With his business, his marriage, and his mental state all leaving much to be desired Hermann hits upon the idea of making a clean break with his past when he meets a tramp who, he thinks, looks exactly like him. He will murder the tramp and then start a new life with the insurance money that Lydia will collect when 'his' body is found. But the plan misfires, for not only was he mistaken in thinking the tramp looked like him, but he had also forgotten to take away the tramp's walking-stick, which is engraved with his name. Hermann is arrested in the Swiss retreat to which he had withdrawn to begin his new life.

This plot in outline is intriguing, but outwardly no more complex than many Fassbinder had used before. DESPAIR is, however, certainly his most complex film: to have someone else write his script was a new departure for Fassbinder, and the choice of Tom Stoppard meant compounding Nabokov's sophistication with still more intellectual wit, and with much play on images and words. One major problem had to be faced from the outset: the crucial revelation that the tramp is decidedly not Hermann's double is only made at the end of the novel; in the visual medium of the film such information clearly cannot be withheld from the audience. And so it is not withheld: instead we are made both witnesses to and partners in the delusions of Hermann, his voluntary and involuntary journey through and into madness, a 'Journey into the Light', as the film's German title puts it. The film, which begins in the art-deco interiors, the cafés and streets of Berlin, and ends in the peace of the Swiss Alps, traces, according to Fassbinder, 'the itinerary of a man who escapes from the jungle of an honourable existence and penetrates the free and beautiful world of madness'.[14]

Hermann is a man who is plagued by a confusion of images. He suffers, to use the pat psychological jargon, from an 'identity crisis': he is an exile, his papers are false, his history invented, his origins unclear. He suffers from 'schizophrenia', from a 'split personality', from 'dissociation': hence his repeated visions of himself, visions even of himself looking at himself, and his vision of the tramp as his double. Stoppard and Fass-

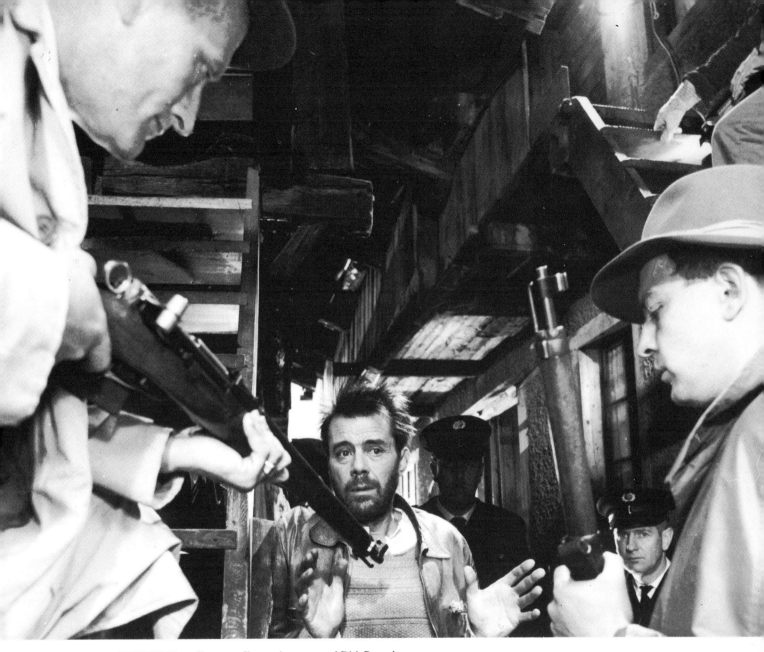

DESPAIR 'I'm a film actor. I'm coming out now.' Dirk Bogarde as Hermann Hermann

binder are, however, sceptical of easy psychologizing (as indeed was Nabokov). Hermann's problems are presented ironically, and when psychology does rear its intellectualizing head it is soon cut down to size with rapid strokes of verbal and visual wit. 'What do you know about dissociation?' Hermann asks a doctor in a cafe, and goes on to elaborate the term as 'split personality', adding 'I'm thinking of writing a book about the subject – maybe two books.' But the 'doctor' is in any case an insurance broker, and it is he who sells Hermann the fateful life policy.

The mirror imagery that had for some time been becoming an increasingly obtrusive hallmark of Fassbinder's style reaches its apogee in DESPAIR. Here, however, it is no longer merely a virtuoso mannerism, it has instead become thematic, for DESPAIR is a film about reflections, about distortions, about reality and illusion, above all a film about images. And inasmuch as the cinema is the supreme creator of images it is a self-reflective film, questioning the 'truth' it conveys, looking both *through* and *at* a distorted consciousness, and defying us to distinguish the two perspectives. Hermann has got the idea of his crime from watching a film – a film about two identical twins; at the end he retreats from the 'reality' of his life into a 'fiction', the 'fiction' that he is in a film. The house is surrounded by police: 'We're making a film here,' Hermann calls out, 'I'm a film actor. I'm coming out now. . . . I'm coming out.' Thus we are drawn into the 'distortions' of Hermann's 'madness': the 'fiction' into which he has retreated turns out to be our 'reality', for Hermann is indeed an actor, and this is indeed a film.

DESPAIR constantly plays tricks on the viewer, things rarely turn out to be what they seem to be, everything is a game of reflections and doubles – even Hermann's name, 'Hermann Hermann' (itself reminiscent of the 'Humbert Humbert' of *Lolita*) repeats itself. What exactly lies behind the scintillating surface is never clear, however. DESPAIR seems to be a film without a centre. Some of its jokes are gratuitous: the sequence in the chocolate factory in which everything possible is garbed in the emblematic lilac colour of Hermann's firm, or another factory sequence where lines of naked chocolate dolls process past on a conveyor belt, for instance. Other jokes are more integrated into the film's overall concern with images, but still lack point and necessity, as in a hazy sequence where Lydia goes to meet Hermann to begin their new dream life, and 'Hermann' turns round, revealing himself as the tramp. In general there is too much self-indulgence here on Fassbinder's part, the cleverness is overstretched, and there is a lack of pace and variety that is only made up in the last thirty minutes or so where a more traditional suspense and concentration are allowed to take over.

Fassbinder's concerns have previously been German concerns. DESPAIR's links with Germany are tenuous: not only are its author, scriptwriter, and leading player foreign, but it was even filmed in English. Its setting is admittedly the Weimar Republic: it opens with a men-tion of the Wall Street Crash, we see Nazi uniforms, brownshirt vandalism, posters of Hitler and Hindenburg, and there are references to Müller, Brüning, and the occupation of the Ruhr. Just how integral are these attempts at establishing a historical context, though? Is it not just a bit too easy to explain Hermann's 'journey into the light' as an allegory of the journey into madness entered on by Weimar Germany? For all its brilliance, DESPAIR does make one wonder how much Fassbinder has abandoned in his move from the outward-looking didacticism of his provincial melodramas to the rootless self-reflection of international sophistication.

x Postscript and Conclusion

To keep abreast of Fassbinder's work is a daunting task; to reach comprehensive conclusions about it is even more difficult. He produces films at such a rate and in such variety that definitive assessments are impossible, and any summarizing survey soons becomes outdated. In the year and a half following the release of DESPAIR he has made three more films, and work proceeds apace on his long-awaited mammoth serialization of Döblin's *Berlin Alexanderplatz*. All of these recent projects testify gratifyingly to the fact that the rootless internationalism of DESPAIR was not, after all, the token of a 'new departure' in Fassbinder's work: Fassbinder has, in the intervening films, returned with a vengeance to the peculiarly German settings and concerns that typify his best work, and that are the greatest strength of the New German Cinema.

This was particularly the case with THE MARRIAGE OF MARIA BRAUN (DIE EHE DER MARIA BRAUN, 1978), in which the fortunes of the eponymous heroine reflect the social history of the first decade of post-war West Germany. Hanna Schygulla's performance as Maria Braun won her the Best Actress award at the 1979 Berlin Film Festival, and the film's evocative reconstructions of life in the broken Germany of the late forties and amid the 'get-rich-quick' bonanza of the 'Economic Miracle' in the early fifties brought it some of the biggest audiences of any recent German film – audiences, moreover, who in many cases would not normally regard themselves as devotees of Fassbinder's work. His two other recent films were much more personal, and, for many, much less approachable. The title of IN A YEAR WITH 13 MOONS (IN EINEM JAHR MIT 13 MONDEN, 1978) refers to an astrological belief that people of an emotional bent are liable to suffer personal catastrophes in those exceptional years in which there are thirteen new moons. 1978 was such a year. It was the year in which Armin Meier committed suicide: the man Fassbinder had been living with for four years, who had played in a number of his films, to whom, along with 'all the others', FOX had been dedicated, and who was seen in GERMANY IN AUTUMN being bullied, berated, and assuaged by a panic-stricken Fassbinder. A few weeks after Meier's death Fassbinder made IN A YEAR WITH 13 MOONS, a brutal, direct, and shocking portrait of the fate of a lonely transsexual in the nightmare city of Frankfurt – a film that lifted to a new pitch the old Fassbinder theme of the yearning for love, and took up again in its setting the expressionistic desolation of SHADOWS OF THE ANGELS. THE THIRD GENERATION (DIE DRITTE GENERATION, 1979) was equally uncompromising, but even more daring in that it not only openly confronted the taboo topic of terrorism, but actually implicated both the anarchic mindlessness of the young 'third generation' of revolutionaries *and* the capitalist establishment, who find a little terrorism is good for business. Turbulently burlesque, but almost documentary in the precision of its satire, THE THIRD GENERATION was too much for the *Westdeutscher Rundfunk* and the Senate of West Berlin, who hastily withdrew their promised financial support when they realized just what sort of film they had let themselves in for.

Fassbinder has come a long way in the decade (and, amazingly, it *is* only a decade) since the gangster films and domestic melodramas of his *anti-teater* beginnings. He has not only made far more films than any other of the New German Cinema's major directors, he has also tried his hand at a far greater range of subject matter and genres. It is in fact in this respect, more than in any other, that Fassbinder differs from the other directors of the New German Cinema: the breadth and variety of his work mean that he is different in a *qualitative* sense, and not just by virtue of the mere *quantity* of his output. It is thus much easier to assess what is characteristic of the work of the other six directors discussed in these chapters than it is to pinpoint 'typical features' in Fass-

binder's work. Fassbinder himself, never one to be backward in coming forward about his ambitions, has set his sights high: 'I want to be to the cinema what Shakespeare was to the theatre, Marx to politics, and Freud to psychology.'[15] But even – indeed, perhaps *above all* – geniuses give to their work an unmistakable individuality. What, then, are the elements of the 'Fassbinder touch'?

At the technical level the distinctiveness of Fassbinder's films derives from the mingling of stylization and realism that was evident in his work from the outset – a combination in which stylization is invariably the more prominent element. In the early *anti-teater* films the *mise en scène* was often stage-like and minimal, with the closed world of the protagonists reflected in the heavily framed and constricted shots. Fassbinder's cameraman then was Dietrich Lohmann; after the turning-point of BEWARE OF A HOLY WHORE Michael Ballhaus took over this role, evolving a style that was technically different, but in its effects very similar to Lohmann's 'imprisonment' of the characters within the frame. Now the camera began to move more, but the characters were, if anything, even more claustrophobically fixated as it swirled and swooped around them, whilst the obsessive use of mirror images that reached its mannered climax in DESPAIR added still more to the sense of a world that is ineluctably closed.

There is stylization too in the décor: again outward realism is belied by the carefully chosen composition and disposition of the objects and spaces among which the characters move. But perhaps most distinctive of all is the stylization of the *acting* in Fassbinder's films. Movement, gesture, and expression are marked by a rehearsed formality that is equally apparent in the language of the scripts. Fassbinder (and this is particularly the case in the proletarian and petty-bourgeois settings of the earlier films) makes much use of the possibilities presented by the interplay of dialect and standard speech that is much more a feature of German – and particularly in Bavaria, where so many of his films are set – than it is of English. Many of his characters whom one would expect to use dialect in real life in fact enunciate their remarks with a strangely stilted clarity that derives from the unnatural combination of a more or less dialect-based vocabulary and syntax with a pronunciation that is much closer to the 'High

German' standard – a technique that is exemplified especially clearly in KATZELMACHER.

The mannered stylization of Fassbinder's work has led many commentators to draw analogies with the Brechtian 'alienation effect'. Certainly the *anti-teater*, like nearly all radical theatre troupes in post-war Germany, was much indebted to Bertolt Brecht, but Fassbinder has been wary of conceding more than a partial debt to him:

> With Brecht you see the emotions and you reflect upon them as you witness them but you never feel them. That's my interpretation and I think I go farther than he did in that I let the audience *feel and think*.[16]

It is a questionable interpretation of the workings of Brecht's drama, but it does draw attention to the very major – and decidedly un-Brechtian – role of *feeling* and *identification* in Fassbinder's films. These are elements that have much more to do with melodrama than with Brecht's 'epic theatre', and the mood and manners of melodrama are perhaps the strongest and most persistent common denominator in Fassbinder's work. Fassbinder has repeatedly expressed his admiration for the classic melodramas of the Hollywood cinema, and in particular for the work of Douglas Sirk. His ambition is no less than to do for West Germany what they did for America: to create a 'German Hollywood Cinema', in fact. Asked in 1974 about the implications of this, and taxed in particular with the accusation that the Hollywood cinema lacked the critical thrust that seemed so important in his own work, Fassbinder replied:

> The best thing I could imagine would be to make films that on the one hand are as beautiful and powerful and wonderful as Hollywood films, and yet at the same time do not necessarily approve and affirm. That would be a dream come true for me, to make a German film like that, as beautiful and fantastic and wonderful and yet at the same time critical of the system, especially as there's a vast number of films from Hollywood that are in no way such facile affirmations of the way things are as is always superficially claimed to be the case.[17]

It is not the most elegantly formulated of programmes, but it is an important one, for it describes not only Fassbinder's work and ambitions, but those of many other directors in the New German Cinema. There are many ways in which Fassbinder's work typifies (often in an exemplararily exaggerated form) salient features of the New German Cinema: his employment on film after film of a crew and cast made up of faithful 'regulars'; his reliance on a mixture of public and private sources of finance; his frequent use of television; the anti-establishment provocativeness of much that he does. But perhaps most importantly of all, Fassbinder's attitudes to Hollywood are the very epitome of the love-hate relationship with the American cinema – and with commercialism in general – that has played such a formative role in the development of the New German Cinema. Fassbinder grew up watching Hollywood movies, and then went on to make use of their subject matter and mannerisms in his own early work in a half parodistic, half infatuated way.[18] The Hollywood influences have persisted, indeed, in some respects they have grown even stronger, and now, like other directors, Fassbinder is looking to the 'New Hollywood' cinema for inspiration in the search for a critical, yet popular and commercially successful New German Cinema.

Thematically, Fassbinder's films are indebted as much, it has often been asserted, to his own autobiography as to the influences of Hollywood. Certainly his choice of themes has been highly selective. He is concerned above all with personal relationships: typically the relationship between two people, and more specifically the patterns of domination and dependence that lead ineluctably to emotional blackmail, exploitation, and betrayal. In practically every film he has made Fassbinder has returned to this circumscribed subject matter – material that is the essence of Hollywood melodrama. It could all be very trivially private, yet time and again his work points up the wider social, cultural, and political ramifications of his ostensibly psychological focus of attention. His characters' crises and tragedies are private reenactments of the public patterns of power and manipulation that surround them in society at large, and that they themselves have internalized by virtue of being members of that society.

Hence the unusual stress placed in Fassbinder's

work on the importance of childhood and education. And hence the sense of constriction and claustrophobia that prevails in his world: there is no way out for his characters; their personal relationships are predetermined by impersonal factors that they cannot, and will not, acknowledge or recognize. Hence too the brutal killings, the sudden, savage eruptions of violence, the slaps and cruelly protracted beatings that punctuate the irritable resignation in which most of them pass their lives, a resignation that is verbalized in repeated invocations of 'Fate', or, in the more articulate, a desperate sophistry that prowls round and round the periphery of their elusive dilemmas. Language as real communication seems almost impossible in Fassbinder's world. Inarticulacy is the normal condition of many of his protagonists, a condition surmounted only in lying, deception, vagueness, and, above all, cliché – for cliché is the essence of this world, a world bounded and shaped by pre-formed norms of behaviour and attitudes of mind.

'The one thing I acknowledge is despair,' says the production manager in BEWARE OF A HOLY WHORE. He was played by Fassbinder himself, and the remark, apart from curiously anticipating the title of one of his later films, reflects most starkly the pessimism and bleakness that seems to dominate his world. But it would be a mistake to overlook two elements that repeatedly pierce this apparently unremitting gloom: a utopian vision, and an anarchic humanism. The vision belongs to Fassbinder's characters: often kitschy, trite, vulgar, and sentimental, it nonetheless speaks of resilience in the face of despair, of the principle of hope that gives an inkling of a better world. The humanism is Fassbinder's. He has often been accused of cynicism, and certainly in his bleaker moments his pessimism carries him to the borders of nihilism. But Fassbinder's despair is occasioned by the world, the society, the conditions in which people live, not by the people themselves. If his films have a message, then it is that that world must be changed.

7 WIM WENDERS

'What's wrong with a cowboy in Hamburg?' asks Tom Ripley, the 'American Friend' of Wim Wenders' 1977 film of that title. The question is posed with the indignant defensiveness of one who is riven with doubts about the image he now cuts. It is one of the first remarks in the film, and is followed, after a pause, by the title. It is a remark that is heavy with significance, not only for the character of Ripley, not only because it points to a central theme in THE AMERICAN FRIEND, but also because it goes to the heart of all of Wenders' work, and ultimately reflects on the history of the whole of the New German Cinema.

The cowboy is the archetypal American hero: in real life he conquered the West; in his celluloid form he conquered the world. And with the cowboy came

Hollywood and all that it stood for in film economics and aesthetics. Wim Wenders is acutely aware, perhaps more so than any other German director, of American 'cultural imperialism' as an inescapable and fundamental fact of life not only in the cinema, but in every other aspect of life in post-war West Germany. 'The Yanks have colonized our subconscious,' as another of his characters puts it in KINGS OF THE ROAD. His films reflect this 'colonization', attempting to raise it to a conscious level. 'All of my films have as their underlying current the Americanization of Germany,' he says.[1] It is a colonization that has been mediated to an important extent by the almost total economic domination of the West German cinema by American interests. In their contents, Wenders' films explore the Americanization of West Germany; in their technique and subject matter they consciously emulate Hollywood stereotypes. All in all, their response to Ripley's question is ambiguous: a cowboy doesn't really belong in Germany, and yet . . .

The uneasy fascination with all things American goes back to the early years of Wenders' life. Wilhelm Wenders – to give him for once his full first name – was born in Düsseldorf on 14 August 1945: three months after the end of the war, the end of the years that the Germans now tried desperately not to think about. It was, according to Wenders, this peculiarly German break with the past that provided an unusually strong foothold for American 'colonization':

> The need to forget 20 years created a hole, and people tried to cover this . . . in both senses . . . by assimilating American culture: much more than French or Italian or British people did. . . . the fact that U.S. imperialism was so effective over here was highly favored by the Germans' own difficulties with their past. One way of forgetting it, and one way of regression, was to accept the American imperialism.[2]

Wenders has claimed that in his case it was American culture in the shape of pinball machines and rock'n'roll music that diverted him from his early teenage ambitions of becoming a priest. Today the fascination is as strong as ever: his house in Munich is decorated with Americana, he chews gum, still plays pinball machines and jukeboxes, is addicted to rock'n'roll, and listens, so he says, to only one radio station – the American Forces Network.[3]

Wenders is the only one of the major new German directors to have had a formal training in film. Abandoning the courses in medicine and philosophy that he initially embarked on, he attended the Munich *Hochschule für Fernsehen und Film* from 1967 to 1970. Here he made seven films: six shorts, and then a feature with which he graduated from the Academy. These early works of Wenders', which have never gone into commercial distribution, are essentially non-narrative, 'experimental' films. Their titles are already indicative of an interest in American culture. His second film (the first one – 'LOCATIONS' (SCHAUPLÄTZE, 1967) – is lost) took its title from the world of pintables: SAME PLAYER SHOOTS AGAIN (1967). Then came SILVER CITY in 1968, and in 1969 ALABAMA – a film containing much pop music, and itself named after a piece by John Coltrane. ALABAMA was followed by more pop music in 3 AMERICAN LPs. In fact, the only film that does not have major American references was POLICE FILM (POLIZEIFILM, 1970), which dealt with the tactics used by the Munich police to handle the student demonstrations of 1968.

Wenders' first feature again exploited pop culture, and again it had an English title: SUMMER IN THE CITY (1970) took its name from a song by the Lovin' Spoonful, and was dedicated to the Kinks, who are frequently heard, and once even seen, during the course of the film.[4] SUMMER IN THE CITY, the story of a man trying to find his feet again after being released from prison, is what Wenders describes as a 'documentary about the end of the sixties', reflecting the disappointment and sense of powerlessness that followed the failure of the revolts of 1968, a film about 'a longing for better times', for summer, in fact.[5]

Although SUMMER IN THE CITY runs for over two hours, Wenders still regards it as the last of his shorts. Certainly for the world at large it belongs to the unknown early Wenders, a fact that actually enabled him to get a grant for his next film – THE GOALIE'S ANXIETY AT THE PENALTY KICK (DIE ANGST DES TORMANNS BEIM ELFMETER, 1971) – from the *Kuratorium junger deutscher Film* on the assumption that *this* was the young director's first feature. The film was based on a story of the same title published in 1970 by the Austrian writer Peter Handke, an old friend of Wenders', who had worked with him on 3 AMERICAN LPs, and who was later to write the script of WRONG MOVEMENT. Handke's book, which makes some heavy nods in the direction of Camus' *L'Étranger*, Sartre's *La Nausée*, and Kafka's *The Trial*, tells of the meandering existential crisis of Joseph Bloch, an ex-goalkeeper who, for no apparent reason, has murdered a cinema cashier. It is a very intellectual book, concerned with a derangement that occurs when, to reverse Sartre's formula, 'names have drifted free from their objects'. (The book's striking title, which is partly a symptom of the wilfully iconoclastic image that Handke revelled in at the time, refers to the link between what is 'signified' – the goalkeeper – and the 'signifier' – the ball that is pointed in his direction and that he must catch if things are to work out right.)

Out of this unpromisingly cerebral material, Wenders (assisted by Handke, who wrote the dialogues) made the first film that brought him international attention. The plot is basically that of the original story, and much of the film was shot in the Austrian village of Jennersdorf, close by the Hungarian border, where Handke worked on the book. As in the book, the theme of communication – and its absence – is central, and the film abounds in sequences involving trains, planes, trams, buses, telephones, radios, televisions, and newspapers. The disintegration of Bloch's world as he waits for the police net to close in on him is transposed from the thoughts and mental imagery of the book into uncommented shots of the world around him: outwardly a banal, ordinary world, but one where the camera lingers just long enough to suggest sinister significance in the most incidental objects. (The effect is underlined – but all too heavily – by a frequently over-done music track.) In this uncomfortably alienated world the plot recedes behind the overall pattern of images; it is not, Wenders insists, a film to be 'explained', least of all in psychological terms. Thus one is perhaps absolved of the need to explain the mysterious intrusion into Bloch's life, at every turn of events, of Wenders' personal obsession: America. American coins and banknotes keep appearing; an American couple in a hotel are overheard talking about Arizona; the Austrian cinema cashier has received a postcard from someone called Bill in St Louis, who has also sent her a quarter dollar; on the radio snatches of AFN are heard; and there are American pop records aplenty, often from the ubiquitous juke-boxes that, together with numerous pin-tables, decorate the various bars that Bloch drifts through.

Wenders' next two films had American settings, but the first of them, quite uniquely in his work, is concerned not with *modern* America, but with the early settlers of the seventeenth century. THE SCARLET LETTER (DER SCHARLACHROTE BUCHSTABE, 1972) is based on Nathaniel Hawthorne's novel of 1850 about the witches of Salem. (Victor Sjöstrom had made a film version of it in 1926.) Wenders shot the film in Spain, with a set made up of wooden houses perched among the dunes on a desolate, rocky coast: an apt location for the theme of the unsteady toehold of civilization on a wild land, the portrait of a people with a paranoiac fear of the uncivilized forces within and without. Wenders' Salem is a society in a state of chronic hysteria, clinging frantically – and thus utterly intolerantly – to the Puritan 'virtues' that define it. All around is the wilderness: the wind blows constantly, mention is made of the Indians who still control all but this tiniest edge of the continent, distances are great, journeys dangerous, overland routes non-existent. It is not surprising that hysteria constantly erupts in the form of repressed passion, violence, mysterious illness, and witchcraft.

THE SCARLET LETTER is also unique in Wenders' work in the emphasis it gives to the women characters: the women here are the positive figures, representing naturalness, vitality, and life, opposed by the repressive hypocrisy of the male-dominated 'civilization' about them. This is above all the case with the powerful, proud, and tragic figure of Mistress Hibbins, who, with her glinting superciliousness and her barely suppressed mad laughter, constantly sees more and admits more than her fellow citizens. Mistress Hibbins' scepticism about this new America offers an intriguing parallel to the desperate insecurity of the 'old' American Ripley in THE AMERICAN FRIEND. It is almost as if the uncertainties of the seventeenth-century 'witch of Salem' come full circle in the twentieth-century 'cowboy in Hamburg'. The New England colonizers are too early, and Ripley has come too late, to enjoy that swaggering American self-confidence that reached a

ALICE IN THE CITIES Yella Rottländer as Alice

peak in the 1950s and then burnt itself out in the Vietnam War.

Significantly, Wenders finds THE SCARLET LETTER his least satisfying film, and the reasons he gives include precisely those two features that make the film distinctive in his work: the leading character was a woman, a mother, 'the only lead character in any of my films for whom I did not, either at the beginning or the end, have any feelings'.[6] It was, moreover, a historical costume film, which ruled out the improvised glimpses of contemporary reality that are, for Wenders, the stuff of film-making. 'And of course,' he wryly added, 'Puritans had no pinball machines. So I lost interest . . .'[7]

But one character did attract his interest: a seven-year-old girl called Yella Rottländer, who played a major role as Pearl, the daughter of the lead character. Two years later she was to become the Alice of ALICE IN THE CITIES, a film that Wenders wrote on the strength of Yella's performance in THE SCARLET LETTER.

ALICE IN THE CITIES (ALICE IN DEN STÄDTEN, 1973) was the first of a trilogy of 'road movies' that Wenders was to make with Rüdiger Vogler – who had already appeared in GOALIE and SCARLET LETTER – playing lead parts. In ALICE Vogler plays Philip Winter, a German photo-journalist who returns to Europe after an abortive attempt at completing a feature article about the United States. The 'Alice' of the title is a little girl who, as a result of a chance encounter, returns with him. Alice's mother fails to turn up to collect her as arranged, and much of the film is then taken up with

Philip and Alice's search for her grandmother, who lives at an address that Alice can't quite remember somewhere in the Ruhr.

ALICE IN THE CITIES, like so much of Wenders' work, is the story of people on a quest, but here, for once, the quest has a clear ostensible goal in the shape of Alice's elusive grandmother. Nonetheless, it is clear that Philip Winter is at the same time another of those Wenders heroes whose whole life is made up of a much more indeterminate and much more fundamental quest, a quest, to put it in its most hackneyed formulation (and one that Wenders himself uses), for identity.[8] At the beginning of ALICE IN THE CITIES the camera zooms in on Philip on an American beach; at the end it zooms away from him as he journeys on a German train: during the course of the film we have quite literally focussed on one brief stage of the quest that makes up his life.

It is, of course, an important stage: not only has his permanent quest taken on a more concrete form, but he has also moved from America back to Germany, a fact that enabled Wenders to say much about the two countries whose relationship so fascinates him. The America of the film's first half is an unprepossessing place: a land of endless car journeys along busy roads lined with neon signs, hoardings, motels, used-car lots, and petrol stations; an offensively noisy world that bristles with the vulgar sights and sounds of pop and commercial culture. It is pure hell, and one appreciates the sentiments of Alice's distraught mother when she says, 'I've just got to get to Germany.' Germany, the setting of the second part of the film, seems increasingly friendly and agreeable, and Wenders creates a sense of escape, of coming home to sanity and civilization in the Old World as the story develops. As if in confirmation of this overall development the film has a happy ending: Alice's grandmother and her mother have been located in Munich. We last see Alice and Philip on a train speeding towards the reunion. 'What will you do in Munich?' Alice asks. 'Finish this story,' comes the reply. And then the camera pulls back from the train, which is now passing through the Rhine Gorge, rises in exultant release high into the air, and pans across the open fields of the plateau above.

The Rhineland was to be the setting for the central part of Wenders' next film. WRONG MOVEMENT (FALSCHE BEWEGUNG, 1974), for once, leaves behind the exploration of 'American imperialism', reflecting instead on the melancholy resignation of European intellectuals in the mid seventies. This is Wenders' most German film: German in theme and subject matter, German in its setting, and German in its roots, for Peter Handke's script is an adaptation of one of the classics of German literature, *Wilhelm Meister's Apprenticeship*. Goethe's novel of 1795 is the story of a journey, of a young man's quest for his vocation in life. Wenders' 'road movie' trilogy is informed by similar preoccupations, and in WRONG MOVEMENT we watch a young man journeying across the length of West Germany from Glückstadt near the mouth of the Elbe to the summit of the Zugspitze, the country's highest point, in southern Bavaria.

Wenders' Wilhelm (played by Rüdiger Vogler again) is, like Goethe's, an aspiring young writer. Fleeing the confines of his provincial home he sets off in search of self-discovery and inspiration. En route he is joined by further latter-day reincarnations of Goethe's characters: an old singer called Laertes and his mute adolescent companion, a juggler called Mignon (played by Natassja Nakszynski, the then fourteen-year-old daughter of Klaus Kinski), and then later by the actress Therese (Hanna Schygulla) and the poet Landau (Peter Kern). The motley group spend the night at the house of a melancholy industrialist who, the following day, like his wife before him, commits suicide; Wilhelm and his companions move on to Therese's apartment near Frankfurt, where Therese finally manages to seduce the brooding and withdrawn young Wilhelm. At the end Wilhelm stands alone on the Zugspitze surveying the Germany he has now traversed, musing over his 'false movements': 'It seemed to me as if I had missed something, and as if I were still constantly missing something, with every new movement.'

Wilhelm Meister's Apprenticeship is regarded in Germany as the classic example of that peculiarly German genre, the *Bildungsroman*, the novel that shows a talented young person's character taking shape under the influence of the people and experiences he encounters as he journeys through life. Where Goethe's Wilhelm on the whole succeeds, Wenders' fails. The possibilities for self-realization that the original Wilhelm Meister optimistically symbolized at the dawning of the age

WRONG MOVEMENT Natassja Nakszynski as Mignon, Rüdiger
Vogler as Wilhelm, and Hanna Schygulla as Therese

of bourgeois individualism are atrophied and thwarted
in the chastened affluent society of West Germany.
The Germany that Wenders' Wilhelm and his companions move through is a melancholy land, with its
concrete cities and crowded highways; even its most
beautiful landscapes – and there are plenty of them in
the film – are never free from the sights and sounds of
industrial and commercial exploitation. In a much-
cited speech (and speeches abound in WRONG MOVE-
MENT – a mark of Handke's sententious formality) the
suicidal industrialist talks of loneliness in Germany, a
peculiar loneliness that is 'more hidden and at the same
time more painful than elsewhere'. It is a loneliness
that is 'masked by all those deceptively lifeless faces
that waft through the supermarkets, community

recreation areas, pedestrian precincts and keep-fit
centres. The dead souls of Germany.' In these lines,
where Handke is limbering up for the onslaught on the
paraphernalia of suburban affluence that he was to
make in the story (though not so much the film) *The
Left-Handed Woman*, the full potential bleakness of life
in modern West Germany is expressed. So too is a
favourite theme of Wenders': loneliness. The industrialist's response is suicide; Wilhelm's is to seek
but not find the companionship he needs, to be left
musing on his Olympus about the false movements that
he cannot avoid.

WRONG MOVEMENT was well received by the German
critics. Hans C. Blumenberg, writing in *Die Zeit*,
ranked it with Fassbinder's EFFI BRIEST as 'the first
authentic masterpiece of the German cinema of the
seventies',[9] whilst *Der Spiegel*'s Siegfried Schober went
so far as to call it 'one of the most important German

films since Lubitsch, Lang, and Murnau'.[10] For the public at large it was, however, Wenders' next film that was to hold the greatest attraction. Its German title had been anticipated early in WRONG MOVEMENT where a brief shot of Wilhelm in restless sleep had shown him, apparently apropos of nothing, muttering 'In the course of time'. Called KINGS OF THE ROAD in English (after the song by Roger Miller), shot in black and white, lasting some three hours, it is a film in which, on the surface, very little 'happens', but it was a film that was to become, both in Germany and abroad, one of the great cult movies of the New German Cinema.

If anything deserves the title 'road movie', it is KINGS OF THE ROAD (IM LAUF DER ZEIT, 1976). The setting for most of the film is one of West Germany's most notorious depressed areas: the eastern fringes of the country hard up against the GDR border that the boom years of the 'Economic Miracle' passed by. KINGS OF THE ROAD explores the relationship that develops between Robert Lander, a runaway husband, and Bruno Winter (the surname he shares with the hero of ALICE – also played by Rüdiger Vogler – is just one of many references to Wenders' earlier films), an itinerant repairer of cinema projectors, as they travel in the latter's converted removal van around the countryside and the backwater villages between Hof and Lüneburg. The two men first meet when Robert, in despair at the recent break-up of

Rüdiger Vogler with Hans Christian Blech as Laertes

his marriage, drives his car pell-mell into the river beside Bruno's parked lorry. (The River Elbe here being the border with the GDR, whose frontier fence can be seen on the opposite bank: like Bloch in THE GOALIE'S ANXIETY AT THE PENALTY KICK, Robert responds to the crisis in his life by heading for a border, but a closed border – the furthest extent of 'American imperialism' – beyond which, forbiddingly inaccessible, lies a system proclaiming the community and coherence that is lacking in his life.) Robert and Bruno take to the road together. Both are taciturn, withdrawn, lonely men; they say little to one another, but slowly a kind of relationship develops between them. And then one day they part again: once more on the GDR border, in a deserted United States Army observation hut, which they have stumbled on late one night after losing their way. In the morning Robert leaves, pinning a note to the door for the sleeping Bruno: 'Everything must change. So long. R.'

KINGS OF THE ROAD is a quiet and gentle film, but a film that is rich in allusions and implications. Three interlinked concerns are woven into it: the psychology of the two men, the fate of the German cinema, and the Americanization of German life. 'My film,' Wenders says,

is about the fact that the two men like one another, and why they get on better with one another than with a woman.

. . . They separate again . . . because in the course of this journey through Germany they've suddenly got too close to one another. That's the story that never gets told in films about men. The story of the absence of women, which is at the same time the story of the yearning for them to be there nonetheless![11]

KINGS OF THE ROAD Bruno (Rüdiger Vogler) and Robert (Hanns Zischler) about to set out on their journey to the Rhine

Women, the family, and children in fact play a major role in this film where, on the surface, they are singularly lacking. The men in KINGS OF THE ROAD long for the company of women, and yet in practice their relationships have remained broken and unfulfilled – and that goes not only for Bruno, who confesses to being unable to feel anything but utter loneliness when making love to a woman, but also for Robert and his failed marriage. It applies also to the man they find one night, in a strange, bleakly expressionist sequence, throwing stones as if in a trance down a giant loading-hopper: his wife has just committed suicide by driving her car into a nearby tree. And it also applies to Robert's father, the editor of a small-town paper, whom he visits after ten years' separation, berating him with the way he had mistreated his mother, and formulating his accusations against the exhausted and pathetic old man in a special edition that he sets up himself with the headline 'How to Respect a Woman'.

Bruno, meanwhile, strikes up a sad and brief liaison with a lonely cinema cashier, who lives alone with her daughter. Shortly after this, Bruno and Robert take time off and travel to the Rhine on a borrowed motorbike, to visit Bruno's now deserted childhood home. (As in WRONG MOVEMENT, the 'romantic' Rhine turns out to be a very noisy place.) Bruno weeps at what he finds, and yet derives comfort from the fact that now his life seems at least to take some shape, to have a 'story' to it. These two central episodes, in which both men seek out the haunts of their youth, are part of a wider pattern of references to childhood: there are various encounters with children in the course of the film, and Robert, it turns out, is a pediatrician specializing in language disorders.

The sorry state of the West German film industry, and in particular the plight of the rural cinemas, is the most explicit of the themes touched on in KINGS OF THE ROAD. The conditions encountered by Bruno at the run-down and poorly attended cinemas he visits in the course of his work speak for themselves, but to make the point even clearer Wenders allows the cinema owners to express their own laments. The film is in fact framed by two monologues: at the beginning a confused old man talks nostalgically to Bruno of the heyday of the silent films, and at the end an old woman speaks with disgust of the vicious exploitation that has led her to close her cinema – a speech that reflects exactly Wenders' own sentiments:

> My father used to say that film is the art of seeing, and that's why I can't show these pictures that – that just exploit anything that is left to exploit from people's eyes and minds. And I won't be forced to show films where the people stumble out benumbed by stupidity, that destroy their very lust for life, that force them to kill their feelings for themselves and the world.

The final sequence shows Bruno outside the cinema in the cab of his lorry. The camera moves up to the sign above the cinema entrance: 'WEISSE WAND' it reads, 'White Screen', but the sign is broken, and only the letters 'E ND' are illuminated. It is a rather gimmicky visual pun (Wenders is fond of these little games with signs and their meanings, as is Handke), but it does more than merely close the film. Not only is it the 'End' of KINGS OF THE ROAD, but it points too to the 'End' of the cinema that the old woman had lamented, as well as to the 'End' of her particular cinema. In all cases the result is the same: a 'white screen'. But there is another point here: the German for 'end' is *Ende*; the word we see here is English, or, more to the point, American.

The old woman had gone on to decry the dominance of the American majors among the distributors, and Wenders' old hobby horse certainly plays its part in KINGS OF THE ROAD. The film itself is very much in the Hollywood tradition not only of the 'road movie' (even functioning as a kind of prototype European 'trucker movie'), but, in its study of two lonely men, it echoes also the cowboy genre of the 'buddy movie'. (More than one critic has noted the film's echoes of John Ford's TWO RODE TOGETHER.) Evidence of the American presence in West Germany abounds, ranging from the Texaco service station where Bruno pulls in early in the film, through the pop records that Bruno plays – and both men sing to – in his cab, to the sequence in the US Army hut, whose walls are littered with American graffiti, and where Bruno, fiddling with some loose telephone cables, suddenly gets a connection to AFN Munich. Here, in this last outpost of the American empire, Robert – referring to Bruno's statement that he can't get the lyrics of certain songs out of his head –

makes the much-quoted remark that sums up Wenders' assessment of the extent of American influence in West Germany: 'The Yanks have colonized our subconscious.'[12]

KINGS OF THE ROAD is a remarkable achievement, using as it does the paraphernalia of Americanization – right down to the very form of the film itself – to create something very European, very German that is at one and the same time a nostalgic celebration and a regretful critique of that process. In THE AMERICAN FRIEND (DER AMERIKANISCHE FREUND, 1977) the critique is much stronger, the celebration more muted. Stylistically this was to be a new departure for Wenders: after the gently rambling KINGS OF THE ROAD with its leisurely sequences shot on old-fashioned-looking soft monochrome, THE AMERICAN FRIEND is a tightly-structured, tense thriller shot on an almost garishly vivid new Eastman Colour filmstock.[13] The plot is based on Patricia Highsmith's novel *Ripley's Game*, and deals with the last weeks in the life of a quiet, gentle Hamburg picture framer called Jonathan Zimmermann. Jonathan is suffering from a rare blood disease, and, at the instigation of Tom Ripley, an American exile involved in shady deals with forged paintings, eventually agrees to carry out two murders in exchange for a handsome sum of money for his wife and son after his apparently imminent death. The murders are carried out: the first by Jonathan on his own in the Paris Metro, the second with Ripley's help on an inter-city train. Jonathan and Ripley successfully ward off an attack on the latter's house by a mafia gang; but after having helped Ripley dispose of the bodies by burning them in an ambulance on a deserted beach, Jonathan, his wife at his side, dies at the wheel of his car – eerily, weirdly reverting for his last words to the otherwise abandoned Swiss dialect of his childhood: 'Marianne, it's getting so dark.'

THE AMERICAN FRIEND went through a number of provisional titles, including 'Rule Without Exception', 'The Frame', and 'The Broken Frame'. The title finally chosen comes from a remark made by Jonathan's wife: 'I haven't the slightest desire to know what you're getting up to with your American friend.' It is a well-chosen title, for it goes to the heart not only of this film but of Wenders' more general concern with the wooing and exploitation of Europe by what politicians used to

call 'our American friends'. In ALICE IN THE CITIES Wenders had portrayed a German in America; in THE AMERICAN FRIEND for the first time he portrays an American in Germany. The 'American friend' Marianne refers to is of course Tom Ripley. Ripley wears a stetson, but he cuts a sorry figure. Jon Voight's Midnight Cowboy had been incongruous, but still uneasily at home in New York; in Hamburg, Wenders' Ripley is a total outsider. Lost, lonely, and bewildered, he is a fatigued, nervous, almost tragic individual with a tortured existentialist conscience. He is far removed from the self-assured figure of the US colonizer of the post-war years. Ripley is a post-Vietnam American abroad, isolated and adrift in a Europe that his civilization has moulded, but that now has no place for him. He lives in a decaying white villa furnished with little more than a pool table and an illuminated advertisement for Canada Dry. His house looks decidedly like a seedy, run-down White House that has fallen on hard times.

Ripley the American shatters the domestic idyll of Jonathan the European. He wants to make Jonathan his buddy. In doing so he estranges Jonathan from his wife Marianne. A triangle develops that reaches a climax of tension towards the end of the film. The development of the relationship between the two men comes over most strikingly in a sequence that begins with Ripley giving Jonathan a present – early on Jonathan had given him one. Ripley's present to Jonathan is an old collection of pictures of naked women each exposed in a different way as an example of lighting technique for film-makers (one of many passing references to the cinema in the film). At this almost sacred moment they laugh: they laugh more than anywhere else in the film. A third male is present: Daniel, Jonathan's little son, who now adopts an exaggeratedly 'manly' stance. Then suddenly Marianne arrives. Her appearance shatters the idyllic moment of all-male communion: quietly, innocently, in an almost classic act of 'intrusion', she has broken a moment of 'buddy-hood' that is quintessential Wenders.

THE AMERICAN FRIEND Directors as mafiosi: Wim Wenders and Sam Fuller

The buddy motif is derived consciously from the Hollywood tradition, and not only by Wenders, but by the two men themselves. When Ripley woos Jonathan with a present he does so in a voice that affects the quotation of a corny line. He does this again much later when he brings Jonathan something to eat as the latter stands guard outside Ripley's besieged house. 'You must be freezing out there,' says Ripley, 'I'm thinking about you all the time.' But he says it with an ironic laugh, as if quoting but nonetheless meaning. Ripley, in his attraction to Jonathan, is fighting against the hard-man stereotype of the all-American male, for whom expressions of affection have been taken over by Hollywood and can no longer be made unselfconsciously. Ripley seems in fact to have adopted the cowboy persona because it is permissible, indeed almost obligatory, for cowboys to have buddies. Thus he is able to profess manliness, to identify with a stereotype, but also to indulge his craving for companionship.

Despite Wenders' assertion that 'EASY RIDER had nothing to do with it',[14] the choice of Dennis Hopper for the part of the melancholy American Friend seems singularly appropriate, for EASY RIDER, which Hopper directed and in which he co-starred, was a kind of epitaph for the road movie, a disillusioned comment on the American dream turned sour, a lament for those ideals of life, liberty, and the pursuit of happiness that had been twisted into the destructive happiness of pursuit. Equally appropriate was the choice of two other established American directors – both also 'outcasts' from the Hollywood system – to play prominent secondary roles: Nicholas Ray and Samuel Fuller. Nor does the cinematic casting end there: other directors – Jean Eustache, Peter Lilienthal, Daniel Schmid, and Sandy Whitelaw – also appear, as does Wenders himself on a number of occasions. Indeed, the habit of cropping up in one's own films is a little in-joke that one associates in particular with Alfred Hitchcock, and Wenders certainly also makes clear nods in Hitchcock's direction on a number of occasions, not least in the murder sequence on the train (a murder, moreover, as in STRANGERS ON A TRAIN, committed by a substitute assassin), and also in the flock of cackling gulls that seem to drop on Jonathan in one of his attacks of dizziness. (Wenders also pays homage to another grand old man of the cinema in dedicating THE AMERICAN FRIEND to Henri Langlois, the founder of the Paris *Cinémathèque*.)

In general, however, the acknowledgments of anything positive that may have come out of America are outnumbered in THE AMERICAN FRIEND by evidence of the damage that Europe, like Jonathan, has suffered from American influence. Hopper, Ray, Fuller, and Hitchcock may meet with Wenders' approval, but one suspects that his view of the bulk of American films, already presented via the old lady at the end of KINGS OF THE ROAD, is reflected more in the activities of the mafia men and their pornography racket; it is clear that they are doing their bit towards the takeover of the German film industry: one of them is overheard on Munich station talking of 'wrapping up the German co-productions'. Their activities – misusing and degrading the film medium for commercial ends – are paralleled by the art forgeries with which Ripley is involved.[15] Even the settings for much of the action have succumbed to that anonymizing process of 'modernization' that is at the same time a process of Americanization. This is nowhere more true than of Paris, which Wenders chooses to show in the shape of the futuristic Metro station at La Défense, the American Hospital, and the vast high-rise development that cynical Parisians have dubbed *'Manhattan sur Seine'*. This Paris is indeed almost indistinguishable from the New York with which, in the opening and closing sequences, THE AMERICAN FRIEND is, most aptly, 'framed'.

THE AMERICAN FRIEND is the culmination of Wenders' exploration of the wooing and exploitation of Europe by transatlantic culture, epitomized in the wooing and exploitation of Jonathan by Ripley. It is also a film that takes the matter a stage further by exploring the effects on the 'American friend' himself of what he and his country have to answer for.[16] The effects of American friendship are presented in all their personal, economic, and cultural ramifications. Much of the dialogue of THE AMERICAN FRIEND is in English: the plot requires this – Ripley's German is, he claims, 'lousy' – but so too do the exigencies of international filmmaking in an American-dominated market. THE AMERICAN FRIEND thus is itself what it is talking about: an instance of the relationship between America and

Europe, America and Germany, Hollywood and the New German Cinema. There is, Wenders seems to be proposing, a great deal that is wrong with a cowboy in Hamburg.

'Film is the art of seeing.' In an interview in 1977 Wenders picked up the remark of the old lady from KINGS OF THE ROAD, and added: 'I want to help people to see again. It's ambitious. But I can try.'[17] His earliest films are now looked on as classic examples of 'Neuer Sensibilismus', that highly visual, contemplative, essentially non-narrative 'Munich School' of filmmaking, which enjoyed a certain vogue in the late sixties and early seventies, in which the camera quietly but insistently observes more or less everyday, unremarkable sights, settings, and events. 'Showing' is the ideal for Wenders, film as 'a form of perception which no longer hurls itself blindly on meanings and definitions, but allows the sensuous to take over and grow':[18] an ideal that he finds epitomized in the work of his 'only master', Yasujiro Ozu.[19] 'Showing' involves the incorporation into his films of what Wenders calls 'trouvailles', the sights and sounds that crop up unexpectedly in the course of filming, a technique most clearly exemplified in KINGS OF THE ROAD, where little more than the itinerary was planned in advance, the script being developed from day to day as filming proceeded.

Wenders believes passionately in the power of the cinema for good and evil:

> The cinema is concerned with life, . . . the cinema is a more accurate and more all-embracing documentation of our age than the theatre, music, or the visual arts . . . cinema can harm people by alienating them from their longings and their fears . . . cinema can benefit people by opening up life to them, showing them new forms of freedom . . .[20]

His films abound with cinematic references, no more so, of course, than in the story of Bruno Winter, the roving projector repairer, who at one point even delivers a brief, incidental, but heartfelt ovation on the Maltese Cross, the mechanism 'without which there wouldn't be a film industry'. In ALICE IN THE CITIES the implications of John Ford's cinematic renderings of the all-American ideals provide a recurrent sub-theme: early in the film Philip watches YOUNG MR LINCOLN on television in a motel, but – an ironic comment on the American Way that the film celebrates – the performance is ruined by the commercials that interrupt it. At the end of the film the end of the American Dream seems heralded in the newspaper article that Philip reads on the train to Munich: an article that announces the death of John Ford.[21]

In WRONG MOVEMENT another film is seen playing on a television set, this time a German film on German television, uninterrupted by commercials: Straub's CHRONICLE OF ANNA MAGDALENA BACH. Television as a whole, though, is presented in an unfavourable light in Wenders' films: for Alice television is already a drug that she must take whenever the opportunity presents itself, whilst Philip vents his disgust with American television by doing violence to the set in his motel room. Almost by way of revenge the television in Jonathan Zimmermann's Paris hotel gives him an electric shock. In WRONG MOVEMENT another television set – that of the suicidal industrialist – is, with heavy symbolism, literally plastic-wrapped as it flickers away long after close-down. Television in fact is just one of the media of communication that figure so largely in Wenders' films: the telephones, the newspapers, the photographs, the pop songs, the trains, cars, lorries, buses, boats, and planes that his protagonists are so often using. The importance that communication in all its forms has assumed in the modern world is reflected in his films, and the fact that so much modern communication is American in inspiration, ownership, control, or ideology lies at the heart of Wenders' recurrent concern with the American 'colonization of our subconscious', with the role of the 'cowboy in Hamburg': his concern, in short, with the cinema.

8 HANS JÜRGEN SYBERBERG

'A manic egocentric beset with a persecution complex, sniffing out conspiracies all over the place; a maker of gargantuan films, who can't restrain the flow of his ink when he writes.'[1] Such is the popular image of Hans Jürgen Syberberg – or at least the image the West German press likes to play with. Syberberg is the outsider in the West German film scene, a man who has conducted a long and bitter running feud with what he regards as a philistine, cliquish, and petty film establishment; a director who is the extreme example of the general rule that the New German Cinema is better appreciated abroad than in the Federal Republic.

Syberberg has always found it difficult to get his films distributed and exhibited in West Germany. In the early days he actually bypassed the distributors and telephoned various cinema owners (with some success,

as it happened) to offer them his work; later he switched to the 'hard-to-get' tactic, declaring that his monumental HITLER would only be shown abroad, because German film culture had decayed beyond the point where such a film could be appreciated. It is certainly true that Syberberg's films have gone down much better outside Germany, and nowhere more so than in France. If, as Syberberg claims, the West German film critics have an automatic aversion to all he creates, the French critics positively idolize him. For the French his films seem to embody and confirm the popular conception of all that is most exotically German: a *furor teutonicus* epitomized in grandiosely Romantic Wagnerian visions. His first major feature, LUDWIG, REQUIEM FOR A VIRGIN KING, was largely ignored in Germany; in Paris it ran for seven months, stealing all the thunder from the simultaneous release of Visconti's sumptuous LUDWIG, and becoming the most successful post-war German film to be shown in France. Some devotees claimed to have seen it up to thirty times, and it made so much money for the cinema concerned – the Marais – that it was able to install three new mini-cinemas on the profits. The French critics' continuing willingness to give the highest acclamation to new works by Syberberg is further attested by *Le Monde*'s description of the Hitler film as 'Faust Part III'.

Syberberg's attacks on the West German film establishment have been caustic and virulent, at times petulant, and always underpinned by a self-righteous and imperturbable confidence in the quality of his own work. As far as he is concerned, criticism in Germany is at best misguided, at worst evidence of a rancorous conspiracy, whereas praise in France is evidence of the discernment and high standards of French film culture. A substantial part of *Syberbergs Filmbuch* is devoted to polemical attacks on the West German critics, coupled with accounts of the enthusiastic reception he has enjoyed abroad: glowing praise from Henri Langlois, a photograph of Giscard d'Estaing and Andréa Ferréol toasting him at a LUDWIG reception, and some forty pages of favourable reviews from the French press in which, to make things quite clear, the most 'discerning' passages have been carefully italicized. The '*Filmbook*' also contains a 36-page 'Dictionary of the German Film Critic', in which key terms from German reviews of his feature films are (rather audaciously) held up for ridicule.

Syberberg has at various times lashed out at most aspects of the film scene in West Germany. His disgust at the prostitution of the cinema to commercial expediency is shared by many directors, and is not unfamiliar. Much more unusual, and unfortunate, have been his back-biting attacks on his fellow directors. ('Wenders . . . is popular because he worships Hollywood, the great whore of showbusiness.'[2]) But his real *bête noire* is the German critic, or at least the critics who work for the big newspapers and magazines, and whom he sees as setting the tone of West German film culture; a film mafia who, to add insult to injury, also sit on the bodies that award official prizes and subsidies. These are the 'self-appointed arts-page judges', the 'language terrorists',[3] the perpetrators of a 'highly refined form of *Berufsverbot*'.[4] They are beneath contempt, and Syberberg dismisses them – by means of a peculiar misuse of the English language – as 'buffs', stressing that the word should be made to rhyme with '*Puff*', a German term for 'brothel'.[5]

What, then, is Syberberg actually in favour of? The faults of the commercial cinema could, he feels, be remedied by what he calls a 'public-democratic cinema and film structure'. This would mean nationalizing not only the production of films, but also their distribution and exhibition. He points out the absurdity of the present system in West Germany, where films are *produced* to artistic criteria with public money, but are then cast out to fend for themselves in the distribution and exhibition market, where only commercial criteria apply: something that would be unthinkable (in West Germany, at any rate) in the case of opera and theatre.[6] Like many others, Syberberg has been quick to point out the vast discrepancy between the generous state subsidies given to opera and the theatre in the Federal Republic, and the comparative pittance granted to the cinema. But Syberberg goes much further than others in justifying this complaint.

Syberberg is a man with a vision of the cinema that is far more exalted than that of any of his fellow directors. For him there is no doubt that the cinema is not just important, but absolutely vital. It is not just one art among many, but *the* art form of our age, and it must flourish and survive just as cathedrals, paintings,

statues, and the theatre have survived as monuments to earlier stages in our civilization. Throughout his writings certain rousing images recur as expressions of his obsession with the cinema: images of film as 'the music of the future', film as 'the continuation of life by other means', as 'the total work of art (*Gesamtkunstwerk*) of our age'. 'We who make films are the heirs of Western culture,' he says. 'There's more than a grain of truth in the statement that Wagner and Schiller would have made films if they were alive today.'[7] Or again, and even more grandiosely, 'He who has film has life.'[8]

According to Syberberg, the film is a product and expression of the age of democracy. Only if we create an active film culture, educating our children to appreciate the cinema, and supporting it in every way possible, can the survival of democracy itself be at all assured. Again like many others, Syberberg admires the earliest stages of the cinema: Méliès (with whom he likes to be compared), Griffith, Eisenstein, Stroheim, the German Expressionists. But after its revolutionary beginnings, the cinema has stood still for fifty years, indeed it has slipped back to a point where today it is dominated by two basic categories of film, both of which Syberberg despises: vulgar entertainment, and shallow didacticism.

And so, for the salvation of Western culture, the cinema must be reinvigorated. And this is where Syberberg comes in. His films, his writings make quite clear, are to be seen as models for the regeneration of a decaying art. His writings are notably lacking in approbatory references to the work of other contemporary directors, which is after all not surprising, for Syberberg's work is indeed quite unique, quite unlike anything else that is being done in the cinema. Behind all his theoretical writings, and behind all his recent films, there is the idea of *music*, 'film as the music of the future', in fact. The key to the cinema is montage, and the art of the cinema consists in the interweaving of the visual and oral elements of that montage into something akin to a musical composition. It is not a new idea (there are, for instance, many unacknowledged echoes of Eisenstein here), but it is one that Syberberg develops to new extremes. He insists that film, through its musicality, can give us not only the highest aesthetic *pleasure*, but also *insight*, an understanding of the world that goes beyond anything attainable by discursive argument. The film provides 'fun', 'insight', and 'a heightening of life'.[9]

Syberberg has described his cinema as the result of a combination of Brecht and Wagner, a fusion, in other words, of the rational and Romantic traditions that have conventionally been regarded in German cultural history as polar opposites. It is a pairing that leads to what he has oxymoronically described as an *'aufklärerische Trance'*, an 'enlightening trance', where the eighteenth-century rationalism of the *Aufklärung* – the Age of Enlightenment – mingles with the mysticism of the nineteenth-century Romantics.[10] Wagner looms large in Syberberg's universe; his spirit is fundamental to the films of the 'German Trilogy', though, interestingly enough, he is not the central figure of any of them. (He is however now working on a film about the last years of Wagner's life, as well as on a film about Wagner's *Parsifal*.)

Syberberg has called Brecht his 'foster father';[11] he knew him, and filmed him at work in Berlin in the early fifties. He sees cinema in terms akin to those that Brecht applied to the theatre. Thus there is the traditional 'Aristotelian' film, which, in a debased form, thrives in the commercial cinema today. But there is also another type of film, with German roots in the classic cinema of the early 1920s, a film that used effects akin to those of the 'non-Aristotelian' theatre that Brecht was to develop. Brecht used this theatre, with its 'alienation effects', its use of narrators, of addresses to the audience, its 'epic' structure, its open-endedness, in the cause of rational analysis, against the obfuscations of metaphysics. It is here that Syberberg parts company with Brecht: there is no inherent or necessary link between epic theatre and rationalism, he claims:

Irrationality with all its kindred concepts such as surrealism etc. is possible and reconcilable precisely here, where music is of importance as the principle that supplies aesthetic and dramatic order, as this whole aesthetic tradition proves, as witness such disparate phenomena as Greek tragedy, the mystery plays, Bach's oratorios, and Wagner's *Ring*.[12]

The formula 'Brecht + Wagner' is, as Syberberg himself admits, an 'aesthetic scandal', in which he has attempted 'to combine Brecht's theory of the epic theatre with the musical aesthetic of Richard Wagner, to join in film the epic system as anti-Aristotelian cinema with the laws of a new myth'.[13] It is a formula that attempts to overcome a classic duality of German culture, thought, and politics. Syberberg seems to have no fear of the enormousness of the undertaking, for he is convinced that it is precisely through the non-discursive medium of film that the 'dualities', rooted as they are in verbal logic, can be overcome.

It is here that another of his mentors seems to have left his mark: in this case an unacknowledged mentor in the shape of Friedrich Dürrenmatt. Syberberg wrote his doctoral thesis on the Swiss dramatist, and he seems to have picked up a great deal from him in the process. Not only do his films share the baroque theatricality that typifies many of Dürrenmatt's plays, but his theoretical writings too have a polemical restlessness very reminiscent of Dürrenmatt's essays and 'monster speeches'. When Syberberg talks of the cinema's ability to surmount the paradoxicality of the world, it could be Dürrenmatt himself talking of the theatre:

Perhaps it is the opportunity to portray the truth of our age, that essence made up of the ambivalence of events and the many-layered nature of human beings. . . . Just for once the luxury, so often denied us in real life, of playing the game of 'both . . . and', just for once not having to decide, but to tolerate the For and Against . . .[14]

The grandiosity of Syberberg's conception of film is something quite unique in the New German Cinema. He tells how Henri Langlois, the director of the Paris *Cinémathèque*, had intuitively stumbled upon the key to his childhood, the reason why Hans Jürgen Syberberg was different from the other boys – or at least from the ones who became film directors. It was, he says, his 'Prussian-conservative upbringing . . . without chewing gum and pin-tables, not for nothing in the Stalinist epoch'.[15] Be that as it may, he does seem peculiarly innocent of that Hollywood heritage so evident in the work of directors who grew up in the West.

Syberberg was born in Pomerania in 1935, and remained in what after the war became East Germany until the 1950s. His first impressions there, he says, were *Faust* and Brecht.[16] Before he left, he chanced to meet Bertolt Brecht in person, and obtained his permission to film some rehearsals of the Berliner Ensemble. The result, obtained with a Heath-Robinson 8mm sound camera, is the only film record in existence of the Berliner Ensemble during the Brecht years. Syberberg actually put the film away and forgot about it, only to rediscover it many years later when moving house. He blew it up to 35mm, added intertitles and a commentary, and issued it in 1970 under the title AFTER MY LAST MOVE (NACH MEINEM LETZTEN UMZUG) – a unique and fascinating document of rehearsals for *Mother Courage* and *The Mother*, and of a complete performance of *Urfaust*.

After this early and unusual beginning, Syberberg's career in film went through three different stages before he emerged into the international limelight in the 1970s as the director of the 'German Trilogy'. He began as a maker of current-affairs and documentary shorts for Bavarian television, and in a hectic three years from 1963 to 1966 completed 185 films of between three and thirty minutes in length. (The 'Oberhausen directors', as he is quick to point out, 'made an average of one or two 12 to 20-minute films a year'.[17])

As a development of this television work he moved on to the making of five feature-length documentary 'character portraits'. The first of these, made in 1965, was about one of the grand old men of the German theatre, the actor and director Fritz Kortner, about whom Syberberg made another film in 1966. Syberberg's second 'character portrait' was of Romy Schneider. Made in three days in 1965, it caught her in the middle of a personal crisis, and led to Syberberg's first major brush with the film and legal establishment: it was cut and altered into something so far removed from the original that he was obliged to totally disown it. An affectionate portrait of a run-down and eccentric family of Bavarian aristocrats followed in 1967. The last in the series was more caustic. SEX-BUSINESS MADE IN PASING (1969 – originally to be called 'Until Smoke Comes out of Your Trousers'), a not unsympathetic study of the Bavarian 'pornography king' Alois Brummer, was at the same time a commentary on the current state of the West German cinema: 'The cinema as brothel, with much to laugh at, if it weren't so serious.'[18]

SEX-BUSINESS MADE IN PASING was sandwiched between two other films that made up the third component in Syberberg's early career. These were his first features, 'SCARABEA – HOW MUCH LAND DOES A MAN NEED?' (SCARABEA – WIEVIEL ERDE BRAUCHT DER MENSCH?, 1968), and SAN DOMINGO (1970), both of which – a portent of future developments – were well over two hours long. SCARABEA was based on the Tolstoy story about a man who enters a wager that will give him as much land as he can run round in a day; when he arrives at sunset back at his starting point, he drops down dead. Syberberg transposed the setting from Russia to Sardinia, and changed Tolstoy's peasant into a German tourist. It was a colourful, often bizarre and surrealistic film, with some violent and shocking sequences that led the distributor to insist that a gong be sounded in the cinemas before incidents that might upset sensitive members of the audience.

SAN DOMINGO, an updating of a *Novelle* by Heinrich von Kleist, was set in the milieu of Munich's young drop-outs, a semi-documentary story of pot-smokers, rockers, motor-cycle gangs, and student revolutionaries. The film, which was provided with German subtitles to help non-Bavarians over the hurdle of the Munich dialect, can be seen in retrospect as a rather remarkable, and almost unique, record of some of the origins of terrorism in the Federal Republic; it ended with an alarming and rousing quotation from Eldridge Cleaver, a warning of the anarchy and violence that would be unleashed if these young people were ignored.

It was a prophetic warning, and one that was to lead Syberberg on to that exploration of the German psyche that lies at the root of his best-known films – the 'German Trilogy':

That our history is, in everything, of necessity our most important heritage, both for good and evil, that is our fate, laid upon us at birth, and something that we can only work our way through with an active effort. When SAN DOMINGO finished with the warning that the consequences would be disastrous if we don't watch out, do something, and take seriously the things that happen there – things happening all around us at the end of the sixties and the beginning of the seventies – then a lot of people laughed or got themselves into a rage. Baader and Meinhof confirmed what was meant in the worst possible way. I chose the way back into the past of our last hundred years, to see if I could seek out the origins of many contemporary developments . . .[19]

Syberberg's 'German Trilogy' is made up of the films LUDWIG – REQUIEM FOR A VIRGIN KING (LUDWIG – REQUIEM FÜR EINEN JUNGFRÄULICHEN KÖNIG, 1972), KARL MAY (1974), and HITLER, A FILM FROM GERMANY (HITLER, EIN FILM AUS DEUTSCHLAND, 1977). In addition, two 'by-products' of the Trilogy have been released: LUDWIG'S COOK (THEODOR HIERNEIS ODER: WIE MAN EHEM. HOFKOCH WIRD, 1972), and THE CONFESSIONS OF WINIFRED WAGNER (WINIFRED WAGNER UND DIE GESCHICHTE DES HAUSES WAHNFRIED VON 1914–1975, 1975).

In his search for 'the origins of many contemporary developments' Syberberg has concentrated on the irrational side of the German tradition, the side that flowered in German Romanticism and in the music of Richard Wagner, the side that the democracy of Weimar never managed to tame before it erupted again in the malignant shape of National Socialism. This dark, brooding, introspective tradition was what Thomas Mann called '*Kultur*', as opposed to the '*Zivilisation*' of the West, and in particular of France. *Zivilisation*, Mann said, was democratic, progressive, rational, and found its expression in verbal communication.[20] *Kultur*, on the other hand, was undemocratic, conservative, irrational, afraid of words – but excelling in *musical* expression.[20] And so it is that in his 'German Trilogy' Syberberg seeks to tackle German *Kultur* on its own terms, with a series of films that eschew verbal discourse in favour of the associative logic of music.

The question 'Where did Hitler come from?' is a key one in modern German history, but none have attempted to answer it in the way Syberberg has. And it is not only his methods that are different. He ignores the well-trodden paths that lead back to the great writers and thinkers in search of symptoms of the apocalypse to come, and concentrates instead on two apparently peripheral figures, the mad king of Bavaria, and the most popular German novelist. The motto for all three films, Syberberg says, could be 'In search of paradise lost' – the subtitle the French gave to KARL MAY.[21] This was the driving force that all three of these figures,

Ludwig, May, and Hitler, had in common: a universal desire to return to the womb-like security of a vaguely remembered innocence, purity, and wholeness; a desire that reached extreme, and ultimately tragic, dimensions in the history of the German people. SCARABEA had taken its title from the beetle that, Sisyphus-like, pushes its ball of dung before it: a symbol of the German tourist on Sardinia in vain search of paradise – he too a trivial heir to the same tradition.

LUDWIG – REQUIEM FOR A VIRGIN KING sets the tone, both in form and content, for the whole of the 'German Trilogy'. Running for some two and a quarter hours, the film is divided into two parts, each in turn subdivided into titled episodes. Part I, 'The Curse', telescopes events from the King's life into a single night (a 'day in his life', in fact, as he rose at 6 p.m. and went to bed at 7 in the morning). Part II, 'Once Upon A Time I Was', portrays his downfall and death, and the legend that surrounded him. Syberberg's budget was small (300,000 DM), and the film was shot in eleven days. (Favourable comparisons are often drawn with Visconti's LUDWIG, which cost forty times as much and took six months to shoot.) In making a virtue of these necessary limitations, he created one of the New German Cinema's most distinctive and remarkable film styles. The film was made indoors, on stage-like sets, the sequences as stylized tableaux in front of backdrops and projections, the camera predominantly static, and using a bare minimum of editing. Many actors play two or more parts, whilst, by contrast, some characters are played by two actors. No attempt or pretence is made at realism, and the overall effect is exultantly theatrical.

Syberberg's ambition is enormous: to portray the life and legend of Ludwig II as a nexus of implications that radiate out into the whole of modern German history and culture. The central issue the film raises is the question of Ludwig's undoubted popularity: 'He took drugs, was a homosexual, a fanatical pacifist, contemptuous of the people, francophile, anti-militarist, lived in an opera world – yet today it is the reactionaries

LUDWIG – REQUIEM FOR A VIRGIN KING Harry Baer as Ludwig

who defend and love him.'[22] And, as the film shows, so did the ordinary people, *his* people, the peasants of Bavaria, who saw in him a symbol of their own yearnings and dreams: 'If you kill him, you will kill the best in us,' as one old man puts it.

Syberberg's original intention was to make a pastiche about Ludwig along the lines of Warhol's LONESOME COWBOYS, but the more he read about Ludwig the more compelling and complex he found him to be. The film he finally made, for all its bizarrerie, is a sympathetic portrait of the Dream King, who comes across as a sad, lonely, and pathetic figure, epitomized in the most memorable image of all: the little child with the beard and moustache of the adult, wiping away two big tears that roll down his cheek.[23] It is an image that is part too of the film's deliberate mingling of time levels, for Ludwig not only symbolized the future, he foresaw it too. He anticipated with horror the new age of the masses, industrialization, cities, pollution of the environment, the rise and dominance of Prussia and all that it stood for. Ludwig was a reactionary inasmuch as he opposed progress, but such was the future that lay ahead that it is the plotters who want Bavaria to march into that industrialized brave new world who come across as Syberberg's real villains. The film's final caption, 'Requiescat in pace', accordingly has a ring of heartfelt sincerity to it; yet we know that the memory and the legend of Ludwig would never be allowed to rest in peace.

True to the principle 'All human life is there', LUDWIG is by no means dominated by sadness and pathos. Much of its humour in fact derives from the exaggerated and mannered settings, the make-up, the clothes, the refreshing shock of Syberberg's alienation effects. The sight of Hitler dancing a rumba with Röhm, of Bismarck riding a bicycle, of camera-girt tourists being guided round a Bavarian castle as Ludwig holds court, snatches of post-war American radio programmes, a casual remark by Wagner, who identifies a quotation as being 'by Brecht or Goethe': these are jokes, but not just light relief, for they point to things to come, suggesting links and consequences, patterns that transcend time yet work themselves out within it.

LUDWIG begins with three Wagnerian norns proclaiming the curse of Lola Montes, as Lola herself walks towards the camera. On the soundtrack we hear Marlene Dietrich's 'I'm naughty little Lola', the song then fading to Wagnerian tones. Wagner's presence dominates the film, just as it dominates the world of Ludwig himself. His music fills the soundtrack, swelling at times to outrageous proportions. Wagner himself appears in two guises: as a dwarf, and as a tall muse-like creature of indeterminate sex.[24] He was to remain the guiding spirit behind Syberberg's world.

While he was working on LUDWIG, Syberberg came across the memoirs published, almost unnoticed, in 1953 by Theodor Hierneis, then eighty-four years old, and a former member of the kitchen staff at the court of King Ludwig. On the basis of this text he made the film LUDWIG'S COOK, a pendant to the Ludwig film, and, like that other 'spin-off' of the Trilogy, THE CONFESSIONS OF WINIFRED WAGNER, a return to the 1960s style of Syberberg the maker of documentary 'character portraits'. LUDWIG'S COOK is everything that LUDWIG – REQUIEM FOR A VIRGIN KING is not: calm, simple, undemonstrative, and verbal.[25] The Bavarian actor Walter Sedlmayr plays the part of a somewhat garrulous Theodor Hierneis who returns as a middle-aged man to take the audience on a guided tour of the castle where he worked in his youth.

It is a nice idea: history quite literally from below; the rumours, the gossip, and, of course, the menus that for the court staff were the only means they had of building up a picture of the man who dominated their lives. It is again a film about Ludwig: his presence pervades every room that Hierneis brings to life with his anecdotes, the vivid 'downstairs' viewpoint being neatly thrown into perspective when it unexpectedly encounters the 'upstairs' survey recited by an 'official' guide taking round a party of tourists. But being a film about Ludwig, it is also a film about the legend, the aura, the myth that was inextricably bound up with the reality of his existence. We see the effects of this myth in the character and views of Hierneis: a little scepticism, but predominantly respect, reverence, even awe, characterize his attitudes to Ludwig. The hierarchy is not questioned, indeed Hierneis has used it to make his way in later life, trading on the fact that he is a 'Court Cook, ret'd.' (as the German title has it) to set up in business on his own. So LUDWIG'S COOK turns out to be not just a film about Ludwig, his castles, his eating habits; nor is it merely a piece of *marxisant* history-from-below: it is much more a portrait of the emergence of that order-loving German bourgeoisie that, fatefully, made the grade by acquiescence rather than rebellion. The attitudes of Theodor Hierneis are not very far removed from those of Winifred Wagner, nor from those of the millions of others who helped German history along the path from Ludwig to Hitler.

During his work on LUDWIG, Syberberg also came across another book that was to lead to a film: this time it was the six-volume novel about the Bavarian king written by Karl May shortly after Ludwig's death. Karl May, who lived from 1842 to 1912, is one of the most important German novelists. Yet one would be hard-put to find his name in any self-respecting literary history, for his importance lies not in the quality of his work, but in its immense popularity. He is the classic example of what in German is dismissively called 'Trivialliteratur' – 'trashy literature', unrefined, simplistic, but in terms of sales immensely successful. The effect of *Trivialliteratur* on popular opinion is immeasurable, for it depends for its very success on reflecting, confirming, and developing stereotyped public attitudes and assumptions. In tackling the subject of Karl May, Syberberg is extending the examination of the debased culture of the trivial, of kitsch, that he had begun in LUDWIG, and that was to play a major part in HITLER. It is at this level, rather than at the level of statesmen and philosophers, that he hopes to find clues to the popular myths that, in the 'age of the masses', have played such an important role in national history.

It is only in recent years that the full significance of the phenomenon of Karl May has come to be appreciated. For most of this century his work has been the most widely read literature in the German language, reaching all groups in the population, and appealing to young and old alike. This fact alone makes him worthy of attention, but awareness of him becomes all the more crucial when one looks at what he actually wrote, at the ethos of his work. This ethos is, to say the least, suspect, and in the context of modern German history, it is profoundly alarming. For although Karl May wrote about exotic places – the East, and the Indian lands of North America – his works incarnate a popular Romantic longing for harmony, simplicity, and a life guided by intuition. Their psychology is primitive, their heroes are noble and just; morally and physically superior beings. It comes as no surprise to learn that Hitler was a great admirer of these books, and that he recommended them as spiritual sustenance to his troops in Russia. As Syberberg himself puts it, in the introduction to his Hitler book:

Anyone who knows the significance of Karl May for the German people, how every schoolboy grows up with his works, also knows how close we are here to a history of German sentiment, to its adventures of the soul and its myths of the Good Man, the German who fights and conquers for all that is noble.[26]

Karl May's life was a chequered and troubled one. Born in humble surroundings, he was blind for the first four years of his life. He became a teacher, but a number of petty thefts and swindles landed him in prison for seven and a half years. It was after this that he began publishing his novels, and quickly became a huge success. But then, twelve years before his death, accusations began to be levelled against him, accusations of obscenity, of corrupting German youth, of being an ex-convict, and, most significantly, of deceit: that his first-person and ostensibly authentic narratives were based on experiences he had never had in places he had never visited. There followed a complicated and protracted series of legal cases, and it was not until the end of his life that May finally managed to win back the respect and acclamation he had enjoyed in his prime.

It is these last twelve years that Syberberg's film concentrates on. He shows Wilhelmine society divided into two camps, the supporters and the detractors of Karl May. Here the links with LUDWIG become apparent: the utilitarian, puritan, Prussian world that Ludwig had foreseen has now arrived; Karl May is virtually an embattled reincarnation of the Dream King, defending his Romantic, heroic, mythical vision against the onslaughts of a shallow rationalism, but, like Ludwig, all too aware of the dangerous perversions to which his Romantic cult of the 'soul' is prone. The uneasy ambiguities of LUDWIG persist: the Romantic world would make an easy villain, but Syberberg resists the temptation; the Wilhelmine Establishment is oddly progressive by comparison, but gets little sympathy. In the end the worst of both worlds results: the

dangerous myth joins hands in reconciliation with the industrial might of the Establishment. In a Vienna doss-house a young man borrows a pair of shoes to go and hear his hero speak. The occasion is historically documented: the hero was Karl May, the young man was Adolf Hitler.

KARL MAY is the odd film out in the 'German Trilogy'. It lacks the baroque exuberance and theatricality of LUDWIG and HITLER. The spirit of Wagner has temporarily receded, to be replaced by Mahler, Liszt, and Chopin. Most of the numerous short scenes are shot in a more or less realistic and conventional cinematic manner. A number of critics felt that it was in fact rather a let-down after the excitement of LUDWIG, and, at over three hours in length, a tedious film. (French critics, as one might expect, insisted that it was well worth the effort.) Certainly the first half reflects all too directly the tedium of May's protracted years of litigation (embattled against his philistine critics, he is intriguingly reminiscent of Syberberg himself waging his endless feud with the West German film Establishment); the film's latter parts have more extrinsic interest, though, as the contexts and implications of Karl May's role in German cultural history are drawn into focus. The choice of cast is also fundamentally different from the familiar young players of LUDWIG and HITLER. For KARL MAY Syberberg selected a quite unique gathering of old UFA stars, leading figures not only from the cinema of the twenties, but also of the Nazi cinema: Kristina Söderbaum, Käthe Gold, Attila Hörbiger, Willy Trenk-Trebitsch, Mady Rahl, Lil Dagover. Karl May himself was played by Helmut Käutner, the leading director of the last years of the Third Reich (and later, in 1953, director of another film about Ludwig II). The casting raised some eyebrows; it was, Syberberg insisted, an attempt to come to terms with the repressed history of the German cinema. It had its irony too, for now these old stars were being confronted with the origins of some of the myths that many of them had so questionably served in their early years.

The confrontation of an elderly German with her complicity in the Nazi past was to be exemplified in Syberberg's next film, THE CONFESSIONS OF WINIFRED WAGNER. This was the second by-product of Syberberg's work on the 'German Trilogy', and, even more than LUDWIG'S COOK, it was a work that harked back to the Syberberg of the quiet documentary 'character portraits'. The film had its origins in Syberberg's research for the Hitler film, which led him to draw up a list of living witnesses of the Third Reich of whom he might make studies on video tape. One of them was Winifred Wagner, and, prompted by her grandchildren Eva and Wolfgang, whom Syberberg knew, the 78-year-old daughter-in-law of Richard Wagner agreed to break her thirty-year silence on her past life – and in particular her acquaintanceship with Adolf Hitler.

Winifred Wagner was born in England, in Hastings in 1897. By the age of two she had lost both her parents; two years later she was sent to Germany to be adopted by distant relations of her paternal grandfather. Her stepfather, Karl Klindworth, a pupil of Liszt and a friend of Richard Wagner, introduced her to Bayreuth society for the first time in 1914. A year later she was married to Richard Wagner's son Siegfried, twenty-eight years her senior, and director of the Bayreuth Festival. After his death in 1930 she took over the running of the Festival, a position she retained right through to the end of the Third Reich in 1945. After the war, Wagner's grandchildren, intent on cleaning up the image of Bayreuth, imposed on her the ban on making any public statements that was finally lifted for Syberberg's film.

Winifred Wagner had first met Hitler in 1923, and had fallen immediately under his spell. From 1933 onwards he began attending the Bayreuth Festival annually, and was received with affection and hospitality by Winifred and her family. In return, Hitler provided personal subsidies for the Festival, and ensured, by string-pulling and special favours, that it was able to continue throughout the war years. (He even obtained exemption for Bayreuth from the ban on Jewish and foreign artists.)

THE CONFESSIONS OF WINIFRED WAGNER lasts some five hours, and was made, in black and white, in the course of five successive days in April 1975.[27] Syberberg's technique was simply to set the camera up and film Winifred Wagner reminiscing in the surroundings of her own home in Bayreuth. The film is made up

KARL MAY Helmut Käutner in the title role, with Käthe Gold and Kristina Söderbaum almost entirely of this gigantic monologue, punctuated by the breaks that come at the end of each roll of film (even then her voice, captured on a tape recorder, often carries on uninterrupted), and interspersed with the odd photograph, and written or spoken captions from Nazis and anti-Nazis alike. It is a technique of extreme self-effacement, an attitude of distanced respect for his subject that Syberberg has called 'tendresse': 'A tender approach to work, from the filming through to the editing and mixing. Tenderness in this context also means calm, care, and patience, being able to wait for echoes of the movements and words, to take people seriously.'[28]

Only the frequently ironic captions imply any external critique of Winifred Wagner's remarks; apart from that they are allowed to speak for themselves. And speak for themselves they do, for the old lady's frankness and volubility conspire to create an unintentional but all-too-clear picture of the frightening capacity for self-deception that the German bourgeoisie manifested in its acquiescence in the crimes of Nazism. These are not, despite the film's English title, 'confessions': Winifred Wagner is redoubtably unrepentant. To her Hitler was a kindly, avuncular friend of the family and a generous benefactor who visited them each year to relax for a while from the burdens of public office. 'If Hitler walked through that door today,' she says, 'I should be just as happy and glad to see him here and have him with us as ever I was.'

Like all too many modern Germans of her generation (and, even more alarmingly, of younger generations too) she admires with gratitude the 'good' things Hitler did – the restoration of order, decency, and purpose to national life. As for Hitler's more notorious achievements, she manages the typical double-think of recalling that 'we never talked about those things', and, at the same time, suggesting that 'those things' have probably been exaggerated in any case – 'all the things he gets blamed for today'. The failure to appreciate the political implications of even the most personal relationships is common enough; Winifred Wagner's story illustrates in a most acute form the way this blindness enabled large sections of the cultural Establishment in pre-war Germany to flirt with and espouse the destruction of the very values that they ostensibly stood for. Describing herself as 'an

utterly unpolitical person', she talks in the film of her amazement at being accused by a de-Nazification tribunal of having been involved in politics. 'I told them that I *hadn't* been involved in politics. Then they all laughed, and said of course you've been involved in politics. I haven't been involved in politics.'

'It's easy not to be a Nazi when there's no Hitler around', reads a closing caption that Syberberg's wife formulated for the film. It was intended as a warning against over-hasty self-righteousness on the part of the younger generation, but it also raised the question of Winifred Wagner's dubious attitudes today now that there *was* no Hitler around. It was undoubtedly the public revelation of these attitudes that led to the ructions in the Wagner family that followed the film's release. Winifred's son Wolfgang, alarmed at the possible damage she had done to the Festival, of which he was now director, barred her again from attending. The friendship between Syberberg and Winifred's grandson Gottfried, who had helped in the making of the film, was abruptly at an end. It was, Syberberg said, the old story of 'the seismograph being held responsible for the earthquake'. It was a sour and unfortunate outcome to what Syberberg had all along seen as a kind of therapeutic psychoanalysis, 'my mourning for Bayreuth'.[29]

In 1977, after four years of preparation, Syberberg completed the final element in his 'German Trilogy'. Although it was made in only twenty days on a budget of less than a million marks, HITLER, A FILM FROM GERMANY is in more ways than one the climax of all of Syberberg's work. It is, with a running time of seven hours, the longest among his many lengthy films. Thematically it is his most ambitious project, attempting to locate the phenomenon of Adolf Hitler in the context not only of Germany, but of the whole of European civilization before, during, and after the Third Reich. Structurally it is his most complex film by far, mingling and interweaving sound and vision, music, dialogue, commentary, and action, documentary and

THE CONFESSIONS OF WINIFRED WAGNER Winifred Wagner sits beneath a portrait of her mother-in-law Cosima, the composer's wife

fiction, past and present, the sublime and the ridiculous, the tragic and the comic, the petty and the grandiose. Technically too it represents the culmination of the special effects – most notably the front projection techniques – that he had been developing over the years.

Syberberg's approach to the phenomenon of Hitler does not take the path of ordered and logical argument; instead, true to his theory of 'film as the music of the future', he builds up a bewildering symphony of ideas, impressions, sights, sounds, and emotions. The film's central thesis is expressed in Max Picard's formula of the 'Hitler in us', which was at one time to be the film's title. 'Hitler was the first person – and the only person – to base his dictatorship on a plebiscite,' Syberberg claims, and suggests that he was able to do this because he emerged in the age of the masses, the age of democracy.[30] But more importantly, Hitler's success lay in his appeal to the deepest levels of the popular psyche, to the dreams and yearnings of the ordinary man and woman. Hitler appealed to the irrational in the German people, and so, in order to appreciate Hitler, and in particular to exorcise the 'Hitler in us', Syberberg proposes that we tackle him on his own terms, by invoking the powers of the *irrational* and of *myth*. And that, Syberberg's aesthetic makes quite clear, is a task for which the medium of film is uniquely well suited.

In an age that has attempted to banish the spectre of Nazism by determined rational analysis, Syberberg's ideas are uncomfortable and unaccustomed. 'It was above all,' he says in the opening words of his Hitler book, 'in the voluntary abandonment of her creative irrationality – perhaps *only* in this – that Germany really lost the war.' The irrational is a vital component of the German tradition that in the post-war world has been denied and suppressed because of its notorious misuse by the Nazis. We deny it at our peril, Syberberg warns, for it then erupts in fanaticism and the violence of the terrorist. Hitler was the incarnation of this tradition in its most negative form; one must tackle him through this irrationalism, but in its *positive* forms:

> We know all about the glory and the wretchedness of irrationalism, but without it Germany is a dangerous nothing, sick, lacking identity, explosive, and a pitiful shadow of its potential. One doesn't fight Hitler

with the statistics of Auschwitz and the sociology of his economic system, but with Richard Wagner and Mozart.[31]

Irrationalism finds expression in *myth*, the myths of the people that Hitler played on, that he promised to realize, and it is those myths that must be grasped: but again by quasi-mythopoeic means, and not through rationalism. In attempting to perfect the fascist aestheticization of politics, Hitler became 'the greatest film-maker of all time', turning the whole of Germany into a giant studio in which to realize his projects: Germany as a 'total work of art', the '*Gesamtkunstwerk Deutschland*'.[32] Here the myths of the German people were to be performed and recorded on film for posterity; it is these myths and their performance that Syberberg has set out to counter in the 'German Trilogy': 'The films LUDWIG and KARL MAY can be understood as positive mythologizations of history, filtered through the medium of film, by means of the spiritual checks of irony and pathos . . .'[33]

'Irony and pathos' make up the final element of the aesthetic that Syberberg has elaborated to validate his Hitler film. It is a paradoxical combination that is closely related to the 'Brecht + Wagner' formula, and one that Syberberg associates with the 'ethics' and the 'truth' of art. Put at its simplest level, the 'pathos' of the film lies in its Wagnerian pretensions to embrace the mythic totality of Hitler's world; its 'irony' lies in the confrontation of the myth with reality, the sublime with the ridiculous. It is this *artistry* of the film that Syberberg invokes in defending his work against the accusation that by emulating the irrationality of Nazism he is in fact dangerously close to an apotheosis of Hitler. It is in part a distinctly old-fashioned view of art, appealing to classical ideals of balance and harmony; in part its ideas seem derived from the world of psychoanalysis – of resubmersion in past afflictions in order to emerge liberated from their domination; at times his imagery even suggests a kind of homeopathic inoculation – the theory of 'the hair of the dog that bit you'.

HITLER, A FILM FROM GERMANY As if rising from Hell, Hitler (Heinz Schubert) emerges from Wagner's grave – an image modelled on a Gustave Doré illustration to the *Inferno*

HITLER, A FILM FROM GERMANY is divided into four parts, each of normal feature-film length. Although, true to the aesthetics outlined above, it has no sustained, discursive argument, it does have an overall pattern within which its associative, 'musical' sequences are located, and numerous images and ideas recur time and again as leitmotifs within the whole. It is framed by the cosmic perspective of the earth – and Germany, and Hitler – in the context of the infinity of the stars. Framed too by an 1844 quotation from Heinrich Heine: 'When at night I think of Germany, I cannot get to sleep' – a quotation to which Syberberg appends his own signature at the end, adding the dateline 'Munich, on the day after Mogadishu-Stammheim-Mulhouse'.[34] Hitler lives, and lived, in everyone, and is accordingly played in many guises by each of the actors in turn, appearing too as a ventriloquist's doll, and symbolized in the ubiquitous little Hitler moustaches.

The setting is a workshop-like stage, often littered with the grotesque and trivial trappings of the Nazi years: the kitsch whose commercial success is for Syberberg the clearest evidence that it is a potent, albeit debased, expression of the deepest myths in the popular psyche, and thus worthy of the most serious attention. Projected backdrops portray landscapes, buildings, paintings, or newsreel films from the Nazi years. The soundtrack mingles recordings of Nazi speeches, radio broadcasts, marching songs, the speeches of the Allied leaders, resistance fighters, news bulletins from America, from Britain, France, and Russia – mingles these and much more with music, German music by Mozart, Mahler, Beethoven, Haydn, and, above all, Wagner, whose dominating presence in Syberberg's work here reaches its ultimate climax, and whose significance is now unambiguously captured in the memorable image of a toga-girt Hitler rising from Wagner's misty grave.

Past, present, and future are all invoked to elaborate the theory of 'Hitler in us'. Hitler was not an accident, but the inevitable result of the meeting of democracy with the old German irrationalism. And Hitler lives today – indeed, if anything, his ideals have been implemented in the modern world beyond his wildest dreams. In the third part of the film a Hitler puppet gloats over Stalinist purges, the UN condemnation of Zionism, Idi Amin, the spread of political oppression, terrorism, torture and brutality, Cambodia, Vietnam, Chile, Brazil, Argentina, South Africa, the Berlin Wall and the mined frontier . . . 'Praise them, praise them, praise them,' he intones as his list rattles on. It is Syberberg at his bleakest and most cynical, painting a picture of a modern hell in which he had earlier found room not only for the cultural functionaries and brainwashers of East and West, but for Hollywood and the film industry that choked and abused its greatest talents, the pornography and commercial cinema of modern West Germany: 'Something for the Human Rights Commission of the Last Judgment; the charge: torture of the human soul.' Here at last Syberberg, like a latter-day Dante, finds the opportunity to put his critics where he feels they belong.

The division of the film into four parts is not arbitrary. Parts One and Four are distinctively more tentative than the rest, the first a protracted beginning that stabs again and again at the implications of the topic, and repeatedly questions the possibility of realizing on film something so enormous as the universal quest for the Holy Grail, which here symbolizes that longing for paradise lost that Hitler promised to fulfil. Here too the many references to film are introduced, with a homage to the medium in the shape of a ubiquitous model of the first film studio, Edison's 'Black Maria'. Part Four is an equally protracted conclusion that works over the ideas that have been thrown up before. In between come more leisurely, less restless sequences (the longest in fact makes up the first 35 minutes of Part Four), sequences in the manner of LUDWIG'S COOK: reminiscences of Hitler's valet, Himmler's masseur and his astrologer, and of a man who imagines he was Hitler's servant and projectionist on the Obersalzberg, and sequences of discourse and analysis, spoken direct to the audience, but discourse and analysis that is suggestive and concrete, quite lacking in deductive, logical abstractions.

Yet even these relatively calm sequences still bombard the audience with a kaleidoscope of visual and acoustic impressions: the changing backdrops, the music, voices, and sounds that compete with and sometimes drown the words of the main speaker. Not that these words are themselves exactly easy to follow: the sentences come in streams of verbosity that leave one's brain reeling, unable to keep abreast of the ideas and images that come tumbling out. It is here that Syberberg's theory seems thinnest: one can accept the 'irrationality' and 'musicality' of the film's sights, sounds, and of its music itself, but *words* . . .? A lengthy discourse that comes too fast to follow irritates rather than enlightens.

In defence of the complexity of good films Syberberg has remarked that 'the supreme law of the quality of art is the category of repeatability': in other words, films, like music, must bear constant re-viewing, yielding something more or something different at every new appraisal.[35] Elsewhere he has pointed out that the 'video revolution' will call for a new aesthetic of the cinema, that films will now be repeatable and analysable to an unprecedented extent, and that they must accordingly develop the complexity and subtlety of the great works of music and literature.[36] Repetition and analysis of HITLER, A FILM FROM GERMANY must lead to a greater appreciation of its artistry, but one cannot help wondering whether closer inspection of its torrents of words – the one element in the film that *does* lay itself open to rational analysis – will not detract from the 'musical' appeal of the whole.[37]

The release of HITLER, A FILM FROM GERMANY was followed by the now familiar skirmishing between Syberberg and the West German film critics. But this time Syberberg was taking no chances: the West German film critics had little to say about the film because most of them had not seen it. HITLER was premiered in November 1977 in England, at the London Film Festival. Shortly afterwards it was given the British Film Institute's award for 'the most original and imaginative film introduced at the National Film Theatre during the year'. It was well received in other countries too, but Syberberg doggedly withheld it from the Germans, even turning down an invitation to show it at the 1978 Berlin Film Festival, because, he said, he knew the German critics would only ruin it. His analysis of what had happened (or hadn't happened, or might happen) was an ironically fitting tailpiece to that creative obsession with the German psyche that lies behind the whole of Syberberg's 'German Trilogy':

The failure of the German film critics in this matter is a sad capitulation of German post-war rationality in the face of the long and great tradition of irrationalism by means of a morbid process of repression. It is a fear of contact that is gradually taking on deadly forms . . .[38]

PART THREE : PECULIARITIES

9 OTHER DIRECTORS: THEMES AND CONCERNS

There is, of course, much more to the New German Cinema than the work of the seven directors discussed in the preceding pages, although it remains true that Kluge, Straub, Schlöndorff, Herzog, Fassbinder, Wenders, and Syberberg are those who have done most to establish its reputation in the world at large. They are also directors who have consistently produced films of quality. A few other directors have had isolated successes abroad with one or two films, and a considerable number have become well-known in West Germany itself; none, however, have yet achieved the international standing of the 'big seven'.

i The First Generation

Little is now heard of most of the directors of the 'first generation' – the immediate heirs of Oberhausen in the 1960s, and the isolated precursors of the New German Cinema in the 1950s. Some of them have stopped making films, others have 'gone commercial'; only a handful have made names for themselves within the New German Cinema proper. These exceptions include of course Kluge, Schlöndorff, and Herzog. Straub, a major figure in the 1960s, has in the meantime become much less of a specifically German filmmaker, whilst Syberberg, despite his early – and substantial – beginnings, remained a peripheral figure until the 1970s. Fassbinder and Wenders, on the other hand, are very much directors of the 'second generation', which was scarcely involved in the birth of the new cinema in the 1960s.

The earliest indications of a new beginning in the West German cinema took the form mainly of 'experimental films', whose novelty lay more at the formal level than in their subject matter. This was the case with the first film of all to break with the commercialized conventionality of the 1950s, Herbert Vesely's 'FLEE NO MORE' (NICHT MEHR FLIEHEN) of 1954, as it was with Ferdinand Khittl's 'THE PARALLEL ROAD' (DIE PARALLELSTRASSE) of 1961, and Vlado Kristl's 'THE DAM' (DER DAMM) of 1964. Interestingly enough, the impetus to do something different within the West German cinema that these three films represent came from outside: none of these directors was a native German, Vesely being an Austrian, Khittl a Russian, and Kristl a Yugoslav.

The only significant 'new' film to be directed by an actual West German in the 1950s was JONAS, made in 1957 by the Stuttgart neurologist Ottomar Domnick. An 'experimental film' inasmuch as it used distorted and unaccustomed camera angles, JONAS asked uncomfortable questions about the price being paid for West Germany's new affluence, showing a man trying to escape a very German past in the midst of a sinisterly futuristic world that on closer inspection is all too clearly the present. The old Germany – authoritarian, bullying, tyrannical – is, the film suggests, being resurrected in the guise of capitalist prosperity. A much more realistic portrayal of social problems in the Federal Republic of the 1950s came in Georg Tressler's 'THE HOOLIGANS' (DIE HALBSTARKEN, 1956), the only notable 'new' film of the decade that did not play with the mannerisms that were later to lead more to the 'underground' cinema, rather than to the New German Cinema proper. (Tressler, who has since become a prolific director of television films and series, was yet another non-German: like Vesely he came from Austria.)

The new cinema of the 1960s was typified by the concerns that Tressler had anticipated: the world of the contemporary Federal Republic, its social problems, its relationship to the Nazi past, and, above all, the difficulties the sceptical younger generation had in coming to terms with their society's stifling conformism and hypocritical materialism. Often private problems of love and marriage, and problems of the 'generation gap', provided the focus of reflection, and most films created a new sense of authenticity by the use of outside location shots, of sequences that at times even bordered on *ciné vérité*. None, however, managed to go much further than a display of the *symptoms* of the malaise that was to lead to the youthful rebellions of the late sixties.

Peter Schamoni's 'CLOSE SEASON FOR FOXES' (SCHON-ZEIT FÜR FÜCHSE, 1966) combined all the elements of the new cinema in the story of the relationship between a young man – the scion of a wealthy family – and a lower-middle-class girl, even managing a reference to Godard's UNE FEMME MARIÉE as a token of its novel cinematic pretensions. It was, however, Peter Schamoni's younger brother Ulrich who made the film that quickly became the first box-office success of the New German Cinema. 'IT' (ES, 1965) looked at the life of a young unmarried couple in West Berlin, but despite its realistic ambitions (which included raising the then ticklish topic of abortion) it was still unable to shake off the ingratiating coyness of much of the West German commercial cinema. This was even more true of the other great box-office success of the early years of the New German Cinema, May Spils' NOT NOW, DARLING (ZUR SACHE SCHÄTZCHEN, 1967), a light-hearted tale of would-be bohemians amid the self-conscious happy-go-luckiness of Munich's 'left-bank' Schwabing.

NOT NOW, DARLING was just one of the many new films that, in most cases aided by the *Kuratorium junger deutscher Film*, made up the first triumphal wave of the New German Cinema that swept into temporary prominence in 1967. By now Straub, Kluge, Herzog, and Schlöndorff had all made their debuts as feature-film directors. For all its disparateness, the New German Cinema was beginning to manifest a distinctive range of thematic concerns that has remained fairly constant in subsequent years. To discuss films in terms of their themes has its dangers: the filmic complexity of the work, the multivalency of its effects, may be obscured by a deliberate homing-in on its 'major concern'. Such an approach – like auteurism, with which it is closely connected – is not inappropriate in the case of the New German Cinema, where, for better or worse, there has always been a decided tendency to produce '*films à thèse*', films with a message, films with a pointed theme. A survey of some of these major concerns certainly provides a convenient insight into the range of work produced in the West German cinema in the 1970s.

ii The New Heimatfilm

The common denominator of practically all the themes tackled in the New German Cinema is the Federal Republic itself: direct and indirect critical references to contemporary society had been the hallmark of the 'new' films of the 1960s; this remained the case throughout the seventies. A whole host of films in the early years attempted to tackle the Federal Republic on its own terms: through the medium of the *Heimatfilm*. By 're-functioning' this staple of cosy sentimentality in true 1968 manner, many directors were able to broach topics unheard of in the genre before. The classic of this 'New' (or 'Critical') *Heimatfilm* was Schlöndorff's THE SUDDEN FORTUNE OF THE POOR PEOPLE OF KOMBACH, which questioned the very bases of the genre: the assumption that life in the country is agreeable, desirable, and essentially unproblematic.

One 'New *Heimatfilm*' was made as early as 1968, and, in its combination of local colour, realism, and probing social analysis, it remains one of the most outstanding. Peter Fleischmann's HUNTING SCENES FROM LOWER BAVARIA (JAGDSZENEN AUS NIEDERBAYERN, based on the 1966 play by Martin Sperr) is a scapegoat parable in the tradition of Dürrenmatt's *Visit* and Frisch's *Andorra*. Set in a Breughelesque village, where mopeds, transistor radios, the scream of jet fighters, and the presence of Turkish *Gastarbeiter* bring a hint of the outside world to an essentially primitive and backward community, it shows what happens when Abram, a twenty-year-old motor mechanic, returns from the big city. Abram, it is rumoured, has been in prison; rumour then has it that he is a homosexual; his final expulsion from village society comes when Hannelore, the village good-time girl, claims he has made her pregnant. Derision turns to anger, and finally Abram is hunted down through the fields and woods by an army of police and villagers after he has stabbed Hannelore in an effort to escape. The film's title had ironically suggested a very different sort of hunt, and it is this false

HUNTING SCENES FROM LOWER BAVARIA Abram (right) is played by Martin Sperr, the author of the play on which the film is based

idyll of romanticized peasant life that returns at the end as the villagers hold a feast in the fields after Abram has been led back to the prison he came from. HUNTING SCENES FROM LOWER BAVARIA was a sharply-observed study of the social psychology of a small community, of the hypocrisy and mass hysteria that a closed world could generate. One wonders what the Bavarian villagers who acted in the film made of it.

HUNTING SCENES was, in both setting and implications, a film about the present. Other 'New *Heimatfilme*', true to the conventions of the genre, were usually set in the past, though their implications were highly contemporary. *The* year of the 'New *Heimatfilm*' was 1971, and of the four main examples of the genre that appeared then, three had historical settings: Schlöndorff's KOMBACH, Reinhard Hauff's MATHIAS KNEISSL and Volker Vogler's Western-style 'JAIDER – THE LONELY HUNTSMAN' (JAIDER – DER EINSAME JÄGER)

Both of these latter films were about folk heroes whose activities as poachers represented a radical challenge to the privileges of the landed gentry: here again, a traditional motif from popular culture was being 're-functioned' into a political parable.

Poaching as a challenge to the authority of the ruling classes also figured in the fourth of the group, Uwe Brandner's I LOVE YOU, I KILL YOU (ICH LIEBE DICH, ICH TÖTE DICH), which, curiously, was actually set not in the past, nor even in the present, but in the near future. Like HUNTING SCENES FROM LOWER BAVARIA it is the story of a young man who returns to his village – in this case to teach in the village school. The setting is idyllic, but sinisterly so, for the villagers, it turns out, are regularly drugged to keep them docile, whilst two sadistic policemen take care of any signs of disorder. The countryside belongs to the mysterious 'Masters', who descend once a year in helicopters to hunt unseen in the nearby forests; after they depart they drop a parcel of toys on a parachute for the loyal villagers. Their agent is the young local gamekeeper, and it is his uneasy relationship – at one point overtly homosexual – with the teacher that provides the film's main focus of interest. In the end the teacher rebels by poaching. He is captured by the keeper, and shot by the policemen; but then the keeper too rebels, and shoots the policemen in his turn. In its distinctive admixture of science fiction, I LOVE YOU, I KILL YOU took the re-functioning of the

Heimatfilm to a new extreme, yet it shared with other examples of the newly critical genre a forthright reappraisal of the stereotype of the 'rural idyll'.

Isolated examples of the 'New *Heimatfilm*' cropped up later in the seventies too – notably in Hans W. Geissendörfer's 1976 version of Ludwig Anzengruber's peasant novel *Sternsteinhof* – but for the most part the directors involved moved on from implicit to explicit criticism of the Federal Republic, to urban settings, and themes that were unambiguously contemporary. In a society that promised equal opportunities for all, and one that had long grown complacent about its achievements, it was only natural that the new cinema, building on the foundations laid in the 1960s, should turn its attention to those who were all too clearly less equal than others. Three groups in particular, making up between them perhaps two thirds of the population, played a distinctive role in the New German Cinema's choice of protagonists: *Gastarbeiter*, old people, and women.

iii Gastarbeiter

When one starts to categorize the new German films under subject headings, one is immediately struck by the ubiquity of Fassbinder: he crops up in almost any list one can think of. This is of course very true of film treatment of the problems of West Germany's vast labour reserve of immigrant workers, the *Gastarbeiter*. Fassbinder's FEAR EATS THE SOUL is still without doubt the best-known film portrait of German attitudes to the *Gastarbeiter*, though the topic had already played a central role in his second feature KATZELMACHER in 1969, and was taken up again in EIGHT HOURS DON'T MAKE A DAY and WILD GAME, where the casual remark 'He's just a foreign worker' typifies the condescension, dismissiveness, and potential inhumanity of popular attitudes towards immigrants. Fassbinder's early concern with the *problems* of the *Gastarbeiter* may be contrasted with the simple registration of their presence as an intriguing *phenomenon* in some other films of the late sixties. Thus in Schlöndorff's A DEGREE OF MURDER the crowds of immigrant workers on Munich's main station, together with the departure board showing trains bound for destinations in Yugoslavia, are little more than superfluous decoration, adding a whiff of cosmo-

FAR FROM HOME Parviz Sayyad as Hasseyin

politanism to the self-indulgent image of 'swinging Munich'.

The largest national element among the West German *Gastarbeiter* are the Turks, of whom there were over a million in the country by the mid seventies. The Turks, because of their very different cultural background, have greater difficulties than most in adapting to life in West Germany, and it was therefore appropriate that their peculiarly acute problems should be the concern of two films that were both made in 1975, and that between them represent the New German Cinema's major contribution to discussion of the *Gastarbeiter* theme. These were Sohrab Shahid Saless's FAR FROM HOME (IN DER FREMDE), and Helma Sanders' SHIRIN'S WEDDING (SHIRINS HOCHZEIT).

Saless was a newcomer to the German cinema: born in 1944 in Iran, where he made shorts and documentaries for the Ministry of Culture, and then two independent features, he began working in West Germany in 1975, making a name for himself as a creator of quiet, unemphatic, but intense observations of the non-events of daily life – films that have attracted comparisons with Chekhov, Bresson, and Olmi. FAR FROM HOME begins with Saless's statement: 'I did not want to make another film about *Gastarbeiter*, but about *das Elend* ['misery'], which etymologically means "in a foreign land"'. The film, whose sparse dialogue is predominantly in Turkish with German subtitles, is a gentle, undemonstrative portrait of the life of a small group of *Gastarbeiter* in West Berlin. The central character, Hasseyin, played in a highly-praised performance by Parviz Sayyad, is seen at his monotonous work in a noisy machine room, in the streets and on the underground on his way to and from work, and with his colleagues in their seedy and dimly-lit flat, with its bare walls, its pin-ups, and sparse furniture. Despite his good intentions and his touching determination to 'integrate', Hasseyin meets largely with indifference or hostility from the Germans he encounters. Like his flatmates, he is an agreeable, simple, almost pathetically naïve character, who cannot admit the horrible truth that it may have been a grave mistake to leave his home for the cold grey world of the Berlin backstreets.

That home is seen in the early sequences of SHIRIN'S WEDDING, which adds two important dimensions to the *Gastarbeiter* theme: firstly by taking the trouble to look for once at conditions in the immigrants' homeland, and secondly in portraying the plight of *women* immi-grants, who suffer exploitation and oppression not only as workers but also as women – and that not only in Germany, but even more in their patriarchal home-lands, in this case the semi-feudal Muslim world of rural Turkey. The film, which is accompanied by a commentary in the form of a dialogue between Shirin and Sanders, is based on a popular Turkish legend about a young man who bores with his bare hands through an iron mountain to find his lover Shirin. Here it is Shirin herself who sets out on a heroic search for Mahmut, her childhood betrothed, after fleeing from an arranged marriage in Turkey. After being 'pro-cessed' by the West German labour recruitment office in Istanbul, Shirin travels to Germany, where Mahmud is a *Gastarbeiter*. In Cologne she is accomodated in a hostel, but has to leave when the factory where she

SHIRIN'S WEDDING Ayten Erten (right) as Shirin

works closes down. She finds a job as an office cleaner, but here too she is made redundant, though not before her boss has raped her. Once more she becomes homeless when the house where she had been living with a Greek family is demolished. Looking for work in a café, she is picked up by a pimp, who sends her out to work in *Gastarbeiter* hostels. Here, at last, she finds her Mahmud: but he must pay first before she can celebrate her 'wedding' in his bunk. In the end she is shot dead by one of the pimps as she attempts to run away one night.

The ending of SHIRIN'S WEDDING is melodramatic, and the story-line hovers between contrivance and documentary realism; indeed, the overall effect is not unlike that of many Fassbinder films, and, like Fassbinder at his best, Sanders manages to carry it off brilliantly. Much of the film's force comes from the performance of Ayten Erten as Shirin, who throughout her degradation and downfall remains unassailably the same gentle, trusting, warm figure that she has always been, an innocent whose very goodness is her tragic flaw. SHIRIN'S WEDDING shows the hollowness of the 'liberation' that the adoption of superficial Western ways can bring for immigrant workers. Shirin's largely involuntary Westernization is entirely superficial – yielding to external pressure she removes her scarf, dyes her hair, exchanges her trousers for a skirt, puts on lipstick, drinks alcohol, and dances – and it leads her only from one form of bondage to another. But the film does have its positive implications, glimpsed in moments of tenderness and loving solidarity that Shirin encounters among the women she meets, and above all in her Greek friend Maria: a citizen of a country that Shirin has been taught to regard as the Turks' deadliest enemy, and with whom she can communicate only in broken German, the language of work, officialdom, and exploitation. When Maria and her friends celebrate the fall of the Colonels, it is the happiest day in Shirin's life, even though she herself will never be freed.

iv Old People

SHIRIN'S WEDDING is clearly more than a '*Gastarbeiter-film*': it is also a '*Frauenfilm*', a film not only directed by a woman, but one with a clear feminist theme. Similarly Fassbinder's FEAR EATS THE SOUL is concerned not only with German attitudes to immigrant workers, but equally with the conventional image of old people, for Emmi, even though she is only middle-aged, is subjected to scorn, ridicule, and ostracism for behaviour 'inappropriate' to her age.[1] The dismissive popular image of the elderly was again taken to task in EIGHT HOURS DON'T MAKE A DAY, where Grandma not only gleefully pronounces Gregor to be her 'lover', but is also in the vanguard of radical action. And again, in MOTHER KÜSTERS Fassbinder shows with much sympathy another resourceful, though more bewildered, elderly woman, who in the end falls victim to the ruthless exploitation of the younger generation.

The neglected setting of the old folks' home was brought to the fore in two West German films of the mid seventies that managed to attract a degree of international attention. JANE IS JANE FOREVER (JANE BLEIBT JANE, 1977), directed by Walter Bockmayer and Rolf Bührmann, mingled documentary realism and bizarre fantasy to tell the tale of Johanna, an old lady who is convinced that she is Tarzan's Jane, and who lives, in a room bristling with potted palms, surrounded by her 'memories': photographs of 'her' and Tarzan, and Tarzan comics. The film opens with Johanna being admitted to a cold and impersonal old folks' home, and closes with her, dressed in a leopard skin, aboard a jumbo jet en route for Nairobi. It is an uneasy film: initially certainly the portrayal of her self-possession, vitality, and resilience in the face of the bemused and shocked world about her is a rebellious and delightful celebration of the rights of the elderly akin to that exemplified in Fassbinder's Grandma. Later, though, Johanna becomes almost pathetic: where at first one laughed with her, towards the end of the film the perspective of the young reporter who has befriended her has taken over, and his attitude is increasingly one of *concern*.

A couple of years after Fassbinder's FEAR EATS THE SOUL, another film appeared in which old people and *Gastarbeiter* unite to flaunt established conventions. This was Bernhard Sinkel's LINA BRAAKE, or, to give it its full title, LINA BRAAKE – THE INTERESTS OF THE BANK CANNOT BE THE INTERESTS OF LINA BRAAKE (LINA BRAAKE – DIE INTERESSEN DER BANK KÖNNEN NICHT DIE INTERESSEN SEIN, DIE LINA BRAAKE HAT, 1975). Lina,

LINA BRAAKE Fritz Rasp as Gustaf and Lina Carstens as Lina

played by the then 81-year-old Lina Carstens (who died in 1978), is, like Johanna, a resident of a hostile and authoritarian old people's home. Here she is befriended by the rascally Gustaf, who tutors her in the art of fraud, enabling her to obtain a substantial loan from the bank that had evicted her from her flat. With the money she buys a farm in Sardinia for a family of *Gastarbeiter*; she is arrested, but the bank finds it impossible to prosecute her, whereupon she and Gustaf decide to go and stay in Sardinia. Despite its almost fairy-tale ending and the improbably idyllic Sardinian sequences, LINA BRAAKE was an important contribution to the New German Cinema's exploration of the way society treats its old people. The outstanding perform-

ance of Lina Carstens won the hearts of a very large audience, and made the film a notable success with the general public.

v Women

It may not be entirely coincidental that when West German directors have portrayed old people, they have generally chosen women rather than men as their protagonists. Feminist implications have been discernible in the New German Cinema from the outset, initially in the work of male directors, and latterly in the films of the growing number of women directors. One of the first films in this category is of course Kluge's YESTER-DAY GIRL, followed later by his OCCASIONAL WORK OF A

THE LEFT-HANDED WOMAN Edith Clever in the title role with Markus Mühleisen as her son Stefan

FEMALE SLAVE. Fassbinder's work contains frequent feminist overtones, and a number of his films are specifically concerned with conventional attitudes to women's roles in society: this is especially the case in NORA HELMER, MARTHA, EFFI BRIEST, and FEAR OF FEAR. The topic also surfaces in a number of Schlöndorff's films, and is a central issue in SUMMER LIGHTNING.

More recently, Peter Handke's THE LEFT-HANDED WOMAN (DIE LINKSHÄNDIGE FRAU, 1977), a cool, meditative, painterly – not to say precious – study of a woman's reaction to the break-up of her marriage, has been cited in the context of feminism. There is much of Wim Wenders in THE LEFT-HANDED WOMAN – he himself produced it, and both his cameraman Robby Müller and his editor Peter Przgodda worked on it – but in the intensity of its perception of the potential vividness of the everyday, in the clean absence of all sentiment, and in the stilted sententiousness of much of the dialogue, it is a remarkably accurate filmic transposition of the mood of Handke's prose writing. It is also very much an autobiographical film, reflecting – much more than his novel of 1976 – Handke's own experience of life as a single parent, and moreover a German-speaker, in contemporary Paris. Feminism, in fact, is by no means such a central issue in THE LEFT-HANDED WOMAN as may on the face of it seem to be the case.

Women directors were few and far between in the early years of the New German Cinema, a notable exception to this general rule – though very much at the commercial end of the spectrum – being May Spils, the director of NOT NOW, DARLING. Meanwhile, Erika Runge had begun, almost in isolation, to make documentaries on women in the late sixties. Of the feature films of that decade, only one stands out as a precursor of the *Frauenfilm* of the seventies: Ula Stöckl's 'THE CAT HAS NINE LIVES' (NEUN LEBEN HAT DIE KATZE, 1968). During the mid seventies, the situation changed considerably, and in 1978 nearly a third of the films shown at the Berlin Festival had been made by women.[2]

The West German women's movement had for some years been active in the production of shorts and documentaries, with an increasing number of female directors turning to feature production as well. There has

been much debate about the nature and function of a possible feminist aesthetic, and about the traditional image and role of women in the cinema, both behind and in front of the camera: a debate conducted in particular in the journal *Frauen und Film*, founded in 1974 by Helke Sander.[3] 1977 saw the making of the two most widely discussed and successful films by women directors thus far. One was Helke Sander's own first feature, THE ALL-ROUND REDUCED PERSONALITY (DIE ALLSEITIG REDUZIERTE PERSÖNLICHKEIT); the other was Margarethe von Trotta's first film to be made without the collaboration of Volker Schlöndorff: THE SECOND AWAKENING OF CHRISTA KLAGES (DAS ZWEITE ERWACHEN DER CHRISTA KLAGES).

The title of REDUPERS – as it has come to be known – is an ironic reformulation of a familiar phrase in the official terminology of the German Democratic Republic, which declares one of the goals of socialist society to be the creation of 'the all-round developed personality'.[4] The film's protagonist, Edda Chiemnyjewski, played by Helke Sander herself, is a freelance photographer, who lives alone in West Berlin with her small daughter, and enjoys watching East German television and imagining, a few miles away across the Wall, an all-round developed socialist personality watching Western tv. Edda and her friends in the Women's Photography Group are asked by the City Council to produce an exhibition of photographs about West Berlin. Their work, which takes the form of photographic 'happenings' that play on jokey juxtapositions of image and reality (a giant picture of a corner of the Berlin Wall, for instance, is positioned in front of that self-same corner of the Berlin Wall), turns out in the end to have little effect and is largely ignored.

Sander describes her film as 'a rather comic contribution to the question of why women so seldom make much of their lives'.[5] She portrays with wit and honesty the way in which so much of Edda's day is taken up with countering the resistance of the 'man's world' in which she lives, as well as fulfilling the responsibilities she feels towards her child, that there is precious little time left to devote to the task of giving her life the shape

THE ALL-ROUND REDUCED PERSONALITY The Berlin Wall is just as incongruous as the giant photograph, but only the image surprises us any more

and purpose of which she dreams, a task that the film illustrates with a quotation from a woman writer from across the Wall, Christa Wolf:

Before going to sleep I think that life is made up of days like this one. Points that, if you are lucky, will in the end be connected by a line. It is also possible that they might fall apart, a heap of meaningless time spent. Only a continuous, unfaltering effort can give meaning to the small units of time in which we live.

As well as being a film about a woman, and about women in general, REDUPERS is also a film about West Berlin: indeed, it is one of the most vivid evocations of life in the island city that the New German Cinema has produced. It shows the phenomenon of Berlin as a constant talking point among Edda and her friends. In their search for images of their life they are drawn constantly to the border, the crossing-points, and the graffitti-covered Wall. The East is repeatedly glimpsed, though never visited, its presence always felt, intruding on the television and the radio, counterbalanced there by the jumble of British, American, French, and West German programmes. The West Berlin that we see in the film is dingy, decrepit, cold, and dreary. It becomes clear that it too, in its isolation and artificiality, has become as much of a 'Redupers' as Edda herself and her friends.

Margarethe von Trotta's film takes as its starting point an actual event that occurred in Munich: a bank robbery committed by a young woman desperate for money to continue running her day-care nursery.[6] The Christa Klages of the title, on the run with the booty from the robbery, loses both her male accomplices, the first immediately after the raid, whilst the second is later shot by a policeman. In Munich she seeks refuge at the flat of an old school-friend, Ingrid, a beautician married to an almost permanently absent soldier whose hobby is collecting and stuffing bats. Ingrid gradually warms to Christa and her cause, and eventually joins her on the collective farm in Portugal to which she flees. But post-revolutionary Portugal, it turns out, still has to liberate its women: they are assigned their tasks, their roles, and their morals just as before, and Christa and Ingrid have to leave as awareness of their lesbian relationship gets abroad, and news of Christa's

criminal background filters through. After a bleak and suicidal interlude in an empty flat, Christa rejoins the women's group that had run the nursery – now to be turned into a sex shop. She is arrested, and in the closing sequence is confronted with Lena, the bank employee she had held hostage during the raid, and who has been obsessively following the hunt for Christa. Lena, asked by the police to identify the prisoner as the wanted woman, stares at Christa. 'No,' she says, 'that's definitely not her.' The camera too in this last shot dwells on Christa's face, as it manifests a mixture of astonishment, controlled delight, and revelation: this, as the closing title makes clear, is the second awakening of Christa Klages, occasioned by the first awakening of the bank-clerk Lena.

Von Trotta's film neither condones nor condemns Christa's action. It simply shows, like KATHARINA BLUM, 'how violence can arise, and what it can lead to'. 'The political situation in Germany today simply provokes individual actions,' von Trotta remarks. 'We don't have any organization, whether it be a union or a political party, to cater at the majority level, rather than in four-percent factions, for the sort of interests Christa is pursuing with her day nursery.'[7] THE SECOND AWAKENING OF CHRISTA KLAGES posits a process of consciousness-formation that derives not so much from rational analysis as from human warmth, tenderness, and affection. The love that develops between Christa and her men and women friends is neither romantic nor erotic, but simply a natural matter of comfort, compassion, and solidarity in a hostile world – the ideals, in fact, of the nursery that Christa so desperately tries to save. It is a bold and hotly contemporary film, which, almost uniquely – and in the tradition of von Trotta's work with Schlöndorff – dares to raise the issue of politically-engendered violence, and more specifically examines the motives of the 'Sympathisant'. The audience cannot escape the questions it asks: so appealing is its foolhardy heroine, so patently just her cause, that they cannot help but themselves become 'Sympathisanten'.

THE SECOND AWAKENING OF CHRISTA KLAGES The closing sequence: the bank assistant (Katharina Thalbach, left) deliberately fails to identify Christa (Tina Engel) as the bank raider the police are seeking

vi Young People

Immigrant workers, old people, women: three groups whose lives one might well expect to find reflected in an alert young cinema. One would, of course, not be hard put to find the rest of society playing at least an incidental role in a number of films as well. The wealthier end of the social spectrum – a favourite milieu in the commercial cinema – has been featured in a limited number of films, notably in Fassbinder's work (FOX and CHINESE ROULETTE, for instance), and more peripherally in much of Schlöndorff's. Young people and children have on the whole been distinctly neglected, especially in more recent years. The 'Young German Cinema' of the 1960s focussed more than anything on the younger generation, but as the directors have grown older, their attention has tended to turn to more adult concerns (Fassbinder, yet again, being a noteworthy exception in such films as WILD GAME).

Today only one director of any standing has regularly made feature films about, and for, young people, and that is Hark Bohm. His well-received 'NORTH SEA = MURDER SEA' (NORDSEE IST MORDSEE, 1975) showed the grimness of children's lives on a modern high-rise estate. MORITZ, DEAR MORITZ (MORITZ, LIEBER MORITZ, 1977), which portrayed the adventures and misadventures, real and imagined, of a fifteen-year-old son of the Hamburg upper classes, was, in box-office terms, the most successful German production in 1978. It had no single story line, simply mingling various threads of Moritz's life at home, at school, with friends, relations, and pets, adding a few contrived horror sequences, raising – though never answering – a whole host of contemporary issues, and in the end bringing salvation to the unhappy hero in the purely fortuitous form of the love of a pretty girl who sings in a church choir in the middle of the red-light district. At least the film did raise one major matter – the perils of road traffic – that has been almost totally overlooked in the New German Cinema: and that in one of the most car-obsessed countries in the world, where the road-accident death rate is among the highest in Europe.

The actual morality of making films with children was raised in Reinhard Hauff's THE MAIN ACTOR (DER HAUPTDARSTELLER, 1977). Here, as a result of his own unfortunate experience in the making of an earlier film with a youthful protagonist (PAULE PAULÄNDER, 1975), Hauff shows a film director who has made a semi-documentary film about a young boy's sufferings at the hands of a brutal father, only to find himself the object of the child's mingled aggression and disguised pleas for help, and ultimately the author of his descent into delinquency and vandalism. As a film about a film, THE MAIN ACTOR asked serious questions of the whole realist movement, and in particular whether films made with amateurs in pursuit of some political, consciousness-raising therapy, might not sometimes do more harm than good. When the young boy Pepe sees the film that has been made about him, the accompanying posters, and the general publicity surrounding it, he sees them as an intruder and an outsider, and it becomes clear that his own life, far from being placed more firmly in his possession, has been alienated from him. The director (and the newsmen who sanctimoniously seek to 'expose' him) has exploited Pepe's misfortunes in the guise of helping him. The film's conceit is of course infinitely extendable: a film might also be made about the effect on the boy protagonist of the making of THE MAIN ACTOR itself. And the implications do not stop at the level of realist documentary: inevitably it brings to mind the accusations of 'exploitation' levelled, for instance, at Herzog's use of out-of-the-way amateurs in his films.

vii The Berlin School

Apart from Fassbinder, few of the directors of the New German Cinema, for all their radicalism, have managed to make any films about the working class. At least that is the case if one concentrates on the mainstream of the New German Cinema, the predominantly Munich-based directors whose films have received the widest publicity, the most international attention, and a modicum of commercial success. In West Berlin, however, a more politically engaged cinema emerged out of the student movement of the late sixties, making films that, unlike the Hollywood-inspired work of the Munich directors, hark back to the brief-lived proletarian cinema of the last years of Weimar. The directors of this 'Berlin School' are in many cases former students of the Berlin Film and Television Academy, and most have been involved in the making of agitational documentaries about, and aimed at, working-class people. Guided by the principles of critical realism, they have worked typically in black and white and on small budgets to make films that eschew the polish and finish of the Munich directors' work, and that substitute political enlightenment for the latter's commercial and aesthetic goals.[8]

A major early example of this realist genre was Erika Runge's 'WHY IS MRS B. HAPPY?' (WARUM IST FRAU B. GLÜCKLICH?, 1968), a study of the wife of a Ruhr coal-miner. Early in the seventies a number of the Berlin directors moved away from the purely documentary approach typified in Runge's film, in the hope of reaching a wider audience with fictional – though still strongly realistic – story lines. The first, and in many ways still the classic, among these 'Worker Films' was Christian Ziewer's 'DEAR MUM, I'M FINE' (LIEBE MUTTER, MIR GEHT ES GUT, 1972), which portrays the development of political consciousness in a young worker in West Berlin at a time of threatened lay-offs and dismissals. Unemphatic, restrained, and almost naïvely traditional in its cinematic techniques, 'DEAR MUM, I'M FINE' set the tone for Ziewer's following films, as well as for a number of other Berlin film-makers.

Among these others, the better-known include the team of Ingo Kratisch and Marianne Lüdcke, who have also tackled the topic of the politicization of working people – though unlike Ziewer they have tended to use professional actors in their films – and Max Willutzki, who in the late sixties and early seventies worked with Ziewer in using film as part of a tenants' campaign in one of the poorer districts of West Berlin. Willutzki's 1976 film VERA ROMEYKE IS NOT ACCEPTABLE (VERA ROMEYKE IST NICHT TRAGBAR) was the first, and still almost the only, West German film to tackle the issue of the *Berufsverbot*. His more recent work has moved away from the restraint associated with the more typical films of the Berlin School, and in 'YOUR FIST IN YOUR POCKET' (DIE FAUST IN DER TASCHE, 1978), he wrapped a radical study of youth unemployment in a package of action, drama, and rock music, in the hope of making it more attractive to the youthful audience he was aiming at.

The intrusion of economic forces into the lives of young people was also one of the themes of THE BAKER'S BREAD (DAS BROT DES BÄCKERS, 1976), made not by one of the established Berliners, but by the Swiss director Erwin Keusch. It is a tender, appealing portrait of a young trainee baker who finds the small family business he has come to work for being overtaken by automation and supermarket selling. At one level it is a genre study of small-town life as experienced by young people in the West German provinces today; at another it is a commentary on the human implications of 'modernization' and 'rationalization'. But, most remarkably, it is above all an utterly absorbing celebration of the rapidly disappearing art of the small-time baker, something about which Keusch, whose father was a baker, obviously cares passionately. As Nigel Andrews very aptly commented: 'What *Moby Dick* is to whaling, this film is to bread-making.'[9]

viii GERMANY IN AUTUMN

To look at the subjects it *has* tackled is one way of getting the feel of the New German Cinema. But, given the economic conditions under which the new directors work, and in particular their almost total dependence on various forms of public funding, it is worth bearing in mind that there are major topics that have on the whole *not* been tackled. One is, for instance, hard put to find among the work of the major directors more than a handful of films that tackle the student revolt, unemployment, terrorism, computerized official vetting of citizens' activities and opinions, the *Berufsverbot*, or the nuclear power and environmental issues. Clearly one cannot prescribe those topics that directors should deal with, but the fact cannot be overlooked that these are all much-debated issues of public life on which nearly all the major directors have taken stands *outside* their films, but which very few have actually elaborated *in* them. It seems, then, that there are today sensitive areas in which one of the original distinguishing characteristics of the New German Cinema – its critical concentration on the problems of life in the contemporary Federal Republic – is no longer so much in evidence.

There are, of course, exceptions, many of them noted above. One remarkable film remains to be mentioned, however, as evidence of how quickly and imaginatively the directors of the New German Cinema *can* react to the most sensitive issues of all, given the right conditions. GERMANY IN AUTUMN (DEUTSCHLAND IM HERBST) is a title that ironically echoes the nationalistic sentimentality of the most banal type of *Heimatfilm*. But the autumn in question was that of the year 1977, the most traumatic in the history of the Federal Republic. Three linked sets of events – the successful storming of a hijacked Lufthansa jet at Mogadishu, the mysterious simultaneous deaths in the purpose-built Stammheim jail of three leading terrorists, and the discovery at Mulhouse in Eastern France of the body of the kidnapped employers' leader Hanns-Martin Schleyer – brought to a head the unhappy tensions that had soured public life throughout the seventies. Within a matter of days a group of film-makers had met in Munich to discuss a unique and unprecedented venture: a joint film, independently funded, to which they would all contribute, without any remuneration, their own reactions to the events of the preceding weeks.

GERMANY IN AUTUMN was speedily completed as a collage of episodes from nine different directors – Fassbinder, Schlöndorff, and Kluge among them – episodes that in their various ways reflect the mood of hysteria, fear, and despair that befell all sections of West German society in the autumn of 1977. Alexander Kluge helped put the whole film into its final shape, adding linking passages and a commentary, and providing its twice-repeated motto: 'When cruelty reaches a certain point, it doesn't matter who is responsible. It's just got to stop.'[10]

Some directors offered fictitious sequences, others were documentary; some were public, others very private. Fassbinder contributed two sequences: on the one hand a frank portrayal of himself, terrified, frenzied, hysterical, as the news from Mogadishu and Stammheim came in; on the other hand his despairing arguments with his mother, who feels the time has now come for 'an authoritarian ruler, who is very good and kind, and decent, respectable, and orderly'. Schlöndorff and Heinrich Böll offered a satirical sketch about the rejection by a television station of a performance of *Antigone* because of the uncomfortably contemporary overtones of Antigone's determination to give a decent burial to her rebellious brother Polynices. The film opens and closes with documentary records of two funerals, which counterpoint backstage preparations

GERMANY IN AUTUMN Police photographers at the terrorists' funeral

with the conventional public face of events. At the beginning comes the state funeral of Hanns-Martin Schleyer; at the end the controversial interment in a Stuttgart cemetery of Andreas Baader, Gudrun Ensslin, and Jan-Carl Raspe. As the film closes, the Stuttgart mourners, many of them masked to avoid identification, move off amidst the vast army of police. The final shot, accompanied on the soundtrack by Joan Baez singing the Sacco and Vanzetti ballad 'Here's to you', shows a young woman, a child at her hand, trying in vain to hitch a lift from the passing cars that have woven their way through the obstacle course of roadblocks and checkpoints.

10 THE OUTLOOK: PROBLEMS AND PROSPECTS

The phenomenon of GERMANY IN AUTUMN is most instructive. In its explicit and partisan treatment of some of the most sensitive issues of recent West German public life it is a most unusual film. In two other respects it is quite unique: firstly in its origins as a cooperative effort by a number of famous and not-so-famous directors, and secondly in its mode of financing, for most of the money for GERMANY IN AUTUMN was provided by one man: Rudolf Augstein, the publisher of the news magazine *Der Spiegel*, and majority partner in the *Filmverlag der Autoren*.[1] These facts about GERMANY IN AUTUMN are not unconnected: between them they throw much light on the economic, social, and political factors that lie behind the New German Cinema today, and that will shape its future.

i Finance

The New German Cinema is almost totally dependent on public money for its existence. The only significant form of private financial support for the West German cinema results from a special provision in the tax laws, and comes in the shape of the rather dubious 'loss-making' investments that are allegedly a favourite device among the country's fabulously wealthy dentists for easing the burden of their income tax payments. These written-off investments have, however, been almost exclusively confined to the more commercial end of the film-making spectrum, the one notable exception being Fassbinder's DESPAIR. Otherwise five principal sources of finance are available to film-makers, all of them public:

1 The Film Promotion Office, either in the form of awards given on the strength of a previous successful film, or awards given on the strength of a promising script for a new film.

2 Television, which may commission or co-produce films, or purchase an option on the later transmission of independent productions.

3 The Federal Ministry of the Interior, which awards prizes both for films and for scripts.

4 The *Kuratorium junger deutscher Film*, whose budget is being raised to a more realistic level as the result of an agreement reached between the *Länder* in June 1977. The *Kuratorium*'s brief is still to give particular help to young, non-established directors.

5 Local schemes designed to attract film-makers to particular centres. The 'Berlin Model' is the most important of these, guaranteeing up to thirty percent of the production risk of films that employ facilities in West Berlin.

Of these five sources, the Film Promotion Office, and, above all, television, play the most important role for the New German Cinema. As the sums available from any given institution are not, however, normally adequate to cover the entire costs of making a film, finance typically involves combining sponsorship from a variety of sources, and making up the balance with private backing and personal investment. On the surface the picture looks rosy: a generous and varied system of public support has, both in terms of quantity and quality, given West Germany a much-admired leading position among the film-producing countries of the world. Yet the attitudes of many West German film-makers do not tally with this favourable view of their situation that is prevalent in the world at large. In what to outsiders, dazzled by the manifest success of the New German Cinema, must look like sheer and bewildering ingratitude, directors and critics in the Federal Republic have for years bemoaned what they regard as the miserable state of the West German cinema. One director, Hellmuth Costard, has actually made a film about it: JUNIOR GODARD (DER KLEINE GODARD AN DAS KURATORIUM JUNGER DEUTSCHER FILM, 1978). Another, Rainer Werner Fassbinder, declared with typical flamboyance in 1977 that if the situation got any worse he would 'rather be a street-sweeper in Mexico than a filmmaker in Germany'.[2]

It is in fact precisely West Germany's elaborate system of public funding that has been the constant butt of the directors' and critics' attacks, and the issue they raise is as old as artistic patronage itself. It is the perennial problem of the extent to which the paymaster may legitimately call the piper's tune. The subsidies and support that the young film-makers so long campaigned for have, so the argument goes, constrained rather than liberated their talents. The New German Cinema has got into a rut, and its distinctive features, both in form and content, are determined not so much by the directors' visions as by the conditions that enable them to make films in the first place.

ii Television and the 'Amphibious Film'

The constraints that have shaped the New German Cinema in the 1970s are both political and aesthetic. After the brief interlude of relative tolerance and liberalism in the late sixties, the seventies have witnessed a growing tendency to caution, timidity, and restraint in the media. Although the Film Promotion Office has sponsored radical films, there are distinct limits to the type of subject matter for which a public body is willing to be held accountable in the Federal Republic today. In television, where the great watchword is 'balance' ('*Ausgewogenheit*'), programme planners have increasingly shied off contentious issues in order not to incur the displeasure of their political paymasters and the disingenuous attacks of the strong right-wing press, which likes to discredit the public broadcasting corporations with a view to furthering its ambition of establishing a competing commercial network. In fact the *Antigone* sketch that Böll and Schlöndorff contributed to GERMANY IN AUTUMN is by no means totally implausible: agonized and frequently ludicrous debates about the political acceptability of programmes are all too common in the controlling organs of West German television.[3]

Film-makers are well aware that the surest way of having a film produced is to tailor the script to the anticipated, and predictable, reaction of the sponsoring bodies: and that means, above all, the television corporations. The aesthetic constraints that this involves are actually more fundamental than the political ones: the political climate may change, for better or worse, but the potential and limitations of the television medium remain constant. One result has been the development of what Günter Rohrbach, the head of tele-

vision entertainment at the biggest broadcasting corporation, the *Westdeutscher Rundfunk*, has dubbed the 'amphibious film': a film that, aesthetically and technically, is equally suited to showing on television and in the cinema. Despite the unattractive name, the concept is not criticized by Rohrbach; indeed, for him it is positive evidence of the necessary symbiosis of film and television:

> Cinema and television will be able to live with one another, because they *must* live with one another. We who work in television and love the cinema will do our best to contribute to this. Long live the amphibious film![4]

The distinction between narrative forms appropriate to television and those appropriate to the cinema has never been as strongly felt in many Continental countries as it has in Britain, where the 'television play' is a long-established and prestigious genre, and where *films* shown on television tend to be old cinema movies. In West Germany the 'television film' fulfils a function analogous to that of the British 'television play', and it will normally be produced technically *as* a film, rather than in the video format of the typical 'play'. The traditions of West German television encourage this: work is much more readily contracted out to private companies than is the case in Britain, where the television organizations normally expect to produce their own programmes; furthermore, union agreements in West Germany place none of the barriers that are familiar in Britain in the way of exploiting television productions in the cinema.

'Amphibious film', in the sense intended by Günter Rohrbach, does in fact neatly characterize many of the products of the New German Cinema. The tendency to make '*films à thèse*', films that demonstrate a topic or a theme, where images *support* dialogue and debate rather than being the primary source of inspiration, the tendency, in short, to create 'illustrated radio plays', is a characteristic of television that has left its distinctive mark on the New German Cinema. It is a characteristic that has often led foreign critics to dismiss recent West German films as 'cerebral', ascribing this over-intellectuality to something typically and incorrigibly 'German' in the directors' temperaments, without appreciating the role played by the simple economic facts of life that the directors have to contend with.

Technically the 'amphibious film' is characterized by an avoidance of wide-screen formats – obviously these are of little use when it comes to transmission on television – and a preference for close-ups and short focal lengths: these too come across better on the small screen. They also, ironically enough, enable the television aerials to be blurred into invisibility when period pieces are shot in modern streets. The general effect, in fact, is that of a low-budget production, which is precisely what most 'amphibious films' are: unlike the producer of a 'block-buster' (who would have the offending television aerials removed), the television corporations have extensive schedules to fill, and cannot put all their money on one major project.

For a few West German film directors the choice of medium seems unimportant: Schlöndorff, for instance, comes across equally well on television and in the cinema. Others, like Fassbinder, make a clear distinction between their television and their cinema productions. But there are also major cinematic talents whose work is almost totally unsuited to television: significantly, these are often the ones who have formed their own production companies. Herzog is the prime example, Wenders is another.

iii Films of Books

The constraints resulting from the public subsidizing of West German films have affected the film-makers' choice of contents in other ways too. A frequently remarked, and often lamented, peculiarity of the New German Cinema has been its apparent infatuation with literature: in particular with modern novels and the realist German writers of the nineteenth century. Virtually all directors have tried their hand at film versions of literary texts, some have done little else, and all the major films of recent years, and many of the minor ones too, have been based on books. The reasons for this are varied, but all derive ultimately from the economic basis of the New German Cinema. In the first place the fact that the New German Cinema has always been something of a cottage industry has meant that film-makers have tended to combine the roles of script-writer and director, and even of producer as well. This

has led to an almost total lack of scriptwriters as such; moreover, having to devote their attention to a number of roles at once has left most film-makers with less time than they would like for scriptwriting. It is therefore only natural that the majority of them have resorted at one time or another to pre-existing texts as the basis for their scripts. As Volker Schlöndorff puts it:

An author usually spends years working on a book, and even when he's not actually writing, then he is constructing it inside himself. . . . When you're writing a film script you take perhaps eight weeks – all right, let's say three months –: the result can't be the same. I'm not trying to rule filmscripts out of court, I'm just saying that I prefer to film literature because I don't know anyone here who could dedicate himself in quite the same way to a film script – I know *I* certainly couldn't.[5]

There are other reasons for the popularity of the 'film of the book' in the New German Cinema. Firstly, the television corporations are particularly ready to accept this sort of material, as it fits in very nicely with their contractual obligations to 'educate' as well as to 'inform' and 'entertain' their viewers. Secondly, literary material, especially if sanctioned by cultural tradition, has the aura of being 'safe'; this has the double effect of protecting the television corporations against accusations of subversion, whilst at the same time enabling directors to 'smuggle in' doses of contemporary relevance by pointing up the traditionally underplayed political implications of the original texts. Thirdly, and more fundamentally, the system of *Projektförderung*, the allocation of production grants on the basis of plans submitted by would-be film-makers – something the directors have long campaigned for – has led to an undue emphasis on the script itself, and in particular on its intelligibility as a text to the grant-awarding committees. Scripts that can be read and appreciated as narratives are thus at a premium. But, as more and more directors are now pointing out, the script can be little more than a general statement of intent; the creation of films occurs not at the writing desk, but on location and in the editing room. The truly cinematic qualities of a film – and *they* should be its starting point – are by definition not expressible in the verbal medium of the script.[6] The result, once again, has been to confirm still further the popular foreign image of the New German Cinema as 'earnest' and 'cerebral' – not only because of its concentration on literary texts, but because *German* literature, from which most of the texts are taken, has in any case a long tradition of emphasising the ratiocinative at the expense of the sensuous![7]

It is clear, then, that despite favourable outward appearances, all is not entirely well with the New German Cinema. The intricate and sophisticated state-funded system of grants, awards, and subsidies has had its negative as well as its positive effects. Indeed, more than once there has been talk in West German film circles of 'subsidizing the cinema to death'. The *cinéma des auteurs* that state sponsorship was intended to promote runs the risk of blandness and impersonality as directors seek to reconcile the various requirements of their several paymasters. GERMANY IN AUTUMN, produced without public financial support as an unprecedented cooperative, but still highly individual, effort by directors who found both moral and economic strength in numbers, looks more than ever like the exception that proves the rules that have come to shape the New German Cinema.

iv Alternatives to Public Patronage

Enlightened personal patronage of the sort that made GERMANY IN AUTUMN POSSIBLE is clearly not a practical solution for the problems of the New German Cinema. For those directors who wish to escape the dubious embrace of public subsidy three possibilities present themselves. Two of them – emigration, or the production of 'international films' – might be the salvation of individual directors, but would almost inevitably lead to their making films that could not by any stretch of the imagination be accounted products of the New German Cinema. Only a third possibility, the creation of films that are both *good* and *popular*, seems a real alternative.

Fassbinder's outburst about the preferability of being a Mexican road-sweeper to being a German filmmaker came at a time when there was much talk of emigration among a number of West German directors. America seemed the obvious place to go, and Wenders, for one, did go there to film HAMMETT for Warner Bro-

thers at the invitation of Francis Ford Coppola; Herzog has expressed a wish to move to Ireland; Straub, of course, has for some years now lived in Italy; Syberberg, meanwhile, continues his running feud with the whole German film scene.

Just how many directors will, like Straub, become permanent émigrés remains to be seen. On the whole a mass exodus seems less likely now than it did a few years ago. (Such a phenomenon is, of course, not without precedent in the history of the German cinema.) A more insidious threat to the New German Cinema is the possibility that its major directors may be lured by the temptations of the 'international film': films funded and made in various countries, with an international cast, and aimed at an international market. Volker Schlöndorff was one of the first to recognize the dangers of this,[8] and more recently other directors have joined him in stressing the importance of national flavour if the New German Cinema is to remain authentically German. The 'international film' tends, for obvious cultural and economic reasons, to be more than anything an American film. (The 'British' film SUPERMAN is a typical case in point here.) The copying of Hollywood stereotypes in the early years of the New German Cinema was a legitimate element in the exploration of the Americanization of West German life that was such a major concern of young directors in the late sixties and early seventies. Today there is the danger of a less critical adoption of American ways in the West German cinema.

The 'international film' is usually shot, or dubbed, in English. Already a number of major West German films have been made partly or wholly in English. Schlöndorff's MICHAEL KOHLHAAS was an isolated early example, and a salutary experience that he does not wish to repeat. More recently with Herzog's STROSZEK and Wenders' THE AMERICAN FRIEND the plot provided a justification for lengthy sequences in English.[9] But Fassbinder's DESPAIR was made in English with no intrinsic justification, for it is set among Germans in Germany. DESPAIR in fact is the prime example of an 'international film' in the recent New German Cinema. It is heartening to note that Fassbinder has in the meantime returned with a vengeance to making German films again about specifically German topics.

It may well be, in fact, that Fassbinder's method –

the making of a big-budget 'international film' followed by a return to German production – could be of some use to the New German Cinema, provided the 'international film' is largely made in Germany. The 'shot in the arm' effect that can accrue from such films, be they 'international' or 'German', was already being mooted by Volker Schlöndorff in 1972:

It can be a good thing for a country's film industry if each year three or four projects are realized that cost in the order of five to eight million [marks], because in that way a whole team of technicians and people are employed and trained, and the economy has, so to speak, the opportunity to work for once at full capacity. It's really very smart the way those who run the film industry in Italy or France every now and then produce a BORSALINO, or something like that, with which not only can they bring the whole infrastructure of their film industry up to the latest technical standards, but they can also use the product as an advance guard, a 'locomotive', for penetrating the world market.[10]

Apart from emigration and the making of 'international films' there is a third possibility that represents the most promising way forward for the New German Cinema. It is something that has been consistently advocated by Kluge, long sought after by Fassbinder, and – at the end of the seventies – is finally actually beginning to be realized by a handful of directors: the creation of quality films that actually make a profit at the box office. Two factors have hitherto made profitability, and even audience appeal, surprisingly low priorities with many West German film-makers: on the one hand the cushioning effects of public subsidy, on the other a long tradition in the German cinema of concentrating almost entirely on the domestic market, and ignoring the possibilities of exporting films.[11] The daunting (and often unjust) 'teutonic' image of the German cinema has not helped, but there is more than a grain of truth in one of *Variety*'s inimitable verdicts on the German film:

Too often German producers forget the basics of appeal to Joe Miller of Kenosha, Wisconsin. They seem only to be able to think in avant garde terms, which is what flops in Kenosha.[12]

Such sentiments are not unfamiliar, both in West Germany and abroad. One should not be under any illusions about the status of the New German Cinema. Despite the commonplace that it is more appreciated abroad than at home, it is still internationally an 'arthouse' phenomenon, its audiences consisting largely of students, film buffs, and cineastes in a few big cities. In most countries the only German films that reach the high-street cinemas are products of the pornography industry, and anyone outside Germany who reads the regular glowing newspaper reports of the New German Cinema is bound to be disappointed unless he happens to catch the odd television showing, to belong to an enterprising local film society, or to live in London, New York, or Paris. In West Germany itself the New German Cinema has not managed to attract the sort of audiences that would give it anything like a sound economic base. With cinema attendances among the lowest in Europe, the share of the market held by German films (including co-productions) sank in the 1970s to an all-time low of less than ten percent, whilst the number of feature films actually produced in the country (again including co-productions) dropped from 121 in 1969 to 51 in 1977.

Simple commercial viability is the great hurdle that the New German Cinema must surmount if it wishes to revitalize the country's film culture, and at the same time to free itself from the constraints of public subsidy, whilst remaining a distinctive and thriving national cinema, reflecting and exploring life in West Germany today. The dangers are obvious: 'commercialism' is a dirty word in film culture, and with justification. There are those, such as Straub and Syberberg, who have no desire to compromise themselves by 'going commercial': their vital and distinctive forms of cinema must clearly continue to receive the public subsidy without which they would be unthinkable. There are others who have made much of the 'amphibious film': this, with all its limitations, will undoubtedly remain a central genre in the New German Cinema for a long time to come. A few directors have also moved in the direction of international productions. But the most encouraging sign of progress as the New German

Cinema enters the 1980s is the sudden appearance of a number of new films that are not only being well received by the critics, but are also enjoying an unprecedented degree of commercial success.[13]

v The New Optimism

There is, for the first time in many years, a mood of optimism among the directors of the New German Cinema. Despite the embittered opposition of the commercial establishment, which has always contemptuously dismissed the New German Cinema and disingenuously called for the abolition of the 'unfair competition' represented by public subsidy, the new *Filmförderungsgesetz*, the Film Promotion Law that came into effect in July 1979, is more generous still than its predecessors. Apart from raising the level of sponsorship, it also meets the directors half way over their objections to the undue emphasis placed on scripts: now grants of up to 200,000 DM can be applied for without the obligation to present a script 'if it is shown in some other way that the project can be expected to result in a film that seems likely to improve the quality and economy of the German cinema'.[14]

The 1979 FFG furthermore eases the financial burden on small cinemas by replacing the flat-rate 15-pfennig levy on cinema tickets, from which the Film Promotion Office previously drew its funds, with a percentage levy of between 2.75 and 3.75 percent on each cinema's annual turnover – the lower rates being applied to the lower turnovers, with total exemption for cinemas with an annual turnover of less than 30,000 DM.[15] The number of cinemas in the Federal Republic, after decreasing steadily throughout the 1960s from over 7,000 in 1959 to around 3,000 in the early seventies, has shown a slight increase of late. There have certainly been tendencies to concentration of ownership, though the giant chains that dominate in Britain have no counterparts in West Germany, where the biggest by far (owned by Heinz Riech) consisted of a mere 160 cinemas in 1979. Notwithstanding the decline of the rural cinemas lamented by Wenders in KINGS OF THE ROAD, there has been an encouraging expansion of specialist cinemas and film clubs catering to a growing audience of cineastes. Particularly gratifying is the success and spread of the *Kommunale Kinos*:

cinemas run, like theatres, museums, and concert halls, as part of the cultural provision of various local authorities. The initiative in this field was taken in the early seventies in Frankfurt, where the country's first *Kommunales Kino* successfully fought both a legal case brought by local cinema owners and a boycott by film distributors.

The new optimism among West German film-makers is reflected in the confidence with which in early 1979 they turned down the city of Munich's proposals for a pompous, star-studded film festival, and took themselves off to Hamburg to organize their own alternative festival – a confidence, and an unwonted mood of solidarity, echoed in Uwe Brandner's declaration: 'We believe the German cinema has reached a historic turning point'.[16] There have of course been other points in the recent history of the West German cinema where similar sentiments were uttered only to be quickly proved sadly misled: one thinks of the boom in the commercial cinema that preceded its virtual demise in the late fifties, the resounding clarion of the Oberhausen Manifesto that was followed by an awkward silence, the brief-lived heady euphoria of the 'Young German Film' that was quickly drowned by the first Film Promotion Law, and the constantly alternating jubilation and despair that has accompanied the development of the New German Cinema in the 1970s.

Yet, despite the cautionary experiences of the past one and a half decades, there are grounds for sharing Brandner's grandiosely formulated belief in a 'historic turning point'. There are signs in many areas of significant qualitative improvements in West German film culture. More importantly, the New German Cinema has, after the early success of THE LOST HONOUR OF KATHARINA BLUM, begun for the first time to produce films that have not only come to grips with major contemporary issues, but have done so in a way that – without compromising their aesthetic and filmic integrity – has brought them success at the box office. It could be the fulfilment of a vision that Wim Wenders talked of in 1977, in words that stress the most essential quality of the New German Cinema – its *German-ness*:

I speak for all those who, in the past years, after a long period of emptiness, have begun again to produce images and sounds in a country that has an infinite mistrust of images and sounds that speak of itself, a country that for this reason has for thirty years greedily soaked up all foreign images, just as long as they have taken its mind off itself. I do not believe there is anywhere else where people have suffered such a loss of confidence in images of their own, their own stories and myths, as we have. We, the fatherless directors of the New German Cinema, have felt this loss most acutely in ourselves in the lack, the absence, of a tradition that we can call our own, and in the audiences with their bewilderment and their initial hesitancy. Only slowly has this defensiveness on the one side, and the lack of self-confidence on the other, broken down, and in a process that may well take a few more years the feeling is once more emerging here that images and sounds need not be only something imported, but that they can concern themselves with this country, and moreover can come from this country.[17]

Notes

Chapter 1 The Development of the West German Cinema

1 The *Deutsche Film Aktiengesellschaft*, or 'German Film Corporation', was initially a joint Soviet-German concern; in 1952 it passed into East German hands. It has overall control of production facilities in the GDR.

2 Isabel Quigly, writing in the *Spectator* of 24 May 1957, noted that in post-war West German films 'events of the Thirties and Forties are either ignored or treated as something remote, regrettable, and faintly unmentionable, like halitosis or prostitution in Paraguay'.

3 Figures taken from *The German View*, 10 July 1963. The figure of 128 for film production is also given in Manvell and Fraenkell, p. 124, and in Gregor, p. 122. Thomas Elsaesser (in Rayns, p. 6) has 120; *Variety* of 15 July 1959 has 118. At least all agree 1955 was the peak year. The fact should not be overlooked that these are *West German* films; that the market was increasingly dominated by *American* films is made clear by the fact that in 1959, of 566 films released in the Federal Republic, 114 were German, as against 232 American; France accounted for a further 69, Austria for 23, and Italy for 19 (*Variety*, 15 July 1959). For a convenient survey in English of the economic background to the post-war West German cinema see Elsaesser's chapter in Rayns.

4 The FBW – the *Filmbewertungsstelle Wiesbaden* – is not a Federal institution, but is run by agreement between the *Länder*. It should not be confused with the FSK – the *Freiwillige Selbstkontrolle der Filmwirtschaft*, or 'Voluntary Self-Control of the Film Industry'. This is in effect the West German film censorship board, which is operated by the film industry itself. It issues certificates specifying amongst other things the suitability of films for various age groups (above 6, 12, 16, or 18 years). Its decisions do not absolve a film from possible prosecution in the courts, nor is it obligatory to submit a film for certification: in practice, however, it would be very difficult to find commercial exhibitors for a film that had no certificate.

5 In Britain by contrast there were over eleven million tv sets in 1960. For more detailed figures see Sandford, pp. 121–122.

6 A striking indication of the change from family entertainment that the cinema underwent in the sixties is provided by the relative proportion of the different categories of FSK certificates granted in 1959 and 1969 respectively. Whereas in 1959 only 15 per cent of films were barred to children under 18, in 1969 the figure had become 48 percent – and this too during a decade of unprecendented liberalization in the standards applied by the FSK.

7 The *Oberhausener Manifest* has been reprinted in various publications. Probably the most accessible today is Pflaum/Prinzler, p. 9. The word '*Film*' occurs eleven times in the German original; I have preferred the English word 'cinema' in seven instances in my translation. Thus the phrase 'new German cinema' is actually a rendering of '*neuer deutscher Film*'. '*Neues deutsches Kino*' is a phrase one hardly ever hears in German, where the 'New German Cinema' is (or was) normally referred to as the '*Junger deutscher Film*' – the 'Young German Film/Cinema'. Pflaum and Prinzler (p. 151) distinguish between the '*Junger deutscher Film*' of the 1960s, and the '*Neuer deutscher Film*' of the 1970s, though they do not spell out what this actually means in practice.

8 Once it became a *Land* institution, the *Kuratorium* could now openly support the artistic side of the cinema. Federal promotion of the cinema in West Germany has always been limited, in theory if not entirely in practice, to 'economic measures' as a result of a sacred constitutional principle that gives the *Länder* exclusive competence in all matters appertaining to '*Kultur*' – which includes not only the cinema, but also broadcasting: hence the decentralized structure of West German television, from which the New German Cinema has been able to profit.

9 Italy led with 8.1 visits per head; Britain was next to last with 2.1. There were of course other factors affecting this decline: growing prosperity, leading to greater mobility and the development of other forms of entertainment, also played its part.

10 For a full discussion of the West German broadcasting system see Sandford, pp. 61–130.

11 Also in 1974, the levy on cinema tickets was raised from 10 to 15 pfennigs.

12 David Robinson's article (*Sunday Times Magazine*, 31 July 1977) in fact looks at precisely the same seven directors that I have concentrated on in the following pages.

13 Many writers have commented on this. See, for instance, Wolfram Schütte in Jansen and Schütte, *Herzog/Kluge/Straub* , pp. 12–17. For Alexander Kluge the term seems synonymous with all that is good in the New German Cinema, as opposed to the triviality of the commercialized establishment. One example among many is his remark that 'As soon as you abandon this concept you get either commercial cinema or something arty-crafty'. (Ibid. p. 163.)

Chapter 2 Alexander Kluge

1 The 'Institute of Film Art' was set up under Kluge's supervision at the Ulm Academy of Art in 1962 as the first major response to the demands made in the Oberhausen Manifesto. After initially providing training for a number of film-makers it has since 1966 concentrated on research work.

2 'It's all a bit like a building site', as he says in an essay on the 'realist method' (Kluge, *Gelegenheitsarbeit*, p. 220). For an English interview with Kluge, in which he expounds many of his basic ideas, see *Alexander Kluge and the Female Slave*, edited by Jan Dawson, Perth (Australia), 1975. The interview is also in *Film Comment*, Vol. 10, No. 6 (1974).

3 Kluge, *Gelegenheitsarbeit*, p. 216.

4 Jansen and Schütte, *Herzog/Kluge/Straub*, p. 160.

5 Quoted in Bronnen/Brocher, p. 238.

6 Quoted in *Frankfurter Rundschau*, 22 December 1976.

7 Kluge, *Gelegenheitsarbeit*, p. 209.

8 'Die Sinnlichkeit (siehe Feuerbach) muss die Basis aller Wissenschaft sein.' A difficult sentence to translate without elaboration: 'The senses (see Feuerbach) must be the basis of all science', where *Sinnlichkeit* also means 'sense impressions', 'sense perception', 'sensuality', 'sensuousness', 'sentient-ness', as well as 'material nature'; *Wissenschaft* also has overtones of 'organized knowledge'. (Kluge, *Gelegenheitsarbeit*, p. 212.)

9 Kluge, *Gelegenheitsarbeit*, p. 208.

10 Quoted in *Frankfurter Rundschau*, 22 December 1976.

11 Kluge, *Gelegenheitsarbeit*, p. 195.

12 Quoted in *Die Welt*, 14 September 1968.

13 Ibid.

14 Quoted in *Handelsblatt*, 23/24 September 1966. The penultimate sentence reads: 'Das Repräsentative muss aufgehoben sein im Individuellen.' *Aufgehoben* means 'stored up', 'obliterated', and 'raised up'. It is *the* untranslatable word of German philosophy, and one whose purely fortuitous punning potential is disquietingly central to a lot of German thought. I think Kluge here is using it predominantly in the first sense.

15 There are similar implications in the title given in 1963 to a revised version of BRUTALITY IN STONE: 'YESTERDAY GOES ON FOR EVER' (DIE EWIGKEIT VON GESTERN).

16 That Anita is Jewish is not a piece of heavy-handed meaningfulness on Kluge's part: the woman on whose life story the film is based was herself Jewish.

17 Kluge, like other film-makers – Fassbinder and Schlöndorff, for instance – sees the Frankfurt area as somehow epitomizing the ethos of West German capitalism: 'The whole Rhine-Main area is a phenomenon that interests me just as much as Anita G., because the one wouldn't exist without the other.' (Quoted in *Süddeutsche Zeitung*, 11 June 1966.)

18 The *ratlos* of the German title really means 'at a loss as to what to do'. There are strong overtones here of the criticism repeatedly made of the radicals of the late sixties that they knew what they *didn't* like, but had no clear idea of what they wanted to put in its place.

19 Uniforms and parades are a recurrent symbol of totalitarian degradation in Kluge's films.

20 Referring to Leni's flight across the border with her elephants when the circus is being sold off, Kluge said: 'Leni Peickert leads her elephants to safety. We'll probably have to lead a lot more elephants over the border before we've assembled enough of these creatures with their outstanding memories.' (Quoted in *Die Welt*, 14 September 1968.)

21 Quoted in *Die Welt*, 14 September 1968. In an interview with the Munich *Abendzeitung* (31 August/1 September 1968) Kluge was asked to put Leni's story in one sentence. His reply is a vivid little image of the wily film-maker making the most of a hostile situation: 'She behaves like a fish in winter, keeping near the airhole, but not letting herself get caught by the kitchen staff.'

22 Jansen and Schütte, *Herzog/Kluge/Straub*, pp. 172–174.

23 Roswitha's abortion practice is not a very appropriate symbol here: she is not acting out of *hostility* towards other families.

24 Kluge, *Gelegenheitsarbeit*, p. 21.

25 STRONG-MAN FERDINAND seems to confirm a general trend in Kluge's films to present women in a much more positive light than men. In answer to questions about his portrayal of women as 'reduced personalities' Kluge has made the following point: 'On top of the alienation that labour is subjected to in society, women suffer an extra degree of oppression, and it's perfectly legitimate to start your investigations at the most oppressed point in society. In any case these roles are often not women in the sexual sense, but symbols for characteristics of oppression that also occur in non-women.' (*Gelegenheitsarbeit*, p. 223.)

26 Quoted in *Frankfurter Rundschau*, 22 December 1976. The last two sentences are very close to the sentiments expressed by Wenders in the closing sequences of KINGS OF THE ROAD.

27 He has not. At the Hamburg Film Festival in September 1979 Kluge showed a new film: 'THE PATRIOTIC WOMAN' (DIE PATRIOTIN), a development of the episodes he contributed to GERMANY IN AUTUMN that showed a woman by the name of Gabi Teichert 'digging for traces of German history'. 'THE PATRIOTIC WOMAN' is to all accounts a richly complex film in the tradition of Kluge's earlier feature films.

Chapter 3 **Jean-Marie Straub**

1 Quoted in Roud, p. 29.
2 Ibid., p. 40.
3 Ibid.
4 Ibid., p. 64.
5 *Enthusiasm*, No. 1, December 1975, p. 9. (The first, and so far the only, issue of this journal was an excellent number devoted entirely to the Straubs.)
6 Quoted in Jansen and Schütte, *Herzog/Kluge/Straub*, p. 185.
7 *Enthusiasm*, p. 14. (See note 5.)
8 Roud, p. 102. Roud translates *Komödiantin* as 'actress', which loses the flavour of the original gallicism.
9 Monthly Film Bulletin, 43 (1976), 69.
10 Roud, p. 87.
11 *Jump Cut*, November-December 1974, pp. 16–17. Walsh's article, 'Political formations in the cinema of Jean-Marie Straub', is a lucid appraisal of the peculiarities of Straub's earlier films.
12 Quoted in Bronnen/Brocher, p. 40.
13 *Enthusiasm*, p. 26. (See note 5.)
14 Quoted in Jansen and Schütte, *Herzog/Kluge/Straub*, p. 194.
15 *Enthusiasm*, p. 19. (See note 5.)
16 Quoted in programme sheet of 'The Other Cinema', London, December 1977.
17 Martin Walsh in *Jump Cut*, November-December 1974, p. 12.
18 Courtade, p. 20.
19 *Die Zeit*, 5 February 1971.
20 Jansen and Schütte, *Herzog/Kluge/Straub*, p. 206.
21 Roud, p. 23.
22 *Enthusiasm*, p. 31. (See note 5.) Quite what lies at the end of the 'radical elimination' of art is not clear: obviously one cannot whittle away all artifice, otherwise one is left with nothing. It is interesting that Straub's admirers are often at pains to stress the *artistic* merits of his work, and in particular the 'beauty' of what they perceive as its elaborate rhythms.
23 Bronnen/Brocher, p. 40.
24 Quoted in *Enthusiasm*, p. 13. (See note 5.)
25 Straub is quite insistent about this: 'THE BRIDGEGROOM, THE COMEDIENNE AND THE PIMP is a film for railway station cinemas' (*Frankfurter Rundschau*, 26 April 1969); '(BACH) is a film for the man from the Bavarian backwoods, and I really mean that' (*Abendzeitung*, 19 June 1968); 'I don't believe the workers are not mature enough for a film like OTHON' (*Les Lettres Françaises*, 13 January 1971).
26 Quoted in *Enthusiasm*, p. 13. (See note 5.)

Chapter 4 **Volker Schlöndorff**

1 Bronnen/Brocher, p. 81.
2 'I have an antipathy to black and white. I breathe a sigh of relief in the cinema when the curtain opens and the screen is aglow with colour, and so much the better if it's in 'scope as well.' (Schlöndorff in *Die Welt*, 17 December 1966.) Nonetheless, Schlöndorff later made two films in black and white – THE SUDDEN FORTUNE OF THE POOR PEOPLE OF KOMBACH and COUP DE GRÂCE – at a time when other directors were already shooting only in colour.
3 This was far from the case: the mini-skirts paraded so casually in the film would have turned many heads (in both approval and disapproval) even on the streets of Munich long after they had become almost passé in Britain and America.
4 *Die Welt*, 17 December 1966.
5 *Die Welt*, 15 February 1969. Some versions of the film in fact open with shots of the Vietnam War and the events of May 1968 in Paris.
6 *Frankfurter Rundschau*, 29 March 1969.
7 Ibid.
8 Bronnen/Brocher, p. 84.
9 Oddly enough, Schlöndorff and von Trotta's response on first reading Böll's *Katharina Blum* was: 'That's precisely the story about the criminalization of protest that we have been trying to come to grips with for some time'. (*Die Zeit*, 10 October 1975). In fact it is hard to see this as a major theme in *Katharina Blum*, whereas it does apply to KOMBACH.
10 Schlöndorff had not expected the trial of Minouche Schubert to last so long: had he realized it was going to be such a show trial he might not, he said, have made the film. (*Stuttgarter Zeitung*, 24 March 1972.)
11 *Abendzeitung* (Munich), 18 April 1972.
12 The one Italian name heard in the film sums it all up: 'Massimo, vieni,' calls a mother's voice in a village square. Elisabeth is too dazzled to notice what is going on: like 98 percent of German tourists she linguaphonically delivers herself of the obligatory observation 'È bella l'Italia' to the first convenient petrol pump attendant. *We* are obviously meant to notice just how much Elisabeth *fails* to notice: 'Women have got to be made dissatisfied. In any case it's a film that addresses itself in particular to women, to make them understand that, even when they say 'But *I'm* very satisfied', it isn't true.' (Interview with Schlöndorff and von Trotta in *Jeune Cinéma*, 67 (December 1972/January 1973), 17.
13 Two productions for television followed SUMMER LIGHTNING.
14 'Will Ulrike Gnade oder freies Geleit?', *Der Spiegel*, 10 January 1972, 54–57.
15 It is clear that Böll's own experience of victimization by the press lies behind the treatment of the topic in the novel. With typical modesty, and in an attempt to draw

attention to somebody else's plight, he has stated that the story is in fact based on the press campaign against Professor Peter Brückner, head of the Psychology Department at the Technical University in Hannover, who was suspended on 20 January 1972 for allegedly giving shelter to members of the RAF. (Hanno Beth, 'Rufmord und Mord: die publizistische Dimension der Gewalt', in *Heinrich Böll. Eine Einführung in das Gesamtwerk in Einzelinterpretationen*, Kronberg, 1975.)

16 As David Head has pointed out, the structure of the *book* is, paradoxically, decidedly 'filmic'; it was felt, however, that the *film* demanded something less convoluted. ('"Der Autor muss respektiert werden" – Schlöndorff/Trotta's *Die verlorene Ehre der Katharina Blum* and Brecht's critique of film adaptation', *German Life and Letters*, 37 (1979), 248–264). Schlöndorff similarly resisted the temptation to adopt the cinematic 'flashback' technique of Grass's *Tin Drum*: the framing perspective of Oskar the inmate in an institution is dropped entirely in the film.

17 The book, interestingly enough, had been more forthright still, and actually talked of 'similarities with the practices of the *Bild-Zeitung*' in its 'disclaimer'.

18 Thus, for instance, Wolf Donner in *Die Zeit* of 10 October 1975: 'She is so vulnerable that one immediately wants to protect her. She radiates so much natural dignity and moral strength that one cannot help but respect her. . . . She does not resign herself to her suffering, but rebels against it, with an almost archaic sense of justice. Angela Winkler has that innocence and gentle inflexibility that adults find so disconcerting when they discuss with young people. . . . A Star is born.'

19 The article in question, from *Die Welt* of 27 September 1976, is reproduced in Volker Schlöndorff's '*Die Blechtrommel*'. *Tagebuch einer Verfilmung*.

20 *Die Zeit*, 22 October 1976.

21 Schlöndorff, '*Die Blechtrommel*'. *Tagebuch einer Verfilmung*, p. 50.

22 Ibid., p. 38.

23 Ibid., p. 44.

24 Oskar too is a rebel, or, to use Schlöndorff's almost untranslatable term, a '*Verweigerer*', a 'refuser': 'I simply couldn't imagine how anyone could have invented this figure Oskar Matzerath in the fifties, given that his main characteristic is refusal. The word itself didn't even exist in the fifties. I don't know how it was possible to describe Oskar then without this word. But his main characteristic is his refusal, he refuses to progress with his own growth, he refuses responsibility, the world of adults, he refuses to take on any role or function in it.' (Schlöndorff in *Der Spiegel*, 30 April 1979, p. 186.)

25 Schlöndorff, '*Die Blechtrommel*'. *Tagebuch einer Verfilmung*, p. 37.

26 Ibid. This remark – whilst conveying the *lesson* of MICHAEL KOHLHAAS – does overlook the fact that the *film* was made after TÖRLESS.

Chapter 5 Werner Herzog

1 WAS ICH BIN SIND MEINE FILME (1978), directed by Christian Weisenborn and Erwin Keusch.

2 *The Guardian*, 24 November 1975.

3 *Abend*, 6 July 1973.

4 *Radio Times*, 2 December 1976, p. 6.

5 Jansen and Schütte, *Herzog/Kluge/Straub*, p. 115.

6 *Abendzeitung* (Munich), 27 September 1969.

7 Herzog and the redoubtable grand old lady of German film history have often expressed their admiration for one another's work. Yet another of Herzog's legendary feats was the 500-mile walk he undertook from Munich to her home in Paris when he heard that she was dangerously ill in 1974. (Herzog has since written a book about it: *Vom Gehen im Eis*, Munich, 1978.) Herzog attributed her subsequent recovery to his exploit; intriguingly, before the book appeared, reports of the walk gave as its goal the need to arrange the subtitling and the Cannes screening of KASPAR HAUSER.

8 Jansen and Schütte, *Herzog/Kluge/Straub*, p. 124.

9 *Sight and Sound*, 42 (1973), p. 50.

10 Kraft Wetzel, in Jansen and Schütte, *Herzog/Kluge/Straub* , p. 107.

11 Herzog himself seems to have had very untypical qualms about HEART OF GLASS. Alan Greenberg, in his adulatory account of the film, reports him as asking at one point during the shooting: 'Do you think that what I've done will seem ridiculous?'. (Greenberg, p. 95.)

12 *Monthly Film Bulletin*, 45 (1978), p. 31.

13 *L'Express*, 24 March 1979, p. 68.

14 *Die Zeit*, 12 January 1979.

15 Beverly Walker stresses the important role of Herzog's loyal production team in the creation of the distinctive 'Herzog touch': 'KASPAR HAUSER, HEART OF GLASS, NOSFERATU, and WOYZECK are of a piece, reflecting the refined and painterly sensibilities of the Schmidt-Reitwein/von Gierke/Storch triumvirate – very different from AGUIRRE and STROSZEK, shot by Thomas Mauch.' (*Sight and Sound*, 47 (1978), p. 203.) Jörg Schmidt-Reitwein also acted as cinematographer for LA SOUFRIÈRE, whilst Henning von Gierke and Gisela Storch, the production and costume designers, have been with Herzog since KASPAR HAUSER and have never worked on anyone else's films. (Ibid.) Mention should also be made of the major part played in Herzog's work by Beate Mainka-Jellinghaus, who has been responsible for editing every one of his films from SIGNS OF LIFE onwards.

16 Bronnen/Brocher, p. 11.

17 *Time*, 20 March 1978, p. 55.

18 Quoted in Greenberg, p. 174. Herzog sees the passing of illiteracy as by no means entirely a gain for mankind: 'there is another side to illiteracy, it is a form of experience and intelligence that our civilization is of

necessity losing, a cultural value that is disappearing from the earth.' (*Die Zeit*, 24 November 1978 – in a review of the Tavianis' PADRE PADRONE.)

19 WOYZECK met with some unfavourable reactions when it was premiered as the West German entry at the 1979 Cannes Festival: many critics felt it was rather an effete film after the sort of thing they had come to expect from Herzog, though Eva Mattes won the Best Supporting Actress award for her portrayal of Marie. WOYZECK was a low-budget 'quickie' made in an idyllic little old-world Czechoslovakian town immediately after the completion of NOSFERATU. 'Klaus Kinski is Woyzeck', proclaim the distributors' advertisements, and certainly his performance is the central attraction. It is a quiet, restrained film, in which an almost static camera simply observes the succession of Büchner's brief scenes. Despite the intensity of Kinski's acting, much of it comes across as too low-key, making all the clearer the importance in Herzog of camerawork and music: the really impressive moments are precisely those where these come to the fore – the opening title sequence, which shows Woyzeck/Kinski doing forced exercises, and the murder sequence, which is shot in slow motion, again with music over. One cannot help comparing WOYZECK unfavourably with the much richer KASPAR HAUSER – a film whose close thematic links are made even clearer in Büchner's closing lines, the court usher's delighted conclusion: 'A good murder, a real murder, a fine murder, as fine as you could wish; it's a long time since we had one like it,' – lines that echo closely the remarks of the clerk at the end of KASPAR HAUSER.

20 *Time*, 20 March 1978, p. 57.

21 'The man I really love to hate is [the pop singer] Peter Alexander. He's the one I measure myself against, the real object of my aversion. For me he's the great eccentric. And I'm the centre. And that's something people will very soon come to realize.' (Herzog in *Frankfurter Rundschau*, 21 August 1975.)

22 *Abend*, 6 July 1973.

Chapter 6 Rainer Werner Fassbinder

1 Christian Braad Thomsen sees LOVE IS COLDER THAN DEATH as a film that starts from the tabula rasa Godard had created in the cinema with LE GAI SAVOIR: 'One gets the impression of being present at a process of creation in the truest sense, as if the first film in the world is being born right there in front of one's eyes.' (Thomsen, p. 15.)

2 THE NIKLASHAUSEN JOURNEY also owes much to Glauber Rocha's ANTONIO DAS MORTES. It is worth noting in this context that the similar name of Fassbinder's RIO DAS MORTES is also Portuguese, and not Spanish as one might expect of the alleged Peruvian river in question.

3 Franz wears a jacket decorated with the word 'Korea'. Fassbinder had originally wanted to call the film 'Korean Spring' 'because Korea has associations of war for me'. (Quoted in Jansen and Schütte, *Fassbinder*, p. 61.)

4 In the world in which Franz and Hanni live, public confessions of private emotion are, however, sanctioned in one particular sphere: in the realm of the pop song. Pop songs are regularly used by Fassbinder to reflect and counterpoint the feelings of his characters, but at the same time they also *trivialize* those feelings, and the fact that Fassbinder uses pop songs at all in its turn draws attention to the act of trivialization that the emotions have been subjected to in order to become a saleable product. Fassbinder seems to be suggesting that genuine emotions – loneliness, love, dependence – have been usurped by the pop music industry, processed, packaged, and then sold back in their new vulgarized form to the teenagers who are looking for an acceptable way of expressing them. The fact that these are normally American pop songs is not only evidence of the American 'cultural colonization' of West German life, but also compounds the characters' estrangement from their own emotions when they have to be expressed in this way. The characters who half-listen to the numerous juke-boxes in Fassbinder's films will catch very few, if any, of the words they hear, for they are in a foreign language and reflect a foreign culture. Only the most hackneyed, debased words will stick – 'love', 'lonely', 'baby', 'blue' – whilst anything even vaguely approaching subtlety will inevitably be lost on young Germans such as Hanni and Franz.

5 The clash between the father's ideas of 'order' and 'discipline' and the 'waywardness' that he bemoans in the younger generation is reflected in the film's title. 'Wild Game' is a clever but misleading attempt at translating the original German *Wildwechsel*, where '*Wild*', though derived from the idea of wildness, actually means 'game' in the sense of wild boar, deer, and 'game' birds. '*Wechsel*' here means a path traditionally taken through the forest by wild animals, and '*Wildwechsel*' is the warning often seen on German roadsides – usually beneath the international traffic symbol of the leaping deer – to inform drivers that a deer track crosses the road ahead. In the film there is a clear hunting image in the shooting of the father in the wood, but more generally the title '*Wildwechsel*' may be seen as a reference to the 'collision course' between the parents' 'civilization' (the road and its cars) and the children's 'instinct' (the creatures of the forest). Numerous plays have of course dealt with this clash between conventional morality and the force of youthful sexuality, but *the* classic in modern German literature is undoubtedly Wedekind's *Spring Awakening*: there a famously explicit scene takes place in a hayloft – this may well be deliberately echoed in the hayloft sequence in WILD GAME.

6 'All Turks are called Ali' was to have been the title of FEAR EATS THE SOUL. The German title finally chosen – ANGST

ESSEN SEELE AUF – refers to a remark made by Ali. It is ill-served by the distributors' English translation 'Fear Eats the Soul': leaving aside the notorious untranslatability of '*Angst*', which has overtones of anxiety and anguish, the German phrase is deliberately ungrammatical, reflecting the fact that it is spoken by an immigrant worker. Its flavour might be better rendered by something like 'Fear Eat Soul Up'.

7 There is an ironic reference to Fassbinder's own personal life in SHADOWS OF THE ANGELS, where Franz, played by Fassbinder himself, meets a homosexual and asks to be initiated into this other way of life. From then on he is able to liberate himself from his infatuation with, and dependence on, Lily – who is played by Ingrid Caven, from whom Fassbinder had separated after their marriage in 1970.

8 Quoted in Rayns, p. 59.

9 The animal imagery even extends to Fassbinder's use of Döblin's name 'Biberkopf', which literally means 'beaver head': the beaver is exploited to death for its valuable fur. Franz's act at the fair, moreover, involved his head being 'separated' from his body: his new 'friends' also fail to see him as a complete human being, exploiting his body and ignoring his thoughts and emotions.

10 Ingrid Caven, who plays Corinne, went on to develop her talents in real life, and was soon receiving ecstatic press notices for her performances as a *chansonneuse* in Paris night clubs.

11 Fassbinder, interestingly enough, does not feel it necessary to do what Böll and Schlöndorff did and invent a fictitious newspaper: Tillmann is shown to have written in *UZ – Unsere Zeit* – the official organ of the German Communist Party. When it comes to Niemeyer's magazine, however, he is more careful and invents a non-existent journal.

12 Gabriel, an aspiring writer of purple prose who seeks Gerhard's patronage, is, we later learn, writing of the tension of his existence between Man and God, and between Man and Woman: a reference, presumably, to his 'angelic' name, which in turn reminds us of the overtly religious names Fassbinder has given not only to Angela, but to the Christ family as a whole – '*Christ*' in German meaning, incidentally, not 'Christ' but 'Christian'. These religious overtones culminate in the film's mysterious closing shot.

13 *Der Spiegel*, No. 21, 1978, p. 212.

14 Quoted by David Robinson, *The Times*, 26 May 1978.

15 Quoted in *L'Express*, 24 March 1979, p. 68. Fassbinder is fond of feeding journalists (and the authors of film books) with eminently quotable outrageous remarks: his tongue may be in his cheek, but they are often statements that have more than a grain of truth in them.

16 *Cineaste*, Vol. 8, No. 2, Fall 1977, p. 20.

17 Jansen and Schütte, *Fassbinder*, pp. 89–90.

18 The influence of Hollywood was not necessarily always *direct*: the Hollywood-inspired French gangster films of such directors as Melville and Godard also left their mark in the *films noirs* of Fassbinder's early years.

Chapter 7 Wim Wenders

1 *Time*, 20 March 1978, p. 58.

2 Dawson, p. 7.

3 Ibid.

4 That the Kinks were a *British* group attests the fact that for Wenders pop music need not be exclusively American: 'When I started liking rock'n'roll . . . it was . . . British groups that gave me the feeling it had something to do with me.' (Dawson, p. 11.) But pop culture, mediated as it is through the English language, still remains an alien import in Germany.

5 Dawson, p. 19.

6 Ibid., p. 4.

7 Ibid., p. 22.

8 The cinema, the Americanization of Europe, and the motif of the questing journey are all linked for Wenders: 'The theme of the journey intimately concerns the European generation that has been impregnated with American culture, it leads us to a search for identity – the role of the cinema itself.' (Quoted in *Le Monde*, 1 October 1977.)

9 *Die Zeit*, 21 March 1975.

10 *Der Spiegel*, No. 11, 1975.

11 Müller-Scherz and Wim Wenders, (no page numbers).

12 In fact he stumbles over the phrase and says something more like 'colonialized'.

13 Wenders seems to play with the symbolic potential of certain colours in this film – especially the combination red and white, which occurs far more often than could be explained by mere coincidence. Whether this is meant as a repeated reminder of Jonathan's fatal illness – affecting his red and white blood corpuscles – is impossible to say. Certainly these are the colours of the Swiss flag (Jonathan is Swiss), and at the most idyllic moment of family 'togetherness' he is riding with his wife and child on a switchback railway in a red car with a Swiss white cross on the front.

14 Dawson, p. 14.

15 Wenders never misses an opportunity to make his point, showing us not only the name 'Wurlitzer' in Germany, but also the word 'Cadillac' on the Paris Metro: names that now come incongruously home to rest in their countries of origin, so total has been their appropriation by America in our minds.

16 'Pity the poor immigrant,' Ripley sings at the end. The picture he first brings to Jonathan for framing is called 'The emigrant's yearning'. Wenders delights in these little touches: even Jonathan's surname – Zimmermann – is the real name of Bob Dylan, the author of Ripley's song.

17 *The Guardian*, 12 February 1977.

18 Dawson, p. 30.

19 Ibid., p. 8.

20 *Die Zeit*, 21 May 1976.

21 The apparent references in ALICE to another American film, PAPER MOON, are in fact purely coincidental. Wenders first saw Bogdanovich's film just after he had finished writing the script for Alice; the similarities so depressed him that he was at first tempted to abandon the whole project. Samuel Fuller played an important part in helping him to rewrite the script. (Dawson, pp. 22–23.)

Chapter 8 Hans Jürgen Syberberg

1 *Der Spiegel*, 30 October 1978, p. 266.

2 Syberberg, *Hitler*, p. 47.

3 Syberberg, *Filmbuch*, p. 311.

4 Syberberg, *Hitler*, p. 36.

5 Syberberg, *Filmbuch*, p. 112.

6 These ideas are developed in *Syberbergs Filmbuch*, p. 311, and *Hitler*, pp. 53–57.

7 Syberberg, *Hitler*, p. 29.

8 Syberberg, *Filmbuch*, p. 311.

9 Ibid., p. 90.

10 Ibid., p. 60.

11 Syberberg, *Hitler*, p. 33.

12 Ibid., p. 29.

13 Ibid., p. 28. Syberberg did not actually invent the formula himself: it derives from a headline that he saw during the 1972 Edinburgh Festival, in which LUDWIG was described as 'Between Brecht and Wagner'.

14 Ibid., p. 58. 'Ambivalence' is my translation of Syberberg's '*Mehrdeutigkeit*', a key word in Dürrenmatt's scheme of things.

15 Syberberg, *Filmbuch*, p. 307.

16 Ibid.

17 Ibid., p. 111.

18 Ibid., p. 80.

19 Ibid., p. 108. It was not Syberberg's initial intention to make a 'trilogy': this idea came only after the making of LUDWIG.

20 Mann develops these ideas in many different places – in greatest detail in the lengthy *Betrachtungen eines Unpolitischen* of 1918.

21 Syberberg, *Hitler*, p. 22.

22 Syberberg quoted in *Abendzeitung*, 26 April 1972.

23 The image is not actually Syberberg's: he found it on an old postcard (*Sight and Sound*, 44 (1975), p. 7). The postcard is mentioned in the Hitler film (*Hitler*, p. 87).

24 'A woman who doesn't look like a woman but like Jean-Louis Barrault', according to Syberberg. (*Le Monde*, 11 May 1973.)

25 Nonetheless, Syberberg still sees the film in musical terms: 'I can't talk about film style except through musical terms. LUDWIG, as its title indicates, was a requiem in its structure, while COOK is a chamber piece comprising a dominant theme with minor variations.' (*Sight and Sound*, 43 (1974), p. 214.)

26 Syberberg, *Hitler*, p. 25.

27 Syberberg has also prepared a shortened version lasting 104 minutes.

28 *Die Zeit*, 25 July 1975.

29 'Meine Trauerarbeit für Bayreuth' – a phrase Syberberg uses a number of times, including as the title of his notes on the film in the *Filmbuch*. As another reference in the Hitler book makes clear, Syberberg is thinking here of the need of the post-war Germans to come to terms with their Nazi past: to overcome that 'inability to mourn' that gave its title to a much-discussed book on the subject by Alexander and Margarete Mitscherlich (*Die Unfähigkeit zu trauern*, first published in 1967). Syberberg here seems to confuse the beneficial effect the film might have on its *audience* with the effect the *making* of the film may have had on Winifred Wagner herself: 'Winifred Wagner . . . has done Germany a great service. She has taken guilt upon herself, quite openly, for the first time in all honesty. The film shows it, and she must bear this burden. In this way she has redeemed many others from their lie.' (*Hitler*, p. 34.) The film in fact shows quite the opposite: Winifred Wagner remains incorrigible to the end. *That* is the film's most important lesson.

30 *Stuttgarter Zeitung*, 15 March 1977.

31 Syberberg, *Hitler*, p. 19.

32 Ibid., p. 262.

33 Ibid., pp. 20–22.

34 A reference to the events of the autumn of 1977, events that inspired the making of GERMANY IN AUTUMN (see below pp. 147–148).

35 Syberberg, *Filmbuch*, p. 299.

36 Syberberg, *Hitler*, p. 54.

37 The words are, of course, already readily available in print in the Hitler book. To assess them in this *written* form, however, cannot be equated with experiencing them as *spoken* words in the film.

38 Syberberg, *Hitler*, p. 43. Syberberg can be much more pleased with the reception the Hitler film has met with in the United States, where Susan Sontag hailed it as one of the great works of art of the twentieth century, and where Francis Ford Coppola, the American patron *par excellence* of the New German Cinema, has enthusiastically sponsored its distribution.

Chapter 9 Other Directors: Themes and Concerns

1 The loneliness of the old and the isolation of the *Gastarbeiter* are also linked in Saless's FAR FROM HOME, where the pathetic old woman in the flat downstairs tries to adopt Hasseyin as a substitute for the son who has left her to live in America.

2 Figure quoted by Margarethe von Trotta in Pflaum, *Jahrbuch Film* 78/79, p. 79.

3 *Not* Helma Sanders: the similarity of names has more than once led to confusion.

4 'Die allseitig entwickelte Persönlichkeit.' Thus, Erich Honecker at the Eighth Party Congress: 'One of the noblest goals and one of the greatest achievements of socialist society is the all-round developed personality.'

5 Quoted in Pflaum, *Jahrbuch Film 78/79*, p. 225.

6 Margarethe von Trotta was herself imprisoned for a day for interrupting a trial connected with this case at the time of the release of CHRISTA KLAGES.

7 Quoted in programme booklet for the Berlin Film Festival, 1978.

8 Even in the feminist cinema the distinction holds good: CHRISTA KLAGES, in its conventional suspense and use of the heist and cops-and-robbers motifs, is still very much a Munich film; REDUPERS, made in black and white, with a quieter, more quizzical and documentary approach, has by contrast much more of the flavour of the Berlin School.

9 Quoted (from the *Financial Times*) in London Film Festival programme booklet, 1977.

10 The remark is attributed to 'a woman of the people' in 1945.

Chapter 10 The Outlook: Problems and Prospects

1 The *Filmverlag der Autoren* was set up in 1971 by thirteen directors as a co-operatively owned production and distribution company. Financial difficulties led in 1974 to the dropping of the production side of its operations; in 1977 Augstein saved it from a renewed threat of bankruptcy by purchasing a 55 per cent partnership. The *Filmverlag* (whose distinctive name means 'Authors' (or *Auteurs*') Film Publishing House') is the leading distributor for the New German Cinema, and is much involved in the promotion of film culture in West Germany. The Federal Election year 1980 brought a second cooperative work in the tradition of GERMANY IN AUTUMN: 'THE CANDIDATE' (DER KANDIDAT), a study of Franz Josef Strauss, the directors of which included Kluge and Schlöndorff, was again backed by Rudolf Augstein and distributed by the *Filmverlag*.

2 *Der Spiegel*, No. 29, 1977, p. 141.

3 In all fairness, it must be said that there *are* programmes on West German television that would strike most outsiders as remarkably frank and outspoken: quite how long this will remain the case is, however, a matter of some concern.

4 Pflaum, *Jahrbuch Film* 77/78, p. 100.

5 Pflaum, *Jahrbuch Film* 78/79, p. 115.

6 Alexander Kluge has been particularly vociferous on this point. The demand (later withdrawn) that he hand back the project grant awarded for OCCASIONAL WORK OF A FEMALE SLAVE (because of 'deviation' from the script originally submitted) is an illustration of the difficulties film-makers face it they insist too much on the priority of *film-making* over scriptwriting. The new FFG has gone some way to meeting these objections: see p. 154 below.

7 One might contrast in this context Wim Wenders' WRONG MOVEMENT, which is rooted in the German literary tradition, with THE AMERICAN FRIEND, based on Patricia Highsmith.

8 See pp. 39 and 47 above.

9 Wenders at times overdoes the attempt to root THE AMERICAN FRIEND in a German context: the German political graffitti, incidentally but nonetheless deliberately glimpsed in the film, may be an interesting '*trouvaille*', providing a bit of decorative historical local colour, but they remain a superfluous intrusion into an otherwise close-knit film.

10 Bronnen/Brocher, p. 83.

11 A number of factors are responsible for this: in particular the isolation of the German cinema during the Third Reich (which went hand in hand with the creation of an artificial 'export' market in occupied Europe), and after the war the negative image of Germany that made competition with Hollywood doubly difficult. The resulting concentration on the domestic market led to an emphasis on peculiarly provincial genres such as the *Heimatfilm*, which lessened still further any chance of exporting German films.

12 Billy Kocian in *Variety*, 12 May 1976.

13 The two-man team of Alf Brustellin and Bernhard Sinkel have been in the van of this development with such films as BERLINGER (1975) and 'GIRLS AT WAR' (DER MÄDCHENKRIEG, 1977). More recent examples are Fassbinder's THE MARRIAGE OF MARIA BRAUN, Schlöndorff's THE TIN DRUM, and Herzog's NOSFERATU. More recently still, Reinhard Hauff's much praised KNIFE IN THE HEAD (MESSER IM KOPF, 1978), a chillingly convincing picture of a contemporary West Germany that is fast becoming a 1984-style computerized police state, moves – like Fassbinder's THE THIRD GENERATION – into the highly contentious areas first explored in KATHARINA BLUM and GERMANY IN AUTUMN.

14 *Filmförderungsgesetz* of 25 June 1979, paragraph 33, clause 3. (The *Filmförderungsgesetz* is reprinted in *Media Perspektiven*, 1979, 486–502; original text in *Bundesgesetzblatt*, Part I, No. 32, 30 June 1979.)

15 *Filmförderungsgesetz*, paragraph 66, clauses 1 and 2.

16 *Der Spiegel*, No. 25, 1979, p. 181. After neglecting the 'underground' film-makers who have made Hamburg their headquarters for some years, the city's administration is now going out of its way to attract the big names of the New German Cinema. It even looks as though Hamburg could become a serious rival to Munich and West Berlin as 'film capital' of the Federal Republic.

17 *Die Zeit*, 5 August 1977.

Glossary of German Terms

German terms have usually been translated and/or explained as and when they first occur. The following is a rather odd, but, I hope, comprehensive list of terms and abbreviations that subsequently occur without necessarily being explained again. It is in strict alphabetical order (i.e. the first word, even if it is, for instance, a definite article, determines the position in the list). Plural forms and other variants have been included only where they differ substantially from the basic word. The list includes the names of newspapers and periodicals mentioned in the text and notes, but does not include film titles, as these have, where necessary, been translated or explained in the text. Further elucidation of some of these terms can be obtained by referring – via the index– to the appropriate points in the text.

Abend 'Evening' (name of a newspaper)
Abendzeitung 'Evening Newspaper'
Angst anxiety, fear, anguish, apprehension
ARD = Arbeitsgemeinschaft der öffentlichen-rechtlichen Rundfunkanstalten der Bundesrepublik Deutschland Association of Public Broadcasting Corporations of the German Federal Republic
Autoren filmmakers, '*auteurs*'
Autorenkino '*cinéma des auteurs*'

Berufsverbot 'occupation ban', ban on exercising a profession (term applied (usually pejoratively) to the measures adopted by West German authorities to exclude radicals (usually of the Left) from appointments in the Public Service)
Bild (*-Zeitung*) 'Picture (Paper)' (a daily newspaper)
Bildungsroman 'novel of education' (a major genre in German literature, especially in the nineteenth century, typically concerned with the development and socialization of a sensitive individual)

der junge deutsche Film the Young German Film (or Cinema)
Der Spiegel 'The Mirror' (weekly news magazine)
Deutschland Germany
die unbewältigte Vergangenheit 'the unsurmounted past' (term used to describe the Germans' alleged failure to have faced up to, and come to terms with, the experience and memory of the Nazi years)
Die Welt 'The World' (a daily newspaper)
Die Zeit 'The Time/The Times/Time' (a weekly newspaper)

FBW = Filmbewertungsstelle Wiesbaden 'Film Assessment Office at Wiesbaden' (set up by the *Länder* to assess the merits of films with a view to remission of entertainment tax as an incentive to – and reward for – quality)
FFA = Filmförderungsanstalt 'Film Promotion Office' (in West Berlin, responsible for the execution of the Film Promotion Law)
FFG = Filmförderungsgesetz 'Film Promotion (or Aid) Law'
Filmgroschen 'Film Penny' (a *groschen* in Germany is ten pfennigs)
Frankfurter Allgemeine Zeitung 'Frankfurt General Paper' (a daily newspaper)
Frankfurter Kreuz 'Frankfurt Cross' (an important motorway intersection)
Frankfurter Rundschau 'Frankfurt Panorama' (a daily newspaper)
Frauen und Film 'Women and Film'
Frauenfilm 'Women's Film' (term applied to films made by and about women, in particular to the feminist films of the mid and late seventies, though the concept itself is rejected by many feminists)

Gastarbeiter 'guest worker' (term used of the immigrant workers who come (usually temporarily) to West Germany from (usually) the Mediterranean countries)
Gesamtkunstwerk 'total work of art' (term associated in particular with Richard Wagner)

Handelsblatt 'Trade Paper' (a financial daily paper, equivalent of the *Financial Times* or the *Wall Street Journal*)
Heimatfilm 'home-sweet-home film' (sentimental film genre, typically set in rural southern Germany)
Hochschule für Fernsehen und Film 'Film and Television Academy' (in Munich; it and the 'German Film and Television Academy' in West Berlin (*Deutsche Film- und Fernsehakademie Berlin*) are the Federal Republic's two main film schools)

Kinderladen 'child shop' (self-help day-care nursery set up in abandoned commercial premises, associated in particular with the ideals of 'anti-authoritarian education')
Kommunales Kino Municipal Cinema
kritischer Heimatfilm critical *Heimatfilm* (q.v.)
Kuratorium junger deutscher Film 'Board of Curators of the Young German Film' (or 'Cinema')

Land (plural *Länder*) state, province (of the West German Federation)

Mehrdeutigkeit ambiguity (implies having *several* meanings)

Neuer Sensibilismus 'New Sensitivity' (term applied to the highly aesthetic manner of filming popular in Munich in the mid sixties; also known as *Münchner Sensibilismus*)

Novelle novella, short story (a distinctive genre in German literature)

Oberhausener Manifest 'Oberhausen Manifesto'
Opas Kino 'Grandad's Cinema' (term used dismissively by the young directors of the mid sixties to describe the established commercial cinema; in retaliation, the 'young' cinema was occasionally referred to as '*Bubis Kino*' – 'sonny-boy's cinema')

Projektförderung 'Project promotion' (i.e. production advance – the sponsorship of planned films on the basis of promising scripts, etc.)

RAF = Rote Armee Fraktion 'Red Army Group' (the 'Baader-Meinhof Group')
Referenzfilm 'Reference Film' (i.e. a film presented as evidence of one's work as a director when making an application for a grant to make a new one)
Reformzirkus reform(ed) circus (has overtones of the turn-of-the-century 'back to Nature/health and efficiency' movement)

Stuttgarter Zeitung 'Stuttgart Paper' (a daily newspaper)
Süddeutsche Zeitung 'South German Paper' (a daily newspaper)
Sympathisant (plural *Sympathisanten*) sympathiser (term used (normally pejoratively) to denote alleged sympathisers and helpers of terrorists)

UFA = Universum-Film-Aktiengesellschaft 'Universe Film Corporation' (the film production, distribution, and exhibition conglomerate that dominated the German Cinema in the Weimar Republic and the Third Reich)
UZ = Unsere Zeit 'Our Age' (a daily newspaper)

Verfremdung alienation, distancing (the Brechtian 'alienation effect')
Volkstheater 'theatre of the people' (popular form of drama, dealing with working- and lower-middle-class people, associated in particular with Vienna)

WDR = Westdeutscher Rundfunk 'West German Broadcasting Corporation' (serves the *Land* of North-Rhine Westphalia)

Zeitung newspaper
Zweites Deutsches Fernsehen (ZDF) 'Second German Television (Service)'

Filmography

The following is a complete list of the films made by each of the seven directors dealt with in Chapters 2 to 8. In accordance with the practice adopted throughout this book, the dates given indicate the year in which the film in question was *completed*. This may differ from the year in which the film was *premiered*: some filmographies and film books date films on this basis; all too many do not indicate which practice they are adopting, and some mix the two. There may thus be discrepancies between the dates given here and those given in some other publications. English titles are given in accordance with the conventions explained in the Preface.

A thorough and comprehensive collection of one hundred filmographies of directors associated with the New German Cinema may be found in Pflaum/Prinzler. More detailed filmographies of Fassbinder, Herzog, Kluge, and Straub are contained in the relevant volumes by Jansen and Schütte, and there is a filmography of Wenders in Dawson.

Rainer Werner Fassbinder
(born 31 May 1946 in Bad Wörishofen, Bavaria)

1965 THE CITY TRAMP (DER STADTSTREICHER), 10 minutes
1966 THE LITTLE CHAOS (DAS KLEINE CHAOS), 9 minutes (originally 12 minutes)
1969 LOVE IS COLDER THAN DEATH (LIEBE IST KÄLTER ALS DER TOD), 88 minutes
1969 KATZELMACHER, 88 minutes
1969 GODS OF THE PLAGUE (GÖTTER DER PEST), 91 minutes
1970 WHY DOES HERR R. RUN AMOK? (WARUM LÄUFT HERR R. AMOK?), 88 minutes
1970 RIO DAS MORTES, 84 minutes
1970 THE COFFEE HOUSE (DAS KAFFEEHAUS), television play, 105 minutes
1970 WHITY, 95 minutes
1970 THE NIKLASHAUSEN JOURNEY (DIE NIKLASHAUSER FART), 86 minutes
1970 THE AMERICAN SOLDIER (DER AMERIKANISCHE SOLDAT), 80 minutes
1970 BEWARE OF A HOLY WHORE (WARNUNG VOR EINER HEILIGEN NUTTE), 103 minutes
1971 PIONEERS IN INGOLSTADT (PIONIERE IN INGOLSTADT), 84 minutes

1971 THE MERCHANT OF THE FOUR SEASONS (DER HÄNDLER DER VIER JAHRESZEITEN), 89 minutes
1972 THE BITTER TEARS OF PETRA VON KANT (DIE BITTEREN TRÄNEN DER PETRA VON KANT), 124 minutes
1972 WILD GAME (WILDWECHSEL), 102 minutes
1972 EIGHT HOURS DON'T MAKE A DAY (ACHT STUNDEN SIND KEIN TAG), television series in five parts, 101, 100, 92, 88 and 89 minutes
1972 'BREMEN FREEDOM' (BREMER FREIHEIT), television play, 87 minutes
1973 WORLD ON A WIRE (WELT AM DRAHT), two parts, 99 and 106 minutes
1973 NORA HELMER, television play, 101 minutes
1973 FEAR EATS THE SOUL (ANGST ESSEN SEELE AUF), 93 minutes
1973 MARTHA, 112 minutes
1974 EFFI BRIEST (FONTANE EFFI BRIEST), 141 minutes
1974 FOX (FAUSTRECHT DER FREIHEIT), 123 minutes
1974 'LIKE A BIRD ON THE WIRE' (WIE EIN VOGEL AUF DEM DRAHT), television show, 44 minutes
1975 MOTHER KÜSTERS' TRIP TO HEAVEN (MUTTER KÜSTERS' FAHRT ZUM HIMMEL), 120 minutes
1975 FEAR OF FEAR (ANGST VOR DER ANGST), 88 minutes
1976 I ONLY WANT YOU TO LOVE ME (ICH WILL DOCH NUR, DASS IHR MICH LIEBT), 104 minutes
1976 SATAN'S BREW (SATANSBRATEN), 112 minutes
1976 CHINESE ROULETTE (CHINESISCHES ROULETTE), 86 minutes
1977 BOLWIESER, two parts, 104 and 96 minutes
1977 WOMEN IN NEW YORK (FRAUEN IN NEW YORK), 111 minutes
1977 DESPAIR (EINE REISE INS LICHT (DESPAIR)), 119 minutes
1978 contribution to GERMANY IN AUTUMN (DEUTSCHLAND IM HERBST)
1978 THE MARRIAGE OF MARIA BRAUN (DIE EHE DER MARIA BRAUN), 120 minutes
1978 IN A YEAR WITH 13 MOONS (IN EINEM JAHR MIT 13 MONDEN), 124 minutes
1979 THE THIRD GENERATION (DIE DRITTE GENERATION), 110 minutes

WERNER HERZOG
(born 5 September 1942 in Munich)

1962 'HERACLES' (HERAKLES), 12 minutes (new version in 1965)
1964 'PLAYING IN THE SAND' (SPIEL IM SAND), 14 minutes
1966 'THE UNPARALLELED DEFENCE OF THE FORTRESS OF DEUTSCHKREUZ' (DIE BEISPIELLOSE VERTEIDIGUNG DER FESTUNG DEUTSCHKREUZ), 14 minutes
1967 SIGNS OF LIFE (LEBENSZEICHEN), 90 minutes
1968 'LAST WORDS' (LETZTE WORTE), 13 minutes
1968 'MEASURES AGAINST FANATICS' (MASSNAHMEN GEGEN FANATIKER), 11 minutes

1969 THE FLYING DOCTORS OF EAST AFRICA (DIE FLIEGENDEN ÄRZTE VON OSTAFRIKA), 45 minutes
1970 FATA MORGANA, 79 minutes
1970 EVEN DWARFS STARTED SMALL (AUCH ZWERGE HABEN KLEIN ANGEFANGEN), 96 minutes
1970 'IMPEDED FUTURE' (BEHINDERTE ZUKUNFT), 63 minutes
1971 LAND OF SILENCE AND DARKNESS (LAND DES SCHWEIGENS UND DER DUNKELHEIT), 85 minutes
1972 AGUIRRE, WRATH OF GOD (AGUIRRE, DER ZORN GOTTES), 93 minutes
1974 THE GREAT ECSTASY OF WOODCARVER STEINER (DIE GROSSE EKSTASE DES BILDSCHNITZERS STEINER), 45 minutes
1974 THE ENIGMA OF KASPAR HAUSER (JEDER FÜR SICH UND GOTT GEGEN ALLE), 109 minutes
1976 HOW MUCH WOOD WOULD A WOODCHUCK CHUCK?, 44 minutes
1976 'NO ONE WILL PLAY WITH ME' (MIT MIR WILL KEINER SPIELEN), 14 minutes
1976 HEART OF GLASS (HERZ AUS GLAS), 94 minutes
1976 LA SOUFRIÈRE, 31 minutes
1977 STROSZEK, 107 minutes
1978 NOSFERATU THE VAMPYRE (NOSFERATU – PHANTOM DER NACHT), 107 minutes
1978 WOYZECK, 82 minutes

ALEXANDER KLUGE
(born 14 February 1932 in Halberstadt, Saxony)

1960 'BRUTALITY IN STONE' / 'YESTERDAY GOES ON FOR EVER' (BRUTALITÄT IN STEIN / DIE EWIGKEIT VON GESTERN), co-directed by Peter Schamoni, 12 minutes
1961 'RACING' (RENNEN), co-directed by Paul Kruntorad, 9 minutes
1963 'TEACHERS IN TRANSFORMATION' (LEHRER IM WANDEL), co-directed by Karen Kluge, 11 minutes
1964 'PORTRAIT OF ONE WHO PROVED HIS METTLE' (PORTRÄT EINER BEWÄHRUNG), 13 minutes
1966 YESTERDAY GIRL (ABSCHIED VON GESTERN), 88 minutes
1967 'FRAU BLACKBURN, BORN 5 JAN. 1872, IS FILMED' (FRAU BLACKBURN, GEB. 5. JAN. 1872, WIRD GEFILMT), 14 minutes
1967 ARTISTES AT THE TOP OF THE BIG TOP – DISORIENTATED (DIE ARTISTEN IN DER ZIRKUSKUPPEL: RATLOS), 103 minutes
1968 'FIREMAN E.A. WINTERSTEIN' (FEUERLÖSCHER E.A. WINTERSTEIN), 11 minutes
1969 'THE INDOMITABLE LENI PEICKERT' (DIE UNBEZÄHM-BARE LENI PEICKERT), 60 minutes
1970 'THE BIG DUST-UP' (DER GROSSE VERHAU), two versions: 86 and 93 minutes
1970 'A DOCTOR FROM HALBERSTADT' (EIN ARZT AUS HALBERSTADT), 29 minutes

1971 'WE'LL BLOW 3 × 27 BILLION DOLLARS ON A DESTROYER'
(WIR VERBAUEN 3 × 27 MILLA. DOLLAR IN EINEN
ANGRIFFSSCHLACHTER), also called 'THE DESTROYER'
(DER ANGRIFFSSCHLACHTER), 18 minutes

1971 WILLI TOBLER AND THE WRECK OF THE SIXTH FLEET
(WILLI TOBLER UND DER UNTERGANG DER 6. FLOTTE),
96 minutes

1973 'A WOMAN FROM THE PROPERTY-OWNING MIDDLE CLASS,
BORN 1908', (BESITZBÜRGERIN, JAHRGANG 1908), 11
minutes

1973 OCCASIONAL WORK OF A FEMALE SLAVE (GELEGENHEITS-
EINER SKLAVIN), 91 minutes

1974 THE MIDDLE OF THE ROAD IS A VERY DEAD END (IN
GEFAHR UND GRÖSSTER NOT BRINGT DER MITTELWEG
DEN TOD), 89 minutes

1975 STRONG-MAN FERDINAND (DER STARKE FERDINAND), 90
minutes (various versions made)

1977 'THE PEOPLE WHO ARE PREPARING THE YEAR OF THE
HOHENSTAUFENS' (DIE MENSCHEN, DIE DAS STAUFER-
JAHR VORBEREITEN), co-directed by Maxi Mainka, 42
minutes

1977 '"IN SUCH TREPIDATION I CREEP OFF TONIGHT TO THE
EVIL BATTLE"' ('ZU BÖSER SCHLACHT SCHLEICH' ICH
HEUT NACHT SO BANG'), revised version of WILLI
TOBLER AND THE WRECK OF THE SIXTH FLEET,
82 minutes

1978 Contribution to GERMANY IN AUTUMN (DEUTSCHLAND
IM HERBST)

1979 'THE PATRIOTIC WOMAN' (DIE PATRIOTIN)

VOLKER SCHLÖNDORFF
(born 31 March 1939 in Wiesbaden)

1960 'WHO CARES?' (WEN KÜMMERT'S), short, not released
1966 YOUNG TÖRLESS (DER JUNGE TÖRLESS), 87 minutes
1967 A DEGREE OF MURDER (MORD UND TOTSCHLAG),
87 minutes
1967 'AN UNEASY MOMENT' (EIN UNHEIMLICHER MOMENT),
13 minutes, contribution to THE KETTLEDRUMMER (DER
PAUKENSPIELER)
1969 MICHAEL KOHLHAAS (MICHAEL KOHLHAAS –
DER REBELL), 100 minutes
1969 BAAL, 87 minutes
1970 THE SUDDEN FORTUNE OF THE POOR PEOPLE OF KOM-
BACH (DER PLÖTZLICHE REICHTUM DER ARMEN LEUTE
VON KOMBACH), 102 minutes
1971 THE MORAL OF RUTH HALBFASS (DIE MORAL DER RUTH
HALBFASS), 94 minutes
1972 SUMMER LIGHTNING (STROHFEUER), 101 minutes
1973 'OVERNIGHT STAY IN THE TYROL' (ÜBERNACHTUNG IN
TIROL), 78 minutes
1974 'GEORGINA'S REASONS' (GEORGINAS GRÜNDE), 65 minutes
1975 THE LOST HONOUR OF KATHARINA BLUM (DIE VERLO-
RENE EHRE DER KATHARINA BLUM), 106 minutes

1976 COUP DE GRÂCE (DER FANGSCHUSS), 95 minutes
1977 JUST FOR FUN, JUST FOR PLAY (NUR ZUM SPASS – NUR
ZUM SPIEL. KALEIDOSKOP VALESKA GERT), 60 minutes
1978 contribution to GERMANY IN AUTUMN (DEUTSCHLAND
IM HERBST)
1979 THE TIN DRUM (DIE BLECHTROMMEL), 144 minutes

JEAN-MARIE STRAUB
(born 8 January 1933 in Metz, France)

1962 MACHORKA-MUFF, 18 minutes
1965 NOT RECONCILED (NICHT VERSÖHNT ODER ES HILFT NUR
GEWALT, WO GEWALT HERRSCHT), 55 minutes
1967 THE CHRONICLE OF ANNA MAGDALENA BACH (CHRONIK
DER ANNA MAGDALENA BACH), 94 minutes
1968 THE BRIDEGROOM, THE COMEDIENNE AND THE PIMP
(DER BRÄUTIGAM, DIE KOMÖDIANTIN UND DER
ZUHÄLTER), 23 minutes
1969 LES YEUX NE VEULENT PAS EN TOUT TEMPS SE FERMER
OU PEUT-ÊTRE QU'UN JOUR ROME SE PERMETTRA DE
CHOISIR À SON TOUR (also known as OTHON), 82 minutes
1972 HISTORY LESSONS (GESCHICHTSUNTERRICHT),
88 minutes
1972 INTRODUCTION TO ARNOLD SCHOENBERG'S ACCOMPANI-
MENT TO A CINEMATIC SCENE (EINLEITUNG ZU ARNOLD
SCHOENBERGS BEGLEITMUSIK ZU EINER
LICHTSPIELSCENE), 16 minutes
1974 MOSES AND AARON (MOSES UND ARON), 110 minutes
1976 FORTINI/CANI (I CANI DEL SINAI), 83 minutes
1977 EVERY REVOLUTION IS A THROW OF THE DICE (TOUTE
RÉVOLUTION EST UN COUP DE DÉS), 11 minutes
1979 'FROM THE CLOUD TO THE RESISTANCE' (DALLA NUBE
ALLA RESISTENZA), 103 minutes

HANS JÜRGEN SYBERBERG
(born 8 December 1935 in Nossendorf, Pomerania)

1965 'ACT FIVE, SCENE SEVEN. FRITZ KORTNER REHEARSES
KABALE UND LIEBE' (FÜNFTER AKT, SIEBTE SZENE. FRITZ
KORTNER PROBT KABALE UND LIEBE), 110 minutes
1965 'ROMY. ANATOMY OF A FACE' (ROMY. ANATOMIE EINES
GESICHTS), 90 minutes, later reduced to 60 minutes
1966 'FRITZ KORTNER RECITES MONOLOGUES FOR A RECORD'
(FRITZ KORTNER SPRICHT MONOLOGE FÜR EINE
SCHALLPLATTE), 71 minutes
'FRITZ KORTNER RECITES SHYLOCK' (FRITZ KORTNER
SPRICHT SHYLOCK), 11 minutes
'FRITZ KORTNER RECITES FAUST' (FRITZ KORTNER
SPRICHT FAUST), 11 minutes (both extracts from the
above)
1966 WILHELM VON KOBELL, 16 minutes
1967 'THE COUNTS OF POCCI – SOME CHAPTERS TOWARDS THE
HISTORY OF A FAMILY' (DIE GRAFEN POCCI – EINIGE KAPI-
TEL ZUR GESCHICHTE EINER FAMILIE), 92 minutes

'KONRAD ALBERT POCCI, THE FOOTBALL COUNT FROM THE AMMERLAND – PROVISIONALLY THE LAST CHAPTER OF A CHRONICLE OF THE POCCI FAMILY' (KONRAD ALBERT POCCI, DER FUSSBALLGRAF VOM AMMERLAND – DAS VORLÄUFIG LETZTE KAPITEL EINER CHRONIK DER FAMILIE POCCI), 28 minutes (extract from the above)

1968 SCARABEA – HOW MUCH LAND DOES A MAN NEED? (SCARABEA – WIEVIEL ERDE BRAUCHT DER MENSCH?), 130 minutes

1969 SEX-BUSINESS – MADE IN PASING, 100 minutes

1970 SAN DOMINGO, 138 minutes

1970 AFTER MY LAST MOVE (NACH MEINEM LETZTEN UMZUG), 72 minutes
PUNTILA, 13 minutes
FAUST, 52 minutes (both extracts from the above)

1972 LUDWIG – REQUIEM FOR A VIRGIN KING (LUDWIG – REQUIEM FÜR EINEN JUNGFRÄULICHEN KÖNIG), 134 minutes

1972 LUDWIG'S COOK (THEODOR HIERNEIS ODER: WIE MAN EHEM. HOFKOCH WIRD), 84 minutes

1974 KARL MAY, 187 minutes

1975 THE CONFESSIONS OF WINIFRED WAGNER (WINIFRED WAGNER UND DIE GESCHICHTE DES HAUSES WAHNFRIED VON 1914–1975), 303 minutes (shortened version: 104 minutes)

1977 HITLER, A FILM FROM GERMANY (HITLER. EIN FILM AUS DEUTSCHLAND), 407 minutes

WIM WENDERS
(born 14 August 1945 in Düsseldorf)

1967 'LOCATIONS' (SCHAUPLÄTZE), 10 minutes
1967 SAME PLAYER SHOOTS AGAIN, 12 minutes
1968 SILVER CITY, 25 minutes
1968 VICTOR I, 4 minutes
1969 ALABAMA – 2000 LIGHT YEARS, 24 minutes
1969 3 AMERICAN LP'S (3 AMERIKANISCHE LPS), 15 minutes
1970 POLICE FILM (POLIZEIFILM), 12 minutes
1970 SUMMER IN THE CITY, 145 minutes
1971 THE GOALIE'S ANXIETY AT THE PENALTY KICK (DIE ANGST DES TORMANNS BEIM ELFMETER), 100 minutes
1972 THE SCARLET LETTER (DER SCHARLACHROTE BUCHSTABE), 90 minutes
1973 ALICE IN THE CITIES (ALICE IN DEN STÄDTEN), 110 minutes
1974 'FROM THE FAMILY OF THE CROCODILIA' (AUS DER FAMILIE DER PANZERECHSEN), 25 minutes
'THE ISLAND' (DIE INSEL), 25 minutes (both contributions to a television series)
1974 WRONG MOVEMENT (FALSCHE BEWEGUNG), 103 minutes
1976 KINGS OF THE ROAD (IM LAUF DER ZEIT), 176 minutes
1977 THE AMERICAN FRIEND (DER AMERIKANISCHE FREUND), 123 minutes

Annotated Bibliography

The following is a list of books relevant to the New German Cinema, including all those referred to in the notes. A number of important books on other aspects of the German Cinema have also been included.

All – as is in most cases apparent from their titles – are in German, except for Bucher, Dawson, Eisner, Greenberg, Kracauer, Manvell/Fraenkell, Müller-Scherz/Wenders, Petley, Rayns, Roud, and Sandford, which are in English. Courtade and Courtade/Cadars are in French, and the two Thomsen books are in Danish.

Much of the material on the New German Cinema has appeared in the form of reports, articles, and reviews in newspapers and periodicals. Details of many of these can be found in Pflaum/Prinzler, and in the two books by Jansen/Schütte.

Bronnen, Barbara, and Corinna Brocher, *Die Filmemacher. Zur neuen deutschen Produktion nach Oberhausen 1962*, Munich / Gütersloh / Vienna, 1973 (Contains interviews, principally about the economics of filmmaking, with most of the major early directors, including Fassbinder, Herzog, Kluge, Schlöndorff, and Straub.)

Bucher, Felix, *Germany*, London / New York, 1970 (Alphabetical guide to various figures in the German Cinema.)

Courtade, Francis, *Jeune cinéma allemand*, Lyon, 1969 (Critical appreciation of the early years; the first foreign book on the New German Cinema.)
——, and Pierre Cadars, *Histoire du cinéma nazi*, Paris, 1972 (Standard survey of cinema in the Third Reich; also published in German as *Geschichte des Films im Dritten Reich*, Munich, 1975.)

Dawson, Jan, *Wim Wenders*, Toronto, 1976 (Slender but indispensable brochure containing a lengthy interview, assorted writings by Wenders, and a filmography.)

Dost, Michael, Florian Hopf, and Alexander Kluge, *Filmwirtschaft in der Bundesrepublik Deutschland und in Europa. Götterdämmerung in Raten*, Munich, 1973 (Thoroughly researched polemical assessment of the economic state of the industry.)

Eisner, Lotte H., *The Haunted Screen. Expressionism in the German Cinema and the Influence of Max Reinhardt*, London, 1969 (Idiosyncratic study of the 'Expressionist' cinema of the 1920s; together with Kracauer – q.v. – one of the classic books on the cinema of the Weimar Republic. Originally published in France in 1952 as *L'écran démoniaque*.)

Fürstenau, Theo, *Wandlungen im Film. Junge deutsche Produktion*, Pullach / West Berlin, 1970 (A glossy survey of the early years.)

Gmür, Leonhard H., ed., *Der junge deutsche Film*, Munich, 1967 (Together with the volume published by the Verband der deutschen Filmclubs – q.v. –, the first survey of the New German Cinema in the 'breakthrough year' of 1967.)

Greenberg, Alan, *Heart of Glass*, Munich, 1976 (An almost mystically adulatory account of the making of HEART OF GLASS by a devoted Herzogian.)

Gregor, Ulrich, *Geschichte des Films ab 1960*, Munich, 1978 (Contains a sizeable chapter on the New German Cinema.)
——, and Enno Patalas, *Geschichte des Films*, Munich, 1973 (History of world cinema up to 1960, with sections on Germany.)

Hembus, Joe, *Der deutsche Film kann gar nicht besser sein*, Bremen, 1961 (Polemical analysis; anticipates laments of the 'Oberhausener'.)

Jansen, Peter W., and Wolfram Schütte, eds., *Rainer Werner Fassbinder*, second edition, Munich / Vienna, 1975 (Essays, interviews, descriptive analyses of all films, and detailed filmography and bibliography.)
——, eds., *Herzog / Kluge / Straub*, Munich / Vienna, 1976 (Similar format and treatment to the Fassbinder volume above.)
——, eds., *Film in der DDR*, Munich / Vienna, 1977 (Historical survey of GDR cinema and assessment of the work of major directors; filmographies of thirty directors and bibliography.)

Kluge, Alexander, *Gelegenheitsarbeit einer Sklavin. Zur realistischen Methode*, Frankfurt am Main, 1975 (Drafts and script of OCCASIONAL WORK OF A FEMALE SLAVE together with relevant essays.)

Kracauer, Siegfried, *From Caligari to Hitler. A Psychological History of the German Film*, Princeton, 1947 (Classic study of Weimar cinema, seen as a key to the evolution of Nazism in the Germans' collective subconscious; see also Eisner.)

Kreimeier, Klaus, *Kino und Filmindustrie in der Bundesrepublik Deutschland. Ideologieproduktion und Klassenwirklichkeit nach 1945*, Kronberg, 1973 (Marxist analysis of the development of the West German cinema.)

Kroner, Marion, *Film – Spiegel der Gesellschaft? Inhalts-analyse des jungen deutschen Films von 1962 bis 1969*, Heidelberg, 1973 (Arbitrary and haphazard 'content analysis'.)

Kurowski, Ulrich, *Lexikon Film*, second edition, Munich, 1976 (Contains an entry on the New German Cinema.)

Manvell, Roger, and Heinrich Fraenkel, *The German Cinema*, London, 1971 (Historical survey; contains a number of errors.)

Meyn, Hermann, *Massenmedien in der Bundesrepublik Deutschland*, new edition, West Berlin, 1974 (Contains a brief but concise chapter on public aspects of the cinema – finance, censorship, etc.)

Müller-Scherz, Fritz, and Wim Wenders, *Kings of the Road*, translated by Christopher Doherty, Munich, 1976 (Fully illustrated script of the film, plus some ancillary material.)

Petley, Julian, *Capital and Culture. German Cinema 1933–1945*, London, 1979 (Questions the received view that the economics and ideology of the Nazi cinema were qualitatively different from what went before.)

Pflaum, Hans Günther, ed., *Jahrbuch Film 77/78*, Munich / Vienna, 1977

——, ed., *Jahrbuch Film 78/79*, Munich / Vienna, 1978 (The first two volumes of a planned annual series containing articles, essays, and factual material on the contemporary cinema, with special emphasis on West Germany.)

——, and Rainer Werner Fassbinder, *Das bisschen Realität, das ich brauche. Wie Filme entstehen*, Munich, 1976 (An account of the making of I ONLY WANT YOU TO LOVE ME, SATAN'S BREW, and CHINESE ROULETTE.)

——, and Hans Helmut Prinzler, *Film in der Bundesrepublik Deutschland. Der neue deutsche Film. Herkunft/Gegenwärtige Situation. Ein Handbuch*, Munich/Vienna, 1979 (An invaluable compendium of factual information on all aspects of the New German Cinema and film culture in West Germany since Oberhausen.)

Prawer, Siegbert, *Caligari's Children. The Film as Tale of Terror*, Oxford, 1980 (Thoughtful and wide-ranging investigation of the 'horror' (or 'terror') genre; includes many important references to German cinema.)

Rayns, Tony, ed., *Fassbinder*, London, 1976 (Essays, interview, filmography.)

Roeber, Georg, and Gerhard Jacoby, *Handbuch der filmwirtschaftlichen Medienbereiche. Die wirtschaftlichen Erscheinungsformen des Films auf den Gebieten der Unterhaltung, der Werbung, der Bildung und des Fernsehens*, Pullach, 1973 (Meticulously exhaustive and lucid survey of all conceivable aspects of film economics in West Germany since 1945; very big (nearly a thousand pages), and very expensive (over fifty pounds).)

Roud, Richard, *Straub*, London, 1971 (Careful appraisal by an English enthusiast.)

Sandford, John, *The Mass Media of the German-Speaking Countries*, London, 1976 (Contains a detailed survey of the history, structure, and workings of West German television.)

Schlöndorff, Volker, *'Die Blechtrommel'. Tagebuch einer Verfilmung*, Darmstadt / Neuwied, 1979 (The director's diary of the making of THE TIN DRUM.)

——, and Günter Grass, *Die Blechtrommel als Film*, Frankfurt am Main, 1979 (Beautifully illustrated filmscript, with a wealth of ancillary material.)

Syberberg, Hans Jürgen, *Syberbergs Filmbuch*, Munich, 1976 (Contains Syberberg's essays on his films and the cinema in general.)

——, *Hitler, ein Film aus Deutschland*, Reinbek, 1978 (Illustrated filmscript with accompanying essay.)

Thomsen, Christian Braad, *I Fassbinders Spejl. En analyse af Rainer Werner Fassbinders arbejde for film, teater, radio og TV*, Copenhagen, 1975 (The lengthiest monograph so far on any New German director; at times disconcertingly enthusiastic, but in general perceptive and impressively thorough.)

——, et al., *Politisk filmkunst*, Copenhagen, 1973 (Includes an interview with Rainer Werner Fassbinder.)

Verband der deutschen Filmclubs, ed., *Neuer deutscher Film. Eine Dokumentation*, Mannheim, 1967 (A most useful collection of essays and reviews from the early years of the New German Cinema, published for the 1967 Mannheim Festival.)

General Index

Page numbers in italics indicate illustrations

Index of Film Titles

The following index includes all titles referred to in the text, notes, and bibliography. German titles are given only where they differ substantially from the English title, or where there is no obvious or generally accepted English translation. Page numbers in italics indicate illustrations.

Sources Of Illustrations

Illustrations were supplied by the following:

Artificial Eye (Portrait of Straub and Huillet, THE CHRON-
ICLE OF ANNA MAGDALENA BACH, MOSES AND AARON)
Atlas-Film (HUNTING SCENES FROM LOWER BAVARIA)
Basis-Filmverleih (THE ALL-ROUND REDUCED PERSONALITY)
Contemporary Films (THE LOST HONOUR OF KATHARINA
BLUM, WILD GAME, THE CONFESSIONS OF WINIFRED
WAGNER)
Export-Union der deutschen Filmindustrie (Portraits of
Alexander Kluge, Wim Wenders and Hans Jürgen
Syberberg)
Filmverlag der Autoren (STROSZEK, WOYZECK, EFFI BRIEST,
ALICE IN THE CITIES, LINA BRAAKE, THE LEFT-HANDED
WOMAN)
foto studio rama (THE TIN DRUM)
Provobis Film (FAR FROM HOME)
Stiftung Deutsche Kinemathek (ROSES FOR THE STATE
PROSECUTOR)

All other illustrations by courtesy of Mrs. Dina Lom, UK
Representative of the German Federal Film Board, and Frau
Hella Roth of INTER NATIONES, Bonn.